PRAISE FOR *BETTER WITH BOOKS*

"Stories heal, bind, illuminate, and guide us. As an educator always searching for stories to help support and aid my students, I need a guide as thorough and essential as *Better with Books*. This will definitely sit on my shelf adorned with many Post-it notes!"

—AN NA, award-winning author of *A Step from Heaven* and *The Place Between Breaths*

"An essential resource for parents, librarians, teachers, and all who help guide our teens and preteens: the reading list topics speak precisely to the kinds of issues they face every day. Reading fiction and memoir offers them another way to expand their understanding of themselves and develop empathy for others—both of which are vitally important in an increasingly complex world."

—NANCY PEARL, bestselling author, librarian, and literary critic

"Few tweens and teens are willing to expose their vulnerabilities, and that is as it should be. But when they see their struggles in story—when they come upon a character with whom they feel true kinship—their sense of isolation recedes. Kids find *truth* in story, and often they find answers. *Better with Books* is a comprehensive guide for educators, parents, and anyone looking to find just the right book for a preteen or teen."

—CHRIS CRUTCHER, award-winning author of *Staying Fat for Sarah Byrnes* and *Whale Talk*

"Essays about important topics, such as body image, mental health, and race, are brimming with personal stories, author interviews, and other helpful information. You'll also find five hundred recommended books for preteens and teens organized by topic, with summaries of each title. This gem needs to be on your bookshelf!"

—DONNA GEPHART, award-winning author of *Lily and Dunkin* and *In Your Shoes*

BETTER
WITH
BOOKS

**500 Diverse Books to Ignite Empathy
and Encourage Self-Acceptance
in Tweens and Teens**

Melissa Hart

Foreword by Sharon M. Draper

SASQUATCH BOOKS
SEATTLE

Printed in the United States of America

Published by Sasquatch Books

SASQUATCH BOOKS with colophon is a trademark of Penguin Random House LLC

23 22 21 20 19   9 8 7 6 5 4 3 2 1

Editor: Susan Roxborough
Production editor: Rachelle Longé McGhee
Design: Tony Ong
Copyeditor: Rachelle Longé McGhee

Library of Congress Cataloging-in-Publication Data is available

ISBN: 978-1-63217-227-3

1904 Third Avenue, Suite 710
Seattle, WA 98101

SasquatchBooks.com

For my mother, who inspired me to love books, and for young readers everywhere.

CONTENTS

A book must be the axe
for the frozen sea within us.
— FRANZ KAFKA

FOREWORD

It's the first day of class. I look at my students and see a wonderful garden of young people, and no two seedlings are alike. I have tulips sitting next to gardenias, and a water lily beside a cactus. I have geraniums and grasses, foliage and fruits, and even a couple of tough and sturdy weeds. None of them are the same, yet I must reach them all and teach them all to the best of my ability. It's a daunting task. Every single teacher faces this challenge, rises to the occasion, and manages to do just that.

The best teachers know, of course, that books are often the key to opening the door of knowledge for many students. Librarians, therapists, and parents know this too. We know that storytelling is a powerful way for kids to recognize themselves and others, but how can we possibly have knowledge of every book we could offer them? Melissa Hart, who is a journalist, author, and teacher, has taken the time to read and research five hundred diverse books to help us find just the right reading material for the preteens and teens in our lives.

Students today wrestle with a variety of complex issues, and reading stories—both fiction and nonfiction—can offer them insight into themselves and those around them. The chapters in this book are thoughtfully organized by issue, and all close with two suggested reading lists: one appropriate for preteens and one for teens. The chapters deal with difficult themes, such as mental health and body image, learning challenges, sexual orientation, religion, and poverty. And while the books included here aren't the only ones that explore difficult experiences, all of them were published within the last ten years; they speak to contemporary issues and offer a solid starting point for the essential human quest toward greater understanding of ourselves and others.

It's the first day of class. I have a million things to do. But now I won't have to spend hours researching books for my students to read and share because I have them right at my fingertips. They will be the water for my blooming garden of students. I dig into the list, and together we begin our yearlong journey into reading and growing with great books.

SHARON M. DRAPER
Award-winning author and
National Teacher of the Year

INTRODUCTION

When I was a kid, my mother worked as a book reviewer, and I got first crack at the children's and young adult novels that arrived in the mail. Once a month, I knelt on her living room carpet and ripped open the heavy cardboard boxes, yanking off plastic tape to lift out the paperbacks within.

I was a painfully shy middle school student, anxious and depressed after my parents' bitter divorce. Once I hit the high school halls and realized the wealth of extracurricular opportunities available, I morphed into a straight-A honors student who sought refuge from a dysfunctional home life on campus fourteen hours a day, involved in track practice and theater rehearsal and yearbook production. I slept maybe five hours a night. My left eye developed a permanent twitch. My head swam. At three in the morning, I lay awake trembling with fatigue. But I had books, and just as they save millions of children and teens today, they rescued me.

Along with the classics assigned at school, I devoured the contemporary novels from my mother's boxes. They showed me places and people I'd never met—kids in wildly different situations but with emotions I recognized as my own.

Margaret J. Anderson's novel *Searching for Shona* offered unexpected comfort after my parents' divorce. Set in Edinburgh during World War II, it's the story of two evacuees who decide to trade identities. Rich, reticent Marjorie becomes Shona—a shabby intrepid girl orphan who moves in with two eccentric women and finds happiness and purpose in a small Scottish town.

I'm not Scottish, and I wasn't an orphan. But I lived with my wealthy, workaholic father instead of my beloved mother who struggled to pay the mortgage, and—like Marjorie-turned-Shona—I would have happily traded my dad's generous weekly allowance to run wild with the chickens in my mom's vegetable garden.

As it was, I read *Searching for Shona* over and over until the cover fell off, knowing each time that someone in the world comprehended my plight. This intimate understanding is what we offer young readers when we hand them a book. We give them comfort and affirmation packaged within a captivating story. Books show kids new ways to live, how to think for themselves, and how to shape their future lives.

Betsy Byars's novel *The Pinballs* taught me what it means to be a foster child unsure of where they will be living month to month. It's the story of three kids brought together into one home with kindly foster parents who help them to build trust in the midst of their trauma. Twenty years after I read *The Pinballs*, when my husband and I decided to start a family, we adopted our child from the foster care system.

The idea for this book in your hands grew out of our adopted daughter's angst. In her second-grade classroom—overcome by separation anxiety and other learning challenges—she imploded spectacularly. She'd spent her first nineteen months in foster care; at seven years old, she still suffered the effects of early trauma and neglect. All this to say that, for a while, she needed us with her all day every day.

My husband and I were lucky enough to be able to adjust our work schedules to homeschool her for two years. I had been teaching English and creative writing for almost two decades, and I'd worked briefly as a third-grade teacher. I studied the third-grade educational standards and enrolled my daughter in a homeschool support program, then headed for the library and our local bookstore.

I designed a literature-based curriculum that allowed us to focus on a different contemporary children's novel each month. On the couch with our cats and terrier between us, I read her a chapter a day. I helped her with related math and science and history projects. We took field trips that pertained to each book. We watched movies and documentaries with similar themes.

My daughter and I came away with a rich understanding of each story we read together. We grew closer as parent and child. And we discovered an unexpected benefit.

Empathy.

Over the past decade, researchers have shown again and again that the more we read fiction, the more we develop the ability to put ourselves in a character's shoes and feel for them deeply. (See page 265 for a list of fascinating studies that point to a correlation between prolonged exposure to literary fiction and increased compassion for self and others.)

Librarians, teachers, and parents in the habit of reading to their kids daily will likely roll their eyes at me and groan, "No kidding." But I'd wager that, in general, most people haven't considered the fact that reading novels can help us become kinder, more caring individuals.

That connection seems pretty important right now. In the midst of increased bigotry and fear in the United States, as more and more preteens and teens report anxiety and depression brought on by everything from bullying to college applications to concerns about climate change, we *need* books.

It's hard for parents and other caregivers to talk about the big issues with our kids. We see them struggling with current events, with what's happening in their schools, their cities, their bodies, and their minds. The issues feel overwhelming. We don't know how to start a discussion with them about racism, transphobia, eating disorders, the inequality between rich kids who take yearly European vacations and those who live with their families in a car.

Books can help.

The five-hundred-plus books listed in the pages that follow represent a wealth of topics and characters and demographics in middle grade and young adult literature over the past decade. Some of the authors and protagonists are immigrants. Some have physical disabilities. Some have ADHD or severe anxiety. Some are gay, lesbian, transsexual, or genderqueer. Some are fat, some have battled anorexia, some have been bullied, some have been bullies themselves. All of the titles reveal, through story, what it's like to be a young person today.

Some of the chapters include scary statistics. The number of suicide attempts by young people has increased. So has the prevalence of hate crimes in the US. Stories abound of tweens and teens intimidating and humiliating each other on social media. But fictional narratives can address and mitigate even the toughest issues. Books allow for revelation in classrooms, in libraries, at book clubs, at home.

Educators and caregivers can encourage deep reading and discussion in numerous ways. Cindy Hudson, author of *Book by Book: The Complete Guide to Creating Mother-Daughter Book Clubs*, used to meet regularly with her friends and their preteen and teen girls to discuss a novel that everyone had read. They talked about Justina Chen's *North of Beautiful* and how physical appearance can affect both the ways in which we see ourselves and how others see us. They talked about Frank Cottrell Boyce's *Millions* and about how losing a parent can create instability and insecurity in a child's life.

When the girls were eighth graders, about to enter high school, they discussed a book that had particular impact on them—Laurie Halse Anderson's *Speak*. The story of a girl who had been raped at an end-of-summer party before her freshman year resonated with them; they were wary of transitioning to a larger school where they might be pressured to do things they weren't ready for. Hudson explains, "At our meeting we talked about situations they might find themselves in, like parties where friends were drinking, and how they could protect themselves. We also talked about what they could do if they were attacked."

By the end of the meeting, she says, everyone felt better about bringing such a volatile and difficult subject out into the open for discussion.

When kids see their own fears and experiences and struggles represented in the pages of a novel, they become kinder and more compassionate to themselves as well. After my own daughter and I read about a lonely, angry foster child in Katherine Paterson's *The Great Gilly Hopkins*, we were able to process her own adoption story with new insight into her fear of being separated from my husband and me.

As a biracial child, my daughter learned pride and resilience from Rita Williams-Garcia's *One Crazy Summer*. Katherine Applegate's Newbery Medal–winning *The One and Only Ivan* rocked her world and inspired a passionate commitment to homeless cats and dogs, our backyard chickens, and even her giant aquarium full of tadpoles and minnows. Why wouldn't we encourage our kids to experience such powerful epiphany through literature?

Adults are busier than ever before. I get that. Some of us may work two and three jobs, as my mother did, to pay for housing and food. Children may come home after school to empty houses, to daycare facilities, to four hours of homework a night. Still, if we can make time—even ten minutes a night—to read with our kids aloud, the benefits are remarkable.

When we read to our children, and later, when they prefer to read on their own, they learn to calm their bodies and pay attention. They learn vocabulary and sentence structure. Stories drop them into ethical dilemmas in a safe way, increasing their emotional intelligence. Best of all, books offer parents and other caregivers a way to bond with young people through conversations that have nothing to do with who dented the family car or whether the math homework got done and the litter box was scooped.

Worried that your preteen is just a little too focused on body image? Starting on page 33, you'll find reading lists with dozens of contemporary young adult novels featuring protagonists with similar struggles—you can discuss any of them as a way into their feelings of fear and insecurity. Concerned that your newly out teen is the target of school bullies? The books listed from pages 103 to 111 about kids in the same situation explore how the protagonist overcomes negative stereotypes and ultimately triumphs.

My husband and I have been reading to our daughter since we adopted her as a toddler. Even during the most difficult parts of her childhood—when she's cranky and withdrawn, or she's retreated to her bedroom overcome by peer conflict at school—we've carved out a few minutes each day between work and chores and homework and dance class to read novels out loud.

Sometimes these are the only moments of the week in which we feel a blissful parent-child connection. Other times, the promise of a chapter follows us throughout the day—in the car and waiting in the doctor's office and on walks with our dog. We find ourselves talking about the characters as passionately as if they were real-life friends, debating why they do what they do and speculating on what they'll do next.

My friend Merie and I read and discussed stories throughout our undergraduate studies in literature at the University of California at Santa Barbara. Now she's a literature professor at the University of North Dakota and the mother of an avid teen reader. Recently her daughter, Cory, came up with the idea of a reading challenge. Everyone in the family chooses eight books to read themselves over the summer as well as one in common to read together.

Merie says the idea came out of reading to her daughter at night: "When she decided she would rather read to herself, we missed that 'shared story' experience. Often now, Cory will read a book and want us to check it out—like *Simon vs. the Homo Sapiens Agenda*. Sometimes it's a book I'm teaching and she wants to read it too, like *The Hate U Give* or *Eleanor & Park*."

Merie wholehearted recommends the reading challenge to families with kids who have outgrown reading aloud with their parents. Books have inspired her own family to talk about important topics—friendships, hard choices, disabilities, fear, adoption, falling in love, social justice issues, and more. She suggests that kids choose the books; it can be a great way to find out what they want to talk about, what issues are important to them, and how the world looks through their eyes.

These days with my daughter—now twelve—I follow her lead and read the books aloud that she suggests. She's increasingly interested in diversity issues, so we've read Jewell Parker Rhodes's post-slavery novel *Sugar,* and Sharon M. Draper's *Stella by Starlight,* set in the segregated South during the Great Depression. It's hard to talk about the racism in these books with my biracial child. It's also critical to her understanding of race relations in our country and how we can work toward a more equitable future.

Life can be difficult for both fictional characters and real kids; conflict is, after all, inevitable in this business of living. But life is also a tremendous gift, full of wonder and excitement and opportunities to make powerful connections. With this in mind, we can give young readers literature that inspires and delights, that provides opportunities for thoughtful discussion and deliberate action, and that fosters empathy for the way they see themselves and others.

As I learned all those years ago, tearing open cardboard boxes on my mother's living room floor, everything—*everything*—is better with books.

Melissa Hart

October 2018

1

BOOKS ABOUT ADOPTION AND FOSTER CARE

L eyda Garcia-Greenawalt, a university honors student studying social work, entered foster care at age twelve because of neglect and violence in her home. Over the next seven years, the State of Illinois moved her in and out of eight different placements and enrolled her in five different schools, bringing her total up to twelve.

Leyda's admittedly not a huge fan of reading. But her final foster mother gave her Steve Pemberton's memoir *A Chance in the World* and said, "You *have* to read this book."

Leyda read it. She loved it. It was the first time she'd read a book written by a former foster child about the system that they both knew so well.

Pemberton's memoir, subtitled *An Orphan Boy, a Mysterious Past, and How He Found a Place Called Home*, explains how he was placed in an abusive foster home at age five and discovered comfort in a box of books.

Leyda believes wholeheartedly in the power of literature to build connections and heal emotional wounds. Many foster kids are traumatized even before the age that they can read, she tells me, and they psychologically remain the age at which they experienced that mental or physical trauma for a very long time.

"It's hard to address it," she says, "but literature can help. Something about a story gets you to continue reading. It pushes you to feel for characters and makes you want to do something about the issues they're facing."

At any given time, 438,000 US kids live in foster care, removed from birth parents who are often struggling with addiction and/or domestic violence. Children who enter the system often come from backgrounds of profound abuse and neglect. Some are born exposed or addicted to narcotics—and that, combined with the terror of removal from a birth family, can cause mood disorders throughout childhood and adolescence.

Birth parents in this country permanently relinquish tens of thousands of children each year to the state. These kids often bounce around between foster placements; one girl I met had lived in sixteen homes by the time she turned seventeen. Like her, wards of the state wait to be adopted . . . or not.

I learned about the plight of foster children when I was young by reading *The Pinballs*, Betsy Byars's preteen novel about three unrelated traumatized kids taken in by the same kindhearted foster parents. In part, the book inspired me to adopt my daughter decades later.

When my daughter turned eight years old, we read Katherine Paterson's preteen novel *The Great Gilly Hopkins* about a feisty middle schooler who finds unexpected kinship with a folksy foster mom and a painfully shy foster brother until her grandmother abruptly appears to adopt her. Though my child has, so far, shown little curiosity about her birth parents, she's plenty fascinated by her early months in foster care.

Inspired by Gilly Hopkins, we processed how my daughter ended up in a foster home in the first place, and how the Department of Social and Health Services matched her with my husband and me. We looked at her baby photos and watched videos of her as a toddler, all of which were instrumental in creating a story that—to her—is every bit as compelling as Gilly's fictional tale.

Like *The Pinballs*, *The Great Gilly Hopkins* was published in the 1970s. Contemporary novels about foster and adoptive children reflect the message of these earlier books that—with apologies for the cross-stitch cliché—home is where the heart is. Children need a safe and loving environment with adults devoted to their well-being, whether those adults are biological or adoptive or foster parents. It's imperative that foster kids, with their history of trauma, grow up with a sense of security and self-worth. And yet so many do not.

Author Holly Goldberg Sloan knows well the power of a story to inspire empathy for these children and teens. She volunteered as an art teacher for kids taken away from abusive parents by authorities and placed in a county-run facility. The experience helped inspire her preteen novel *Counting by 7s*.

"We'd be doing a painting project, and kids would come up and ask me to take them home," she recalls. "They were so vulnerable, waiting for their court dates, waiting to see what would happen to them."

Counting by 7s is the story of twelve-year-old Willow Chance, a mixed-race girl with a genius IQ who is adopted as a baby, then thrust into bewildered grief after her adoptive mother and father are killed in a car accident. Willow has no idea who her birth parents are, or even if they're still alive. She has just one relative in the world—an adoptive grandmother suffering from dementia.

"People usually find a good place for stray dogs, or for the elderly when they can no longer go up stairs or use a can opener," Willow says. "Finding a good place for a kid seems like a much bigger challenge."

She's taken in by a sympathetic Vietnamese manicurist who lives in a garage behind a beauty shop with her two children. Two other adults help Willow as well: an inept school counselor frustrated by his inability to pigeonhole her into a diagnosis, and a taxi driver who refers to her as his "angel" after she encourages him to go back to school.

Throughout the story, Willow changes the adults' lives and their surroundings in positive—almost magical—ways. Simply by paying attention, she inspires the manicurist to move out of the garage and into an apartment. She gets the slothful school counselor to start running. She plants a flower garden in the stark courtyard of the apartment complex, assisted by the motley community she's created.

In the end, a judge grants the manicurist and the taxi driver permanent custody of Willow. The happy ending in *Counting by 7s* might strike some as a bit of magical realism.

However, anyone familiar with the world of foster care and adoption will recognize the creative blending of caregivers as completely believable. Stories that show the benefits of adopting older children like Willow are critical to their well-being. Fifty-six percent of children adopted in the US are five years old or younger, which leaves older available kids at risk.

As she wrote *Counting by 7s*, Holly Goldberg Sloan recalled a man she met in Cuba who adopted seven- and nine-year-old siblings he and his wife had met at an agency picnic. "They started out as foster parents and ended up adopting this brother and sister. I thought it was a magical way to create a family."

But what does it *mean* to be a family?

This question guides Robin Benway's National Book Award–winning teen novel *Far from the Tree*. Like *Counting by 7s*, the story demonstrates how people create families in infinite ways, and how the definition of family can expand as needed throughout a lifetime.

Three siblings tell their stories in *Far from the Tree*. Two have been adopted separately from one another—sixteen-year-old Grace, who's just given birth and put *her* baby up for adoption, and fifteen-year-old Maya, who lives with a wealthy and dysfunctional family nearby. A third sibling, seventeen-year-old Joaquin, bounces between a dozen-plus foster homes before moving in with an übercool couple who wants to adopt him.

Benway wrote Joaquin as biracial—his father is Mexican and he shares a white mother with the two sisters—to show how racism plays a part in the world of adoption. Most adoptive parents in the US have a preference for white female infants. In some cases, they'll pay $10,000 more than they would for a male infant of another ethnicity.

Joaquin accepts this truth stoically, in the same way that he's accepted his numerous homes over seventeen years; he tries to blend into each of his new surroundings so that no one knows he's a foster child. "Everyone—neighbors, people at school, the person who bagged their groceries—would just think that he was one of the bio kids, as permanent as blood, someone who could never be traded in, swapped out, sent away," Benway writes.

Being adopted or living in foster care can be hell for a schoolkid. Teachers assign family trees and guide children to create Mother's and Father's Day cards each year. We take for granted that we're all having a similar experience because what we know is our own. But asking an adopted child to trace her family line back to her great-great-grandparents, or giving a foster kid an alternative art project while his or her classmates cut out colorful paper hearts for birth mothers and fathers can be incredibly painful and confusing.

Author Chris Crutcher has worked for decades in Washington State as a counselor specializing in childhood abuse and neglect. His experience has long inspired and informed his award-winning teen novels—books like *Losers Bracket*, about teenage Annie who lives happily with her foster parents before getting sucked back into her birth family's drama, which threatens her well-being and her future.

"I've run into kids with really dysfunctional, scary, dangerous families, and they'll still do whatever they have to do to get back to their original homes," says Crutcher. "If their life has been a horror, it's not necessarily a horror to them—it's just life. The power of familiarity kind of blows my mind."

In one case, a brother and sister who had been removed from a violent home couldn't agree on this point: the sister didn't want to return, but the brother was desperate to be with his father. "I don't know why she doesn't want to go back," the boy told Crutcher. "He didn't kill her."

Counting by 7s and *Far from the Tree* inspire readers—adopted or not—to ponder big questions. Who are we in relation to our family? Are we doomed to repeat our parents' dysfunctions? Are we inextricably linked to our siblings who have shared the same roof? Do we need to resemble family members physically in order to feel connected to them? And who are we if we lack the details of our birth story, the story that those of us who remain with our birth parents through adolescence often take for granted?

My daughter is adopted and biracial. She's a thoroughly happy kid who enjoys relationships with some members of her biological family. She knows the stories of her birth and her adoption. Our whole life together, we've fielded clumsy questions like "Why don't you look like each other?" and "Where's her real mom?" and my personal favorite, "Are you her grandma?"

How wonderful to have novels for all stages of her adolescence narrated by empowered protagonists who represent a variety of experiences that can help her identify and process her emotions. It is, after all, a bit too simple to say "Home is where the heart is" and leave it at that. The truth is, many preteens and teens have pieces of their hearts in many homes.

After *Counting by 7s* was published, Holly Goldberg Sloan began receiving letters from adoptive and foster kids who told her how the book reflected their deep fears of being unwanted and unloved, but also offered comfort and affirmation of their emotions. "It's a very scary thing to lose your parents," she says.

Scary, too, that the older her readers get, the less likely they are to be adopted into a permanent home.

Far from the Tree takes a hard look at this truth—at what happens when a kid like Joaquin ages out of the system—a fate that befalls more than twenty thousand real eighteen-year-olds in the US each year. Older foster youth are entitled to a couple years of financial assistance before they're sent into the world completely on their own, but this is often without knowing how to open and maintain a checking account, rent an apartment, or fill out a financial aid application for college.

Is it any wonder that half of former foster youth become homeless six months after leaving the system—why a quarter of them opt for life on the streets? *Far from the Tree* and *Counting by 7s* illustrate just how important it is to ensure that kids of all races, ethnicities, and gender identities have a place to call home.

One of Sloan's goals was to address the strong identity politics she finds influential in the world today: "We've reverted to almost a kind of tribalism. Looking at how we're different is not the answer to creating community—we find humanity by discovering what we share."

She believes children's literature can have a profound affect. "Young people often don't have solidly formed ideas about identity, community, and about what we need to do to make ourselves bigger and better," Sloan says. "When we read a book, we identify with characters who grow and come out the other side of the story with a different understanding of what it means to be human."

For her own part, Leyda Garcia-Greenawalt—now in her early twenties—would love to see more novels about teenagers who go through the foster care system and end up getting adopted. Five years after she walked through the door of her eighth placement—after she received a life-saving memoir with the words "You *have* to read this book"—her foster parents filed for permanent adoption.

The local newspaper printed a photo of Leyda and her mother and father posing in Chicago Cubs caps, smiling broadly. In the photo, they look joyful . . . intimate.

They look like a family.

PRETEEN BOOKS ABOUT ADOPTION AND FOSTER CARE

ALL RISE FOR THE HONORABLE PERRY T. COOK by Leslie Connor (Katherine Tegen Books, 2016). Eleven-year-old Perry lives with his mother at a correctional facility. She is up for parole, but the district attorney opposes it. The attorney insists that Perry move into foster care, and the boy fights to return to his mother and understand her crime, then get the court to grant her appeal.

ALMOST HOME by Joan Bauer (Viking, 2012). Twelve-year-old Sugar moves into a foster home after her father takes off to gamble, and she and her mother become homeless. Sugar learns to deal with loss thanks to a rescue dog, a teacher who supports her, and a new love of poetry.

ASHES TO ASHEVILLE by Sarah Dooley (G. P. Putnam's Sons, 2017). After one of her mothers dies, twelve-year-old Fella is forced to leave her remaining mother and sixteen-year-old sister, Zany, to live with her grandmother. Zany retrieves Fella in the middle of the night, and they journey with a charismatic poodle on a disaster-filled road trip to scatter their mother's ashes in Asheville, North Carolina.

BO AT BALLARD CREEK by Kirkpatrick Hill (Henry Holt, 2013). Two gold miners raise Alaskan orphan Bo with the help of people from the nearby Inuit village in this historical novel set just after the Gold Rush.

COUNTING BY 7s by Holly Goldberg Sloan (Dial Books, 2013). Twelve-year-old nature-obsessed Willow Chance loses her adoptive parents in a car accident and gathers together a surprising new family thanks to her charismatic kindness.

DREAM OF NIGHT by Heather Henson (Atheneum Books for Young Readers, 2010). Eleven-year-old Shiloh, who's been abused and traumatized, bounces around between foster homes and ends up on a farm where she gets to know a former racehorse that was also abused. Together, they learn to trust each other and the woman who cares for them both.

FAST BREAK by Mike Lupica (Philomel Books, 2015). After twelve-year-old Jason's mother dies, he avoids the foster care system and retreats to his favorite place—the old basketball court behind the projects in North Carolina. When he gets caught stealing a pair of shoes, he's forced to move in with a foster family that can help him realize his dream of playing college basketball.

FINDING FAMILY by Tonya Bolden (Bloomsbury, 2010). Twelve-year-old Delana searches for the truth about her family after the great-aunt who raised her dies. With the author's own antique photos serving as inspiration, this story details Delana's grandfather's life after the emancipation of slaves, how her mother died in childbirth, and the discovery that the father she's never met is still alive.

FOREVER, OR A LONG, LONG TIME by Caela Carter (Harper, 2017). Eleven-year-old Flora and her little brother, Julian, who have grown up in a series of foster homes, find adoptive parents at last. When their adoptive mother gets pregnant and Flora reacts with fear and anger, they—along with Julian—take a road trip to visit their previous foster homes and caregivers.

HALF A WORLD AWAY by Cynthia Kadohata (Atheneum Books for Young Readers, 2014). Adopted eleven-year-old Jaden is full of rage and can't seem to stop lighting fires and stealing. When he and his parents travel to Kazakhstan for an infant that's mistakenly been adopted already, he finds himself captivated by three-year-old Dimash, who is in danger of aging out of the orphanage and facing a bleak future.

HOPE IN THE HOLLER by Lisa Lewis Tyre (Nancy Paulsen Books, 2018). After Wavie B. Conley's mother dies, she must move to a poor Kentucky neighborhood and live with her aunt, who only wants the money from her deceased mother's social security check. Wavie relies on her mother's advice to be brave—she makes new friends and defies her aunt's attempts to become her legal guardian.

KINDA LIKE BROTHERS by Coe Booth (Scholastic Press, 2014). Jarrett's mother, who cares for babies in the foster care system, makes him share a room with Kevon, a foster kid his own age. Kevon acts like he's better than Jarrett, and he definitely has secrets to hide, but somehow, the boys must find a way to get along—and even try to like one another.

THE MISADVENTURES OF THE FAMILY FLETCHER by Dana Alison Levy (Delacorte Press, 2014). Two dads and their four adopted kids celebrate life and navigate school adventures as a multiracial family while struggling with the constant complaints of their elderly, miserable next-door neighbor.

MY FAMILY FOR THE WAR by Anne C. Voorhoeve (Dial Books, 2012). Ten-year-old Franziska Mangold is one of ten thousand children taken by train out of Nazi Germany at the beginning of World War II after she is attacked by bullies and her father is beaten. In England, living with a new family, she questions her identity and confusing feelings of guilt and love for her adoptive parents.

NINTH WARD by Jewell Parker Rhodes (Little, Brown Books for Young Readers, 2010). Motherless twelve-year-old Lanesha lives in the Ninth Ward of New Orleans with her caretaker, Mama Ya-Ya, who can predict the future and sees visions of a powerful hurricane. Lanesha must find reserves of strength and optimism to help them both survive Hurricane Katrina.

ORPHAN ISLAND by Laurel Snyder (Walden Pond Press, 2017). Every year, a boat comes to the child-only island on which Jinny lives to bring a new young orphan and take away the oldest. Faced with losing her best friend, Jinny breaks a rule and causes the island—which has previously protected the children—to become inhospitable and dangerous.

PAPER CHAINS by Elaine Vickers (Harper, 2017). Fifth-grader Katie, adopted from Russia as a baby, lives life timidly because of a heart transplant. Her friend Ana—a gregarious athlete—has a Russian grandmother who moves in with her family after Ana's father leaves to become a professional hockey player and her mother sinks into depression.

PATINA by Jason Reynolds (Atheneum/Caitlyn Dlouhy Books, 2017). Twelve-year-old Patina, a competitive runner, leaves her urban neighborhood and moves in with her black uncle and white aunt. She attends a school with wealthy classmates and finds herself challenging her own assumptions after working on a group project about Frida Kahlo and making the relay team.

RED BUTTERFLY by A. L. Sonnichsen (Simon & Schuster Books for Young Readers, 2015). In this story told in verse, Kara—a child with a malformed hand—is abandoned as an infant in China and informally adopted by American parents living in the country. When police discover Kara, they deport her mother and send her to an orphanage for disabled children, where a new family hopes to adopt her.

SARA LOST AND FOUND by Virginia Castleman (Archway Publishing, 2014). Twelve-year-old Anna and ten-year-old Sara are sisters who will likely be separated by the foster care system after their mother leaves and their father is sent to jail. They're caught trying to run away, and Sara finds herself having to take care of her troubled older sister while wondering how to best care for herself.

STRAYS LIKE US by Cecilia Galante (Scholastic Press, 2018). Fred wants to rescue an abused dog from the owner next door, but her foster mother forbids her to go to his house. She tries not to care about the suffering dog or her foster mother—or even her new classmate who wants to be her friend—because she could move back in with her mentally ill mother at any time.

SUMMER OF THE GYPSY MOTHS by Sara Pennypacker (Balzer + Bray, 2012). Eleven-year-old Stella misses her mother; still, she lives happily at her great-aunt Louise's house on Cape Cod. When Louise takes in a tough foster girl named Angel and then dies, Stella and Angel band together to hide the fact of her death with the shared longing for a real family.

THREE PENNIES by Melanie Crowder (Atheneum Books for Young Readers, 2017). Eleven-year-old Marin lives in a series of foster homes, taking three pennies and a copy of the *I Ching* with her as she searches for her birth mother to convince her that they're meant to be together. She finds a family that feels like the perfect fit and discovers the painful truth about her biological mother.

THE WAR THAT SAVED MY LIFE by Kimberly Brubaker Bradley (Dial Books for Young Readers, 2015). In the midst of World War II, ten-year-old Ada leaves her abusive mother's tiny London apartment to move in with her brother and a reclusive woman who cares for them and teaches Ada to read and ride a pony.

THE WAY THE LIGHT BENDS by Cordelia Jensen (Philomel Books, 2018). In this novel in verse, Linc watches with longing as her sister Holly—adopted from Ghana—pleases their surgeon mother with her constant academic success. Linc's photo project based on Seneca Village (what's now Central Park) uncovers a secret that gives her new insight into her mother.

WHEN FRIENDSHIP FOLLOWED ME HOME by Paul Griffin (Dial Books, 2016). Twelve-year-old former foster child Ben doesn't make friends easily; he prefers to read. His life changes when he meets a charismatic dog who leads him to a fellow book lover named Halley. She asks him to coauthor a book with her while she's fighting cancer.

TEEN BOOKS ABOUT ADOPTION AND FOSTER CARE

ALLEGEDLY by Tiffany D. Jackson (Katherine Tegen Books, 2017). Sixteen-year-old Mary B. Addison, incarcerated for the alleged murder of a baby, moves into a group home. A missing birth certificate keeps her from taking the SATs to get into college, and then she gets pregnant; since her boyfriend also lives in a group home, the state insists on putting the child up for adoption.

A CHANCE IN THE WORLD by Steve Pemberton (Thomas Nelson, 2012). This memoir is about the author's experience of being taken from his mother at age three and put into foster care, where he suffers constant abuse. In a box of donated books, he finds inspiration to survive, and eventually goes on a journey to understand his identity and locate his birth family.

COMPROMISED by Heidi Ayarbe (HarperTeen, 2010). After fifteen-year-old Maya's con-man father gets thrown in prison, she runs away from a foster placement and heads for a long-lost aunt's house in Idaho. When she meets up with two other runaways, she finds herself questioning both her passion for scientific laws and her ability to live on her own.

FAR FROM THE TREE by Robin Benway (HarperTeen, 2017). Sixteen-year-old Grace, who has just put her infant up for adoption, meets her fifteen-year-old birth sister, who is dealing with her dysfunctional adopted family. Together they find their biological half brother, seventeen-year-old Joaquin, who has lived in a series of foster homes before finding a couple who wants to permanently adopt him.

GOODBYE, SARAJANE: A FOSTER CHILD WRITES LETTERS TO HER MOTHER by Sequoya Griffin (Key Purpose Books, 2017). The author is a former foster child who writes letters to her birth mother, whom she hasn't seen since she was ten years old. She details what she calls her "spiritual confinement" after she leaves Las Vegas to live with her adoptive family in upstate New York.

GREETINGS FROM WITNESS PROTECTION! by Jake Burt (Feiwel and Friends, 2017). After her father is arrested, Nicki Demere is placed in foster care, and she is asked by FBI agents to participate in a program that matches foster kids with families under witness protection. Nicki develops new friendships and vows to keep her new family safe, but her past actions threaten their safety and hers.

HOW TO SAVE A LIFE by Sara Zarr (Little, Brown Books for Young Readers, 2011). After seventeen-year-old Jill MacSweeny's father dies, she isolates herself from her support system and regards with anger her mother's plan to adopt a baby. Her mother invites pregnant nineteen-year-old Mandy Kalinowski into their home as part of the open adoption process, and Mandy begins to heal from sexual assault.

IF ONLY by Jennifer Gilmore (HarperTeen, 2018). Sixteen-year-old Bridget is pregnant and struggling with whether or not to raise her baby as a single mother. Sixteen years later, her birth daughter Ivy, adopted by two mothers, embarks on a journey to find Bridget, but wonders if finding out the truth about why her mother relinquished her will do her more harm than good.

JANE UNLIMITED by Kristin Cashore (Kathy Dawson Books, 2017). When Jane's aunt dies, leaving her alone, she accepts an invitation from a wealthy and mysterious acquaintance to visit an island mansion. The house offers her the ability to live in a spy thriller, a gothic horror story, a heist mystery, a fantasy realm, and a space opera . . . but each choice is incredibly risky.

THE LENGTH OF A STRING by Elissa Brent Weissman (Dial Books, 2018). Imani Mandel, Jewish and adopted, wants to search for her birth parents. She is troubled by the fact that she is black and almost everyone she knows is white. When she reads her great-grandmother's diary entries about fleeing the Holocaust in Europe and moving in with an adoptive family in Brooklyn, Imani gains a new understanding of herself and her adoptive family.

A LIST OF CAGES by Robin Roe (Disney-Hyperion, 2017). Shy high school freshman Julian reconnects with senior Adam Blake— the foster brother with ADHD whom he hasn't seen for five years. As an aide to the school psychologist, Adam is determined to help the younger boy free himself of an abusive home life . . . and then Julian disappears.

LOSERS BRACKET by Chris Crutcher (Greenwillow Books, 2018). After Annie Boots is removed once again from her biological mother, she signs up for numerous high school sports so that her mother can still see her, causing difficulties for her foster family. When her nephew goes missing, Annie works with her foster brother and social services to place him in a safe home.

LOVE ME, LOVE ME NOT by S. M. Koz (Swoon Reads, 2018). After authorities put Hailey Brown into foster care, she finds herself becoming attracted to her foster brother. But as she acclimates to her new school and develops a vision for her future, the romance threatens both her happiness and her safety.

MY LIFE WITH THE WALTER BOYS by Ali Novak (Sourcebooks Fire, 2014). After Jackie Howard's family dies in a car accident, she must move across the country from New York City to a Colorado ranch to live with a foster family and their dozen wild and annoying children. While there, her type A personality undergoes a transformation, and she falls in love.

ONE FOR THE MURPHYS by Lynda Mullaly Hunt (Nancy Paulsen Books, 2012). When Carly moves in with the Murphys as a foster child, she's dismayed by their loving and perfect household. Just when she begins to let down her guard and feel like she might belong with them, her mother wants her back, and Carly must decide where she wants to live.

ORBITING JUPITER by Gary D. Schmidt (Clarion Books, 2015). Thirteen-year-old Joseph has a traumatic past and a baby he's never seen. After time in a juvenile institution, he's placed with a foster family on a farm in Maine. There he meets twelve-year-old Jack and begins to feel supported thanks to his foster parents and middle school teachers, though he longs to find his child.

PEAS AND CARROTS by Tanita S. Davis (Knopf Books for Young Readers, 2016). White fifteen-year-old Dess and black fifteen-year-old Hope become foster sisters who are resentful of each other at first. Dess worries about being mistaken as racist and Hope feels alone after her best friend moves away. Eventually, the two girls learn to trust and care about one another.

THE PROBLEM WITH FOREVER by Jennifer L. Armentrout (Harlequin Teen, 2016). After a series of grim foster homes, Mallory is placed with kind adoptive parents who homeschool her for years. When she decides to attend public high school, she encounters Rider—her former foster brother who helped her avoid abuse—and finds herself struggling to help him in return.

THIS IS THE PART WHERE YOU LAUGH by Peter Brown Hoffmeister (Alfred A. Knopf, 2016). When Travis's heroin-addicted mother abandons him, he suffers in foster care before being taken in by his grandparents. Violent and economically deprived, he defaults to aggression.

WHEN MY HEART JOINS THE THOUSAND by A. J. Steiger (HarperTeen, 2018). Seventeen-year-old Alvie, who has Asperger's syndrome, runs away from foster care and works at a zoo with a one-winged hawk. She meets physically fragile Stanley, who walks with a cane and falls in love with her. His affection terrifies Alvie so deeply that she loses her job and becomes homeless.

WRONG IN ALL THE RIGHT WAYS by Tiffany Brownlee (Henry Holt, 2018). When AP high school student Emma and her new foster brother fall in love, they must hide their feelings so that he'll be adopted into a good home. Their passionate and secret love affair has echoes of the novel Emma is studying in English class—*Wuthering Heights*.

2

BOOKS ABOUT BODY IMAGE

T he first time my daughter opened an issue of *Kazoo Magazine*, she flipped through the pages for an hour, then looked up at me with her brow furrowed. "Where are the photos?" she asked.

She's used to glossy magazines with full-color photos of kids or adults or animals—not *Kazoo*'s whimsical illustrations of girls and women at work and play in the world. But founder and editor-in-chief Erin Bried, who spent twenty years working for major magazines, knew exactly what she was doing when she opted against photography for the publication that caters to preteen girls.

"We don't show photos of real girls in *Kazoo*, because I want our readers to have the opportunity to get completely lost in their own experiences," she explains. "I didn't want them to have to compare their experience to anyone else's and therefore feel that there's a right—and wrong—way to look or feel or act. So much of our media, print and otherwise, tells girls and women how they should look and act, and our mission is to celebrate them for being smart, strong, fierce and, above all, true to themselves, whatever that may be."

Artists illustrate the articles and stories by well-known scientists, artists, authors, chefs, and others as though the adult experts featured in the pages of *Kazoo* were still girls, with inspiration drawn from their childhood photos. Bried says this helps readers more easily see themselves in these future positions of power. She's hoping preteens will study the pictures and think to themselves, *What does a future astronaut/chef/athlete/artist/engineer look like? She looks just like me!*

Kazoo's website offers stark information about the vulnerability of preteen girls. By age eleven, 30 percent of girls have made themselves diet, and 60 percent stop doing what they love because they're embarrassed by how they look. That sort of self-censorship is heartbreaking.

According to my sixth-grader, the worst thing you can call a girl is "chubby." Somehow, despite the dance school I chose because of the body-positive teachers who embrace all shapes and sizes, despite the focus my husband and I put on people's personalities and actions rather than their appearance, my daughter has gotten the message that fat equals bad. At a sleepover last summer, she and her friends sat around and compared their most disliked body parts. Invariably, these parts were round—the hips and buttocks of pubescent girls.

Where are they getting this message that roundness is ugly and undesirable? Television and movies? Magazines less mindful than *Kazoo* of girls' body image vulnerabilities? Chance comments from family members and friends?

I myself still sting from a careless remark made decades ago by one of my parents when I was twelve: my younger sister asked what cellulite was and received the response, "Cellulite is what Melissa has on her thighs." Is it any wonder that I nearly ran myself into the ground on my high school track and cross-country teams, trying to escape from what I perceived to be a moral failing?

We are a nation that demonizes fat, equating it with weakness and sloth and ignorance. Even very young children show concerns about their physical appearance. In 2015, Common Sense Media released a report based on dozens of studies that examined the connection between mainstream media consumption and body image, finding that the appearance and weight of characters in children's media are generally "gendered, stereotypical, and unrealistic." Many of the studies cited indicate that an alarming preponderance of children—as young as five years old—long to be thinner than they are.

Writer and former psychotherapist Emily Mendez has worked with teens who struggle with body issues and eating disorders. As "therapeutic homework," she recommends K. A. Barson's teen novel *45 Pounds (More or Less)*, the story of a sixteen-year-old girl, Ann, who's a size 17 and decides to lose forty-five pounds for a wedding. Eventually she realizes that she and her size 6 mother have an unhealthy relationship to food. That discovery helps Ann make positive changes and develop a healthier approach to eating; she also learns to feel more comfortable in her own skin. "It's an excellent read," Mendez says, "and a book that I really like for teens who are struggling with body issues and/or eating disorders."

Clients relate in particular to Ann's struggles with emotional eating. "Reading about her experiencing real growth and empowerment by making small changes throughout the book was most helpful and inspirational for my clients," Mendez continues. "Novels that cater to preteens and teens can increase readers' empathy for themselves and their peers when the characters and their struggles are relatable and real. *45 Pounds (More or Less)* does a great job of that."

Author Julie Murphy dedicated her *New York Times*–bestselling teen novel *Dumplin'* to all the "fat-bottomed girls" in a nod to British rock band Queen and their hit song of the same name. Willowdean Dickson, nicknamed Dumplin' by her former beauty queen mother, introduces herself to her handsome coworker Bo as "cashier, Dolly Parton enthusiast, and resident fat girl."

The word *fat*, she observes, causes discomfort in people. "But when you see me, the first thing you notice is my body," she explains. "And my body is fat. It's like how I notice some girls have big boobs or shiny hair or knobby knees. Those things are okay to say. But the word *fat*, the one that best describes me, makes lips frown and cheeks lose their color."

The novel is undeniably body positive. Still, Willowdean struggles with society's stigma against fat. Her best friend's coworkers make mean-spirited comments. Willowdean herself worries about whether the boy she adores will recoil when he touches her lumpy thighs and back fat. Still, ultimately, her self-confidence prevails. She competes in her town's annual beauty pageant and learns to own her body and its desires.

As in so many other novels for this audience, the protagonist triumphs because of self-regard and friendships based on kindness and respect. Willowdean has not only a traditionally beautiful thin bestie but a cadre of other friends—fat girls, girls with therapeutic shoes and bad teeth—who support her. She also finds allies in the star football player and in her handsome coworker. *Dumplin'* shows readers that all of these people, too, have insecurities—they're likewise deeply conflicted as they search for their own intrinsic value.

But weight isn't the only body image concern that plagues kids. Children with a clubfoot or a birthmark, with "Coke bottle" glasses, or who use a cane or wheelchair or hearing aids, or a facial difference—they all cringe at some point or another over having such visible differences from their peers.

At a certain point, most kids just want to blend in. Plenty of contemporary tween and teen novels examine the issue of body image apart from the discussion of weight, offering a much-needed challenge to the prevalence of gorgeous white blemish-free models still dominating mainstream media.

Physical appearance informs every aspect of An Na's novel *The Fold* within the context of a story about racially stereotyped beauty. Na's protagonist, Korean American high school junior Joyce Park, longs to be seen as beautiful like the white girls favored by her crush. Her newly wealthy aunt offers to pay for eyelid surgery so that she'll have a fold instead of a monolid. Initially excited, Joyce feels more and more conflicted as she sees what happens to family members who've been the recipients of her aunt's financial endowments.

Joyce's mother gets permanent eyebrow tattoos and suffers a dramatic allergic reaction that causes her face to swell up. Her brother takes shark liver pills in hopes of growing taller and instead suffers nasty side effects. Her father tries to walk in the elevator shoes gifted by the aunt and sprains his ankle. Throughout *The Fold*, teen readers will think about who determines what's attractive, and what kind of power they themselves give over to media standards of beauty.

Whenever Na speaks with Korean American and Asian American students about her book, she hears nervous and

sympathetic laughter—especially from girls. "They understand the pressure to fit in and assimilate. We will talk about
eye makeup and they will chime in with their own stories.
They move from that place of nervousness to a place of comfort and shared experience."

As a child, Na longed to see herself and her particular
experiences represented in stories. She's now the mother of
two daughters who rejoice when they pick up a novel by Grace
Lin and read about Asian families and culture. When her
daughters' experiences are legitimized in this way, the girls
are better able to engage with their peers and understand how
classmates might feel uncomfortable speaking out loud about
their own uncommon experiences.

This is one of the reasons that early on in my own parenting
process, I chose novels to read aloud to my daughter that would
reflect her experiences as a multiracial adopted child who
looks different—and has a different birth story—from a majority
of her peers. Because of our deep reflection on the characters
in these novels, she's better able to articulate the fact of our
multiracial family and her Central American heritage.

We're lucky as caregivers in this century to have an abun-
dance of middle grade and young adult novels that reflect
almost every physical difference a preteen or teen might
experience. The reading lists at the end of this chapter include
books about kids with birthmarks, kids with canes, short kids
and fat kids, girls with facial hair and boys with acne, and kids
like Cece in *El Deafo*, who relies on a mammoth mechanical
device worn around her neck in order to hear.

Cece Bell wrote the graphic novel *El Deafo* based on her
own experiences of growing up hearing impaired after con-
tracting meningitis at age four. Her characters are rabbits—a
conscious choice she made based on the animal's large ears and
incredible hearing. In the book, Bell describes herself as a "regular little kid" who liked to sing and dance around in a polka
dot swimsuit. But after losing her hearing, rabbit-protagonist
Cece can't find effective hearing aids.

Finally, her parents discover the Phonic Ear: teachers and others hold a microphone to be heard, and Cece wears the aid around her neck. The device is impossible to miss. A diagram in the book details all its bells and whistles and captures just how bulky and embarrassing it feels to a child who just wants to fit in with her peer group. At one point a PE teacher drops her microphone and breaks it, and she has to wait weeks for its repair and return—a debacle that puts her at even more of a disadvantage in school and in her social life.

Cece's search for a best friend shares equal time in *El Deafo* with her humiliation about looking different from her peers. Girls in particular react to her obvious physical difference. One bosses and bullies her. Another speaks too loudly, overenunciating, and refers to Cece as "her deaf friend" around other girls.

El Deafo is the name of Cece's alter ego—an outspoken superhero who flies through the air wearing a red cape and the Phonic Ear, the microphone sailing exuberantly out behind her. Still, Cece does just fine on her own. She defies girls at a sleepover who try to give her a makeover, and—in one hilarious scene—kicks her mother in the leg to protest a sign language class. The lesson for readers is that while kids like Cece might appear physically different from their peers, what they crave is camaraderie—not pity. In the end, Cece finds a best friend; readers will discover with delight that the real friendship on which Bell's story is based has indeed lasted decades.

Another graphic novel, Raina Telgemeier's preteen memoir *Smile*, tells the story of how the author as a sixth-grader injures her front teeth and has to wear both humiliating headgear and a retainer with fake teeth. She struggles with self-image and the criticisms of mean girls, as well as with physical pain. Her descriptions are so vivid that I recall the way the metal ends of my own braces cut the tender back of my mouth, and how my head and jaw ached after appointments with the orthodontist, magnifying my perceived ugliness.

What a gift *Smile* is to kids who are also dealing with humiliating orthodontia work or similar physical outrages:

broken bones requiring a bulky cast, scoliosis necessitating a back brace, or—in the case of my own sixth-grader—bifocals. They'll register how Telgemeier's protagonist learns to stand up for herself, calling out unkind friends and growing much more comfortable with her appearance and talents and interests.

Friends matter desperately to protagonists in tween and teen novels about body image—the characters measure their value through the eyes of their peers, reflecting their real-life counterparts. So many of these stories offer insight into how scared and shy and awkward a kid with an obvious physical difference might feel; they teach children and young adults to look past outward appearances and advocate ferociously for each other.

One of the most talked about of these novels is R. J. Palacio's preteen novel *Wonder*. This is the story of ten-year-old August "Auggie" Pullman, who has been homeschooled his whole life because of a congenital facial difference and resulting surgeries. He's attending public school for the first time, and readers feel his trepidation deeply, along with his desire to blend in and learn and find friends who aren't constantly focused on his face.

Auggie does make friends, but not without struggle and a challenge to his already frail self-image. In the end, he learns to appreciate his intelligence and talents and begins to focus less on his physical appearance and more on forging positive relationships with the people around him.

Young people who read novels with body image as a central focus gain empathy for others, but they also gain empathy for themselves. When they're able to relate to peers with exposed vulnerabilities, they're empowered to reframe their own perceived limitations as well. As An Na says, "Stories are such lifelines for those who feel alone, misunderstood, and marginalized. They allow us to connect with ourselves and with others."

As I write this, my sixth-grader has quite literally surrounded herself with preteen novels. She's built a fortress of sorts on her bedroom carpet, the books stacked six deep. Every evening she sits down in the middle of the square to read until long past her bedtime.

If a fortress is a stronghold, fortified to defend against assault, then the novels she's reading may just keep her safe as she enters the treacherous world of middle school. Hers are books about mixed-race characters, and children with glasses or braces or who use wheelchairs, and kids who choose to sport rainbow-hued hair or no hair at all. Above all, they are stories in which kindness and resilience triumph, regardless of how someone looks.

"So what did *you* name at that sleepover last summer when the girls talked about the body parts they didn't like?" I asked her recently.

She furrowed her brow. "I like my body," she replied. "But I told my friends that sometimes I don't like my clothes." She hugged me. "You know, Mom, I'm old enough to go shopping for my own outfits by myself."

I hugged her back, relieved. All those body-positive conversations, those dance classes, those issues of *Kazoo*, must have paid off.

Still, now she wanted to go clothes shopping? Without me?

But that's a different story.

PRETEEN BOOKS ABOUT BODY IMAGE

BEAUTIFUL: A GIRL'S TRIP THROUGH THE LOOKING GLASS by Marie D'Abreo (Far Out Press, 2014). In this graphic novel, average-looking Lizzy with unruly hair longs to look like a model so she can attract her crush. After she decides to get a makeover with unwanted results, she learns that she looks beautiful just the way she is.

A BLIND GUIDE TO STINKVILLE by Beth Vrabel (Sky Pony Press, 2015). Middle school student Alice is albino and nearly blind, relying on a cane and a guide dog. When her parents move her to Stinkville and start researching schools for the visually impaired, she enters a community writing contest to prove her worth and explores her new city with her dog.

BRAVE by Svetlana Chmakova (JY, 2017). Overweight junior high student Jensen longs to be a hero and help people, but he struggles with friendship and bullies. When two kids from the school newspaper entice him with social-experiment projects and tales of interpersonal relationships behind the scenes, he's called upon to find true courage.

CALEB AND KIT by Beth Vrabel (Running Press Kids, 2017). Overprotected twelve-year-old Caleb, who has cystic fibrosis, finds his world expanding and growing more complicated after he meets a mysterious and exciting girl who says they're destined for friendship.

COSMIC by Frank Cottrell Boyce (Walden Pond Press, 2010). Twelve-year-old Liam—extremely tall and with premature facial hair—struggles with being constantly mistaken for an adult, and ends up chaperoning a group of friends on the first civilian spaceship.

DEAR OPL by Shelley Sackier (Sourcebooks Jabberwocky, 2015). After eighth-grader Opl's father dies, she finds herself gaining weight and works out her grief in a blog. She experiments with both cooking and yoga and resists her mother's pressure to diet until she receives a frightening diagnosis from her doctor that leads her to more healthful eating.

EL DEAFO by Cece Bell (Amulet Books, 2014). In this graphic novel, preteen Cece overcomes the humiliation of having to wear an enormous hearing aid, while struggling against her mother's expectations. She works through a series of failed friendships because of the bulky device advertising her impairment, and then finds a girl who becomes her lifelong friend.

GARVEY'S CHOICE by Nikki Grimes (WordSong, 2016). In this novel told in verse, Garvey is overweight and bullied, but his singing talent provides a way to connect with both his father and his tormentors.

HUSKY by Justin Sayre (Grosset & Dunlap, 2015). The summer before middle school, twelve-year-old opera-loving Davis feels excluded from friends and family in his Brooklyn neighborhood. His mother starts to date again, and he tries to assert his independence from his grandmother while trying to see himself as something other than "the fat kid."

INSIGNIFICANT EVENTS IN THE LIFE OF A CACTUS by Dusti Bowling (Sterling Children's Books, 2017). Eighth-grader Aven Green, born without arms, has never had an issue with her body and her abilities. But when she moves with her family across the country to an Arizona theme park, she finds herself chafing against peers' questions and stares until she befriends Connor, a boy with Tourette's syndrome.

JANE, THE FOX, AND ME by Fanny Britt (Groundwood Books, 2013). Eleven-year-old Hélène deals with her loneliness and negative self-image by immersing herself in *Jane Eyre* until she's humiliated on a class camping trip and then shares a life-changing connection with a fox.

KARMA KHULLAR'S MUSTACHE by Kristi Wientge (Simon & Schuster Books for Young Readers, 2017). Karma Khullar, a middle schooler with an interracial family of Sikh faith, struggles with friendships, bullying, and unwanted facial hair as well as parents too distracted to notice her mounting concerns about body image and her best friend's sudden passion for fashion.

THE SECOND LIFE OF ABIGAIL WALKER by Frances O'Roark Dowell (Atheneum Books for Young Readers, 2012). After Abby ostracizes school bullies for taunting her about her weight, she meets a homeschooled boy and finds hope in helping his veteran father research a poem about the Lewis and Clark expedition.

SHORT by Holly Goldberg Sloan (Dial Books, 2017). After a director casts Julia—several inches shorter than her peers—as a munchkin in a production of Oz, she discovers her true talent with the help of an actress with dwarfism.

SKINNY by Donna Cooner (Point, 2012). Fifteen-year-old Ever Davies, whose mother has died, undergoes gastric bypass surgery in hopes of landing the part of Cinderella in the high school musical and attracting the attention of a boy. As she begins to lose weight, she takes an interest in other people and finds that her feelings of worthlessness are beginning to fade.

SMILE by Raina Telgemeier (Graphix, 2010). This graphic memoir tells the story of the author in sixth grade after she injures her front teeth and struggles with dental work and headgear, friendships, and new romantic interests.

STICKS AND STONES by Abby Cooper (Farrar Straus Giroux Books for Young Readers, 2016). Sixth-grader Elyse has an illness that causes the words that people use to describe her to appear on her skin in a painful rash; when a stranger offers help, she gains self-esteem and accepts herself for who she is.

TAKING FLIGHT: FROM WAR ORPHAN TO STAR BALLERINA by Michaela DePrince (Alfred A. Knopf, 2014). Professional ballerina Michaela DePrince tells of being orphaned and abused because of a skin condition, then adopted by a family who supported her love of dance.

UGLY by Robert Hoge (Viking, 2016). This illustrated memoir by an Australian author describes life as a child born with deformed legs and a tumor in the middle of his face; he deals with bullies, and decides—after multiple surgeries—not to have any more operations.

THE UGLY ONE by Leanne Statland Ellis (Clarion Books, 2013). Twelve-year-old Micay is bullied and ignored in her sixteenth-century Incan village because of a scar that runs from her eye to her lip, but her life changes for the better when a stranger gives her a baby macaw.

WONDER by R. J. Palacio (Alfred A. Knopf, 2012). When ten-year-old August Pullman—born with a congenital facial difference—attends public school for the first time, he navigates gossip and bullies and learns the meaning of true friendship.

ZITFACE by Emily Howse (Marshall Cavendish, 2011). Thirteen-year-old Olivia Hughes lands a national ad campaign that puts her on the path to becoming an actress when she develops a serious case of acne and loses both her boyfriend and her job.

TEEN BOOKS ABOUT BODY IMAGE

BIG GIRL SMALL by Rachel DeWoskin (Farrar, Straus and Giroux, 2011). Sixteen-year-old Judy Lohden is three feet, nine inches tall with a powerful voice and a coveted spot at an arts academy, but she finds her dreams of stardom challenged by misogyny and scandal and flees school to hide from television cameras in a sordid hotel room.

BIGGIE by Derek E. Sullivan (Albert Whitman & Company, 2015). Obese high school student Henry, the son of a baseball star, pitches a perfect game in a PE Wiffle ball match. He's determined to lose eighty pounds and work on his curveball so that he can attract a girl named Annabelle, who flirts with him until she finds out that he's been hacking into her email account.

BURNING BLUE by Paul Griffin (Dial Books, 2012). After Nicole Castro's beautiful face is scarred by an acid attack, her classmate ostracized for his seizures commits to helping her find out who perpetrated the crime and why.

BUTTER by Erin Jade Lange (Bloomsbury Children's Books, 2012). High school junior Butter weighs 423 pounds, and the girl of his dreams won't even look at him. He finds himself part of the in-crowd after he invites classmates to watch him eat himself to death live on the internet, then he begins to realize that the kids supporting his endeavor are just as mean as those who bullied him in the past.

CAMP UTOPIA AND THE FORGIVENESS DIET by Jenny Ruden (Koehler Books, 2014). Sixteen-year-old Bethany tries a bizarre diet that fails and has to spend a summer at a fat camp across the country—until she decides to run away.

THE DARK DAYS OF HAMBURGER HALPIN by Josh Berk (Alfred A. Knopf, 2010). This witty novel is about overweight deaf teen Will Halpin, who reluctantly agrees to help a fellow misfit student solve the mystery of a popular jock's death while on a field trip to a defunct coal mine.

A DIFFERENT ME by Deborah Blumenthal (Albert Whitman Company, 2014). Fifteen-year-old Allie decides—with support of friends in an online chat room—to get plastic surgery on her nose, but she reconsiders after she's asked to mentor a popular girl at school and finds herself targeted by a strange boy who likes to photograph people when they're least attractive.

DUMPLIN' by Julie Murphy (Balzer + Bray, 2015). Sixteen-year-old Willowdean is a fat girl with a domineering mother who heads the local beauty pageant. Willowdean's always been comfortable with who she is until she falls in love with a handsome coworker and loses her best friend. With a group of confidently eccentric girls and help from a drag queen, she reasserts her self-worth.

ELEANOR & PARK by Rainbow Rowell (St. Martin's Griffin, 2013). Sixteen-year-old Eleanor, embarrassed by her weight and her crazy red hair, finds true love—and escape from an abusive stepfather—with a boy after they begin exchanging 1980s mixed tapes.

ELENA VANISHING by Elena Dunkle (Chronicle Books, 2015). Seventeen-year-old overachiever Elena Dunkle battles anorexia in and out of treatment centers, and describes her illness in raw and powerful detail in this memoir cowritten with her mother.

FAT CAT by Robin Brande (Knopf Books for Young Readers, 2009). Fat, brilliant teen Catherine Locke gives up cars and computers and processed foods for a science fair experiment, hoping to get into the college of her choice and outshine the science class rival who broke her heart.

THE FOLD by An Na (G. P. Putnam's Sons, 2008). When an aunt offers high school junior Joyce Park the opportunity to have eye surgery to add folds to her monolids, Joyce must grapple with her desire to look like an Anglo-American beauty along with her fear of pain.

FOOD, GIRLS, AND OTHER THINGS I CAN'T HAVE by Allen Zadoff (Egmont USA, 2009). Fat high school sophomore Andy is recruited for the football team, and his previous life as a bullied teen gives way to popularity and a girlfriend. He abandons his friend's plans to be a team at Model UN meetings but figures out a way to maintain his integrity in the midst of peer manipulation.

45 POUNDS (MORE OR LESS) by K. A. Barson (Viking, 2013). Sixteen-year-old Ann Galardi wants to lose forty-five pounds for a wedding, but she becomes comfortable as she is after failed diet plans and dance lessons—plus revelations about her mother, who isn't as perfect as she seems.

FUTURE PERFECT by Jen Larsen (HarperTeen, 2015). Senior Ashley Perkins longs to go to Harvard for medical school, but her grandmother agrees to pay for college only if she gets weight-loss surgery. Though Ashley is tempted to decline, she finds herself considering who she really is and what she wants to do with her life.

GOLDEN BOY by Tara Sullivan (G. P. Putnam's Sons, 2013). Thirteen-year-old Habo has white skin, yellow hair, and light eyes, unlike the rest of the Tanzanian villagers. When his father leaves and the rest of his family is forced out, they travel across the Serengeti to an aunt's house, where Habo learns he's albino and in danger of being killed by a terrifying man with a machete.

HOLD ME CLOSER: THE TINY COOPER STORY by David Levithan (Dutton Juvenille, 2015). This companion novel to *Will Grayson, Will Grayson* is told through the full script of the musical first introduced there. The story follows fat gay teen protagonist Tiny as he navigates eighteen different boyfriends and a homophobic coach with the help of his straight best friend, Phil.

HOLDING UP THE UNIVERSE by Jennifer Niven (Alfred A. Knopf, 2016). High school student Libby Strout—renown for her obesity and aching over her mother's death—bonds with a popular teen boy after both must complete counseling and community service for a game gone terribly wrong.

NORTH OF BEAUTIFUL by Justina Chen Headley (Little, Brown Books for Young Readers, 2009). Terra Cooper has a birthmark on one cheek and a bullying father; she plans to escape both at college until she befriends a Chinese goth boy with a cleft lip and finds herself in China looking for his birth mother.

ONLY EVER YOURS by Louise O'Neill (Quercus, 2015). Sixteen-year-olds Freida and Isabel must remain two of the most beautiful girls in their year to avoid being concubines in this dystopian story complicated by Isabel's angst and Freida's struggle for survival.

PURGE by Sarah Darer Littman (Scholastic Press, 2009). Sixteen-year-old Janie, who suffers from bulimia, attempts suicide and finds herself in a rehabilitation center. There she finds herself negotiating difficult relationships with other teens who have eating disorders. Supportive parents and friends help her to see that she's genuinely ill and needs treatment.

THE SCAR BOYS by Len Vlahos (Egmont USA, 2014). High school student Harry Jones writes a college application essay in which he describes how he was bullied and badly scarred by fire, and then met a boy named Johnny, who offered him friendship and purpose in the form of a guitar and a punk rock band.

THE STONE GIRL by Alyssa B. Sheinmel (Knopf Books for Young Readers, 2012). Teen Sethie Weiss weighs 111 pounds, and wants to be thinner. She's a perfect student who hides her eating disorders and her cutting until she finds that her boyfriend is using her for sex and drugs. Then, without a best friend and in danger of not getting into college, she must turn to her mother and officials at her school.

THIS IMPOSSIBLE LIGHT by Lily Myers (Philomel Books, 2017). This novel in verse tells the story of fifteen-year-old Ivy, who develops an eating disorder after her father moves out and her mother becomes reclusive. A terrible health scare teaches Ivy her own self-worth.

UNTIL IT HURTS TO STOP by Jennifer R. Hubbard (Viking, 2013). High school student Maggie Camden struggles to heal from junior high bullying about her appearance, but her old fears resurface when the most vicious bully of all returns to town.

THE UPSIDE OF UNREQUITED by Becky Albertalli (Balzer + Bray, 2017). As a fat girl, seventeen-year-old Molly is cautious about her crushes until her twin sister falls for a girl who hangs out with an attractive hipster boy. Molly's relationship with him is complicated by her quirky coworker, Reid.

WILL GRAYSON, WILL GRAYSON by John Green and David Levithan (Dutton Books, 2010). Tiny Cooper, a large gay teen with a passion for musical theater, attempts to find a boyfriend for his best friend, Will Grayson, and discovers another boy named Will Grayson who struggles with depression.

WINTERGIRLS by Laurie Halse Anderson (Viking, 2009). Eighteen-year-olds Lia and Cassie, former best friends, share a long history of eating disorders. After Cassie dies, Lia begins the difficult path toward recovery—a journey fraught with treatment centers and therapy, as well as parental deception and crippling obsession with self-worth.

YAQUI DELGADO WANTS TO KICK YOUR ASS by Meg Medina (Candlewick Press, 2013). Piddy Sanchez doesn't look Latina enough for a neighborhood bully who threatens to beat her up. Piddy tries to focus on honors courses and research the father she's never met, but when the girl's harassment becomes overwhelming, she must hide or run away.

3

BOOKS ABOUT
IMMIGRATION

After Angela Cervantes published her preteen novel *Gaby, Lost and Found*—the story of a sixth-grader whose mother is deported to Honduras—parents who read the book, along with their children, sent her letters and emails. "A couple of times, the mothers confessed that they too were undocumented like Gaby's mom and feared they'd be discovered, arrested, and separated from their children," she says. One told the story of how, like Gaby's mother, she was forced to return to her home country for three months without her young daughter.

What must it feel like to be an immigrant in the United States right now? In January 2017, people of all ages gathered at courthouses across the country to protest new immigration laws that made it difficult for citizens from seven nations—primarily Muslim—to enter the country; activists argued against their deportation as well as President Donald Trump's proposed wall along the US-Mexico border.

As I write this, more than two thousand children have been taken from their families at the border in the months since then–US Attorney General Jeff Sessions announced a "zero-tolerance" policy that charges illegal adult immigrants with a crime and places their kids in border facilities. Babies are pulled from their mothers' breasts. A father from Honduras who was separated from his wife and son and thrown into a Texas jail was so distraught that he committed suicide.

In warehouses around the nation, children slump shoulder to shoulder on metal benches, surrounded by metal fencing. At their feet are bottled water and bags of chips and sheets of foil. The lights overhead never switch off. Staff assigned to care for these kids are not allowed to touch them. Older children comfort sobbing babies and toddlers who are strangers to them and change their diapers.

There has got to be a better way to care for this vulnerable group of kids that doesn't add to their heartbreak and terror.

Prejudice comes easy to those worried about their jobs and schools and culture—especially when the people they perceive as threats look and act and even smell different from what they're used to. We're socially conditioned to fear "otherness," and immigrants have long been maligned as criminals or turned into fodder for popular comedy.

In the United States, 3 to 5 percent of kids identify as first-generation immigrants brought here from their home country. In 2014 that meant 2.8 million children arrived from somewhere else. Many of these kids find themselves bewildered and terrified, the targets of anti-immigration sentiment. Children whose parents arrived illegally from other countries may excel in school and work and sports and friendships—all the while living under threat of deportation.

My own daughter, with a birth mother from Central America, has asked me periodically whether she herself will be deported. She worries for her internationally adopted friends and for her classmates with family in other countries. She and many of her peers attended the January 2017 demonstration in front of our local courthouse, brandishing signs with slogans like "No hate, no fear—refugees welcome here."

Kids are pretty constantly exposed to confusing messages about who belongs in this country and who doesn't. But novels can help articulate the controversies surrounding immigration. Many readers may find themselves empathizing with children and parents who risk everything to upend their life for the chance to embrace a new one.

Fortunately, authors writing for tweens and teens have humanized many, many immigration stories over the past decade. Middle-grade readers have *Amina's Voice* by Hena Khan about an eleven-year-old Pakistani girl who emigrates to Milwaukee, and *The Only Road* by Alexandra Diaz about twelve-year-old Jamie, who escapes Guatemala's drug and gang violence and travels to the United States. There's also Laura Resau's *Star in the Forest* about a girl who finds comfort in helping animals after her father is deported.

Teens can read Nicola Yoon's *The Sun Is Also a Star*, about a North Korean immigrant boy who spends a day in New York City with a girl about to be deported with her family to Jamaica. Or they might try Terry Farish's free-verse story *The Good Braider*, about a girl who escapes with her family from Sudan to Cairo to Portland, Maine. Melissa de la Cruz's *Something in Between* tells the story of a scholarship-winning high school valedictorian who learns that her family is undocumented.

In the 1980s, my best friends were Vietnamese and Mexican immigrants in Los Angeles—kids who had come to the US prior to kindergarten. They never spoke to me of their birth countries or their traveling experiences, and I didn't think to ask. But reading Thanhha Lai's middle-grade novel *Inside Out and Back Again* offers poignant insight into what my classmates' private lives must have looked like.

Lai, born in Ho Chi Minh City, relied on her memories of Vietnam and the war to craft her story of ten-year-old Ha, a girl whose father has been captured by Communists and whose mother struggles to raise four children on her own in a war-ravaged country. In a piece for the *New York Times*, Lai describes how her father enlisted in South Vietnam's army to earn a living wage for the family and never returned—how US soldiers in her home country signified a prosperity that disappeared along with them after the fall of Saigon.

Lai moved with her family to Alabama at the end of the war in 1975. *Inside Out and Back Again* is written in verse that paints a delicate portrait of Ha's love for Vietnamese snacks, her fondness for her best friend who must also emigrate, and her frustration at being the only girl among brothers with a mother who never smiles. "I've lived in the North," her mother says, describing for her children why they must move to the United States.

At first, not much will happen,
then suddenly Quang
will be asked to leave college.
Ha will come home
chanting the slogans
of Ho Chi Minh,
and Khoi will be rewarded
for reporting to his teacher
everything we say in the house.

Inside Out and Back Again is part of the Common Core curriculum for eighth-grade students in New York State; Lai visits their classrooms to talk about the book. "I find that no matter what the students' backgrounds, they easily connect with Ha, be it through her humor, her lunch-in-the-bathroom routine, or her dash to outrun the bullies," she says. When she was a teacher herself, Lai told students that the quickest and most authentic way to gain insight into another person's point of view was through fiction.

Gillian Esquivia-Cohen is a bilingual and bicultural educator working in Bogota, Colombia. While earning her degree from Teachers College at Columbia University in New York City, she taught immigrant children in local schools. She describes her dismay at seeing how only a lone school psychologist was expected to serve the emotional and intellectual needs of all students at a dozen or more of these schools.

Esquivia-Cohen began looking for books about the immigration experience to read aloud to the children in her own classrooms. She'd stop frequently to ask questions and discuss different aspects of each story to promote a deeper understanding.

"I observed a significant positive change in the students' understanding of their own immigration process, and in their acceptance of the feelings they were experiencing in connection with their migration," she explains. Noting that other teachers sought out similar literature to speak to immigrant children, she wrote her 2012 thesis on "Bibliotherapy as a Tool for Helping New Arrivals Adapt and Adjust."

Esquivia-Cohen says that literature can help immigrants make sense of their experiences and know that they're not alone in experiencing racism and discrimination. She believes that novels help remove the stigma that often surrounds these marginalizing experiences along with the sense of responsibility and shame victims may feel; a book can create space for victims to talk about their experiences and seek help.

She has found that most children's literature published in English and Spanish features white middle-class children living in the suburbs or elite urban neighborhoods of North America and Western Europe. "This communicates to children who are not those things that their lives and experiences are insignificant and curtails their ability to imagine different futures for themselves," she says.

As a teacher working in Bogota, Esquivia-Cohen and her colleagues work to create stories about the country's conflicts as a way to help entire communities heal. These stories help break the cycle of violence. Young people from displaced and victimized communities who used to believe that the only futures available to them were as prostitutes, guerrilla soldiers, or paramilitary soldiers—when given the opportunity to witness and imagine different lives for themselves—are better able to construct alternative futures, she explains.

Australian author Randa Abdel-Fattah is an expert on Islamophobia in her country. Her first teen novel, *Does My Head Look Big in This*, tells the story of a sixteen-year-old Australian Palestinian Muslim girl who decides to wear a hijab, which inspires various levels of support and protest from friends and family. Abdel-Fattah wrote her latest novel, *The Lines We Cross*, about Mina, a beautiful Muslim refugee from Afghanistan who develops a love-hate relationship with Australian-born Michael—her classmate and the son of parents who've founded an anti-immigration group.

Mina and her mother come over on a boat after her baby brother dies of starvation. Michael's mother and father worry that immigrants will rob Australians of their jobs and culture. Abdel-Fattah's complex characterization asks readers to delve deeply into the actions and motivations of both immigrants and those opposed to them. "The scariest thing about people like Terrence and my parents is not that they can be cruel," Michael says of his best friend and family. "It's that they can be kind too."

Australia's anti-immigration protesters, as depicted in the novel, share all the same fear and anger of their US counterparts. The story feels relevant to any reader engaged in the debate between those of privileged residency status and those in desperate need of a safe place to live.

Much of the political vitriol in the United States stems from the fear that immigrants will force their unique cultures onto those whose families have lived here for generations. *The Lines We Cross* shows readers that a family can arrive from another country and add their unique food and music and clothing and religion to the region without threatening the culture that already exists.

Angela Cervantes, author of *Gaby, Lost and Found*, hoped the story of a girl whose mother is deported would become an outdated idea—that it would represent a time when our government's treatment of immigrants was less than humane.

Students have asked Cervantes why she didn't bring Gaby's mother back home at the end of the novel. "I would have loved a happy ending," she tells them. "Unfortunately, my research showed a more dismal reality." She explains how when parents are deported—especially to countries like Honduras—the opportunity to return can be tough. The journey is treacherous and oftentimes fatal, while the legal visa process is long, expensive, and often impossible if the applicant has been deported.

Still, her novel provides comfort to readers both young and old. One of the deported immigrant mothers who reached out to Cervantes after returning to the US ended her letter with this note, reminding me of the bond that reading together can create between parent and child: "Thanks to this book I spend special time with my daughter. Thank you very much for this beautiful book."

PRETEEN BOOKS ABOUT IMMIGRATION

AMINA'S VOICE by Hena Khan (Salaam Reads, 2017). Eleven-year-old Pakistani American Amina and her Korean American best friend, Soojin, struggle to assimilate into their Milwaukee suburb against a background of bullying and hate crimes.

ESCAPE FROM ALEPPO by N. H. Senzai (Paula Wiseman Books, 2018). Twelve-year-old Nadia attempts to flee Syria with her family during the Arab Spring after a bomb injury; in the confusion, Nadia is left behind and must make her way to the Turkish border to find them.

FRONT DESK by Kelly Yang (Arthur A. Levine Books, 2018). Ten-year-old Mia Tan lives with immigrant parents who work long hours in a motel while Mia manages the front desk. Her parents hide immigrants from the fierce motel owner, and her mother insists that she study math instead of pursuing her dream of becoming a writer.

GABY, LOST AND FOUND by Angela Cervantes (Scholastic Press, 2013). Sixth-grader Gaby Ramirez Howard volunteers to find homes for cats at an animal shelter after her mother is deported back to Honduras and her father neglects her. Gaby wonders if her mother will ever return home, and identifies with the abandoned cats she's devoted to helping.

GRAPE! by Gabriel Arquilevich (Fitzroy Books, 2019). Argentinean Jewish middle-schooler Grape is a good kid, but he keeps getting into trouble. While his parents adjust to life in 1970s California, Grape struggles with school, falls in love with a Texas girl, and streaks—that is, runs naked—briefly, trying to gain acceptance from friends.

HARBOR ME by Jacqueline Woodson (Nancy Paulsen Books, 2018). When six fifth- and sixth-graders must meet weekly to talk with no adults present, they reveal insecurities about deportation, racism, poverty, and friendship.

I LIVED ON BUTTERFLY HILL by Marjorie Agosin (Atheneum Books for Young Readers, 2014). Eleven-year-old Celeste Marconi lives in Chile until political unrest inspires her parents to go into hiding and send her to live in Maine, where she must adapt to a completely new culture.

INSIDE OUT AND BACK AGAIN by Thanhha Lai (HarperCollins Children's Books, 2011). After her mother and siblings leave war-torn Vietnam and emigrate to Alabama with her, ten-year-old Ha grapples with language barriers and questions about her new culture while learning to rely on family in this novel told in verse.

IT AIN'T SO AWFUL, FALAFEL by Firoozeh Dumas (Clarion Books, 2016). In the late 1970s, many people living in the United States express anti-Iranian feelings, which makes fitting in difficult for middle-school immigrant Zomorod (Cindy) Yousefzadeh.

A LONG PITCH HOME by Natalie Dias Lorenzi (Charlesbridge, 2016). Ten-year-old champion cricket player Bilal moves with his family from Pakistan to Virginia, but his father must stay behind. Bilal struggles with language issues and cultural confusion as he learns to play baseball and befriends his sole female teammate, whose father has been deployed to Afghanistan.

MY FAMILY DIVIDED: ONE GIRL'S JOURNEY OF HOME, LOSS, AND HOPE by Diane Guerrero (Henry Holt, 2018). *Orange Is the New Black* actress and activist Diane Guerrero writes about growing up in Boston and returning home from school one day to find that her loving and supportive undocumented immigrant parents were taken from their home and deported.

THE NIGHT DIARY by Veera Hiranandani (Dial Books, 2018). In 1947, twelve-year-old Nisha must emigrate with her father away from Pakistan toward a new and safer life. Traveling first by train, and later on foot, Nisha struggles with sadness at losing her homeland and her deceased mother, while trying to feel hope for the future.

NOWHERE BOY by Katherine Marsh (Roaring Brook Press, 2018). Fourteen-year-old Ahmed flees Syria and loses his father on the journey to Brussels. He goes into hiding, then meets thirteen-year-old Max, son of a Washington NATO contractor, who arranges with new friends for Ahmed to attend school despite significant risk to them all.

THE ONLY ROAD by Alexandra Diaz (Simon & Schuster Books for Young Readers, 2016). After twelve-year-old Jamie's cousin—his best friend—is murdered, he must leave Guatemala with its threats of gang violence and drugs. Anyone who refuses to work for the powerful gang called the Alphas is injured or killed. Jamie must risk his life to travel to the United States so he can live with his older brother.

PAPER WISHES by Lois Sepahban (Farrar, Straus and Giroux 2016). After the 1942 attack on Pearl Harbor, ten-year-old Japanese American Manami and her family have to leave their home on Bainbridge Island and move to an internment camp in the California desert. She gets caught trying to sneak her dog along, and loses her voice as she struggles to adjust to live in the camp.

THE RED PENCIL by Andrea Davis Pinkney (Little, Brown Books for Young Readers, 2014). In this story told in verse, twelve-year-old Amira finds her dreams of going to school shattered when the Janjaweed attack her Sudanese village. She and her family journey to a crowded refugee camp where the gift of a yellow notepad and a red pencil brings her hope.

RETURN TO SENDER by Julia Alvarez (Knopf Books for Young Readers, 2009). Tyler's family hires Mexican migrant workers to help on their family farm, and he meets Mari—one of their daughters—who begins to adapt to life in the US but worries that she and her family will get deported back to a life of poverty in Mexico.

SAME SUN HERE by Silas House and Neela Vaswani (Candlewick Press, 2012). Indian immigrant Meena, who lives in New York City's Chinatown, becomes pen pals with River, son of a Kentucky coal miner, and the two bond over issues related to immigration, racism, and activism.

SAVE ME A SEAT by Sarah Weeks and Gita Varadarajan (Scholastic Press, 2016). Ravi has just moved from India to the US. He thinks he'll be friends with the other Indian American in the class, Dillon Samreen, but realizes Dillon is a bully. Instead, Ravi befriends Joe, and the two boys decide to take down Dillon and take control of their lives in just one week.

SHOOTING KABUL by N. H. Senzai (Paula Wiseman Books, 2009). Middle school student Fadi emigrates from Afghanistan to San Francisco where his family struggles to find his missing six-year-old sister. After the 9/11 terrorist attacks, Fadi enters a photography competition hoping to win the grand prize trip to India so he can find and bring his sister to the US.

SOMEONE LIKE ME by Julissa Arce (Little, Brown Books for Young Readers, 2018). This memoir tells of growing up in Mexico while the author's parents worked tirelessly to make money in the US. When they moved her to Texas with them, she attended school as an undocumented immigrant and graduated from honors college to become a vice president at Goldman Sachs.

STAR IN THE FOREST by Laura Resau (Delacorte Books, 2010). After eleven-year-old Ziatally's father is deported to Mexico and her mother works endlessly to make ends meet, a dog discovered in the forest provides comfort and intrigue.

STEF SOTO, TACO QUEEN by Jennifer Torres (Little, Brown, 2017). Seventh-grader Estafania Soto has an overprotective father who picks her up from school in his ramshackle taco truck, where she does her homework. Wishing he could have a different job and more money, she finds herself unexpectedly defending the truck after city regulations threaten her parents' livelihood.

THE TURTLES OF OMAN by Naomi Shihab Nye (Greenwillow Books, 2014). Aref hates to leave his grandfather, Sidi, and move with his family from Oman to spend three years in Michigan. Before they leave, Sidi takes Aref camping in the desert and fishing on the Indian Ocean, and then to visit a nesting ground for several species of sea turtles.

THE WEIGHT OF WATER by Sarah Crossan (Bloomsbury Children's Books, 2013). In this novel in verse, twelve-year-old Kasienka moves with her depressed mother from Poland to England in search of her missing father. Kasienka finds solace from peer bullying and academic worries at the local swimming pool and in a first romance with a boy.

WISHTREE by Katherine Applegate (Feiwel and Friends, 2017). Red, a red oak tree, narrates the story of a new Muslim immigrant girl and her family, who become the target of anti-immigration sentiment and racism until the girl's classmates—and the animal inhabitants of the tree—intervene.

TEEN BOOKS ABOUT IMMIGRATION

AMERICAN DERVISH by Ayad Akhtar (Little, Brown and Company, 2012). Pakistani American Hayat Shah finds his passions for baseball and video games diminished when his mother's newly divorced friend Mina arrives from Pakistan to stay with his family. He studies the Quran with her and finds himself falling in love—feelings complicated by Mina's decision to date someone else.

AMERICAN STREET by Ibi Zoboi (Balzer + Bray, 2017). Fabiola Toussaint, an immigrant from Haiti, has to adapt to Detroit and a new school and a fraught political situation without her mother, who has been detained by US immigration.

AMERICANIZED by Sara Saedi (Knopf Books for Young Readers, 2018). A memoir of how the author discovered, at thirteen years old, her status as an undocumented Iranian immigrant in the US, and her subsequent fear of deportation. She worries about cultural stereotypes and whether she'll get a green card, while at the same time wondering if she'll get a date to the prom.

THE DANGEROUS ART OF BLENDING IN by Angelo Surmelis (Balzer + Bray, 2018). Seventeen-year-old Evan Panos has an abusive immigrant Greek mother and a father who works all the time, and so he hides in an abandoned monastery and draws. When he and his friend Henry begin a romantic relationship, Evan realizes he must pull away from his family in order to survive.

THE DISTANCE BETWEEN US by Reyna Grande (Atria Books, 2012). This memoir follows the life of a Mexican American child navigating two countries. After her mother risks her life to cross the Mexican border, Reyna must live with her strict grandmother. Upon her mother's return, Reyna must risk her own life to cross the border and meet up with the father she no longer knows.

DREAM THINGS TRUE by Marie Marquardt (St. Martin's Griffin, 2015). High school junior Alma is an undocumented immigrant worried about grades, friends, and whether she'll be deported. She falls in love with wealthy Evan, the nephew of a bigoted senator. Evan, from a dysfunctional family, adores Alma's family. When ICE raids their town, Alma knows she must tell Evan the truth.

ENCHANTED AIR: TWO CULTURES, TWO WINGS by Margarita Engle (Atheneum Books for Young Readers, 2015). A poetic memoir about a fourteen-year-old girl who lives in Los Angeles and longs for the summers she spends in her mother's birthplace of Cuba—visits threatened by the Bay of Pigs invasion.

FLIGHT SEASON by Marie Marquardt (Wednesday Books, 2018). Vivi Flannigan works as a hospital intern as she grieves her father and navigates an angry nursing student who resents his family's demanding Brazilian restaurant business. Their lives, and their relationship, are changed by an undocumented orphan and heart patient named Angel.

GIRL IN TRANSLATION by Jean Kwok (Riverhead Books, 2010). After Kimberly Chang emigrates with her mother from Hong Kong to Brooklyn to live in poverty, she juggles her life as an ambitious student with her work in a Chinatown sweatshop at night, struggling to learn a new language and a new culture.

THE GOOD BRAIDER by Terry Farish (Marshall Cavendish, 2012). The free-verse story of Viola, who escapes with her family from Sudan to Cairo to Portland, Maine, and struggles with homesickness for her birth country combined with a desire to blend into the culture that surrounds her.

HIDDEN by Miriam Halahmy (Holiday House, 2016). Teens Alix and Samir rescue an Iraqi refugee—a student and illegal immigrant who has been tortured and now seeks asylum on their English island. Samir, a former Iraqi refugee, begs Alix to overcome her prejudices and those of her family and friends to help the man.

HOW DARE THE SUN RISE by Sandra Uwiringiyimana (Katherine Tegen Books, 2017). The true story of a girl from the Democratic Republic of the Congo who watches rebels gun down her mother and sister, then escapes to the US. In New York, she deals with trauma and cultural disconnect and eventual finds healing through activism and art.

ILLEGAL by Eoin Colfer and Andrew Donkin (Sourcebooks Jabberwocky, 2018). In this graphic novel, Ebo's brother Kwame leaves Ghana, as their sister did, and sets out on the long and perilous journey to Europe. Ebo joins him, traveling across the Sahara Desert, navigating the hazards of Tripoli, and heading out to sea with the hope of joining their sister.

LIFE, AFTER by Sarah Darer Littman (Scholastic Press, 2010). When her family relocates from Argentina to New York City after a terrorist attack that kills her aunt, Dani Bensimon tries to be the perfect daughter, but misses her old school and her boyfriend while struggling with life as a new Latin American immigrant in a city still in mourning from the 9/11 terrorist attacks.

THE LINES WE CROSS by Randa Abdel-Fattah (Scholastic Press, 2017). Mina, a beautiful Muslim refugee from Afghanistan, develops a love-hate relationship with Australian-born Michael—her classmate and the son of parents who have founded an anti-immigration group. Michael must come to terms with his family's racism and with his own goals for the future.

MY NAME IS NOT EASY by Debby Dahl Edwardson (Skyscape, 2011). When Luke Aaluk and his younger brothers are sent to a Catholic boarding school hundreds of miles from their tiny Alaskan village, they find Inuit and Native American cultures sublimated by white traditions and values. The youngest brother is sent to foster care, and the other boys battle homesickness and anger.

NORTH OF HAPPY by Adi Alsaid (Harlequin Teen, 2017). Eighteen-year-old Carlos lives a wealthy life in Mexico City with a father who's planned his future. But when Carlos's brother is killed, he buys a plane ticket to the United States to visit a restaurant his brother told him about. On an island near Seattle, he falls in love with the chef's daughter and begins to realize his dream of cooking.

THE RADIUS OF US by Marie Marquardt (St. Martin's Griffin, 2017). Seventeen-year-old Gretchen, traumatized by assault, meets an eighteen-year-old El Salvadorian immigrant named Phoenix in danger of being deported after he accompanies his brother on a four-month journey to the US to escape gang violence.

THE RED UMBRELLA by Christina Diaz Gonzalez (Knopf Books for Young Readers, 2010). Fourteen-year-old Lucia Alvarez must leave her town in Cuba when the revolution becomes oppressive, and her parents send her alone to the US. In Nebraska with strangers, she navigates the new country and a new language, wondering if she'll ever see her parents or her homeland again.

THE SECRET SIDE OF EMPTY by Maria E. Andreu (Running Press, 2014). High school senior Monserrat Thalia lives in the US as an undocumented immigrant, which no one guesses because of her pale skin and blond hair. She earns straight As but hides her fears for the future and whether she'll be deported.

SOMETHING IN BETWEEN by Melissa de la Cruz (Harlequin Teen, 2016). Jasmine is valedictorian of her senior high school class and wins a coveted scholarship, but her plans change when she discovers that her family is undocumented.

THE SUN IS ALSO A STAR by Nicola Yoon (Delacorte Press, 2016). Natasha and her family are about to be deported from Brooklyn to Jamaica when she meets Daniel, whose parents emigrated from North Korea, and spends her final day in the city with him.

WE NEED NEW NAMES by NoViolet Bulawayo (Reagan Arthur Books, 2013). After Darling's home in Zimbabwe is destroyed by police and her school is closed, she escapes to an aunt's house in the United States, where she discovers new issues in a country ravaged by economic turmoil.

4

BOOKS ABOUT LEARNING CHALLENGES

My friend Jamie has a sixth-grade daughter who regards a trip to the public library like a day at the county fair. Her fourth-grader, not so much.

Jamie's younger daughter found out at age eight that she has dyslexia. In a family of bibliophiles—and as a book lover herself—she's cried and raged in despair over her inability to read fluently.

"We are a family of stories, of books piled upon books piled upon magazines on most surfaces in our house," Jamie writes in a parenting essay for the *Washington Post*. "My ten-year-old's bedside lamp is on long past bedtime most nights, and my husband and I mostly ignore this because we're in bed reading too."

She goes on to describe how her younger daughter feels left out and longs to share this part of their lives.

And so, on a Saturday in May, they headed once more for the public library. There, Jamie told a youth services librarian named Jennifer ("J," for short) that she needed recommendations for just the right books—not simplistic early readers about animals, but thick books about adventurous and spirited girls. The librarian approached her younger daughter. She got down on her knees and introduced herself, and then she told Jamie's daughter that she, too, had dyslexia.

When J recounted the story later, she had a hard time holding back her tears. "Reading was such a struggle for me when I was young," she tells me. "It was only when I was an adult that I found my love of books and reading."

The 2.4 million public school students diagnosed with learning challenges in the United States have dyslexia, dysgraphia, auditory or visual processing disorders, or related issues stemming from attention deficit disorder. They may also be on the autism spectrum, which—while not a learning disability—can create barriers to a child's education.

Jamie's younger daughter isn't keen on reading novels about protagonists with learning challenges such as hers. But craving insight, her older sister studied Rick Riordan's dyslexic hero in the preteen novel *The Lightning Thief* and Lynda Mullaly Hunt's *Fish in a Tree* about a troubled middle school girl who hides her inability to read until a kindhearted teacher discovers her dyslexia and offers to help. "She's such a helpful older sister," Jamie says. "She's always asking me questions about dyslexia."

As a girl growing up with a younger brother who has Down syndrome, I had plenty of questions as well. Why did he get on a small orange bus each morning and go to a special institution, while my little sister and I walked half a mile to the public school? Why couldn't he read and write, when he was perfectly capable of teasing us until we shrieked with outrage?

For a time, I tried to teach my brother to read with flash cards, rewarding him with chocolate candies. He could remember a handful of words for a day or two, but then he'd shake his head in confusion. I was bewildered too, since aside from his learning disability, he acted just like the younger brothers of my friends . . . which is to say, equal parts lovable and annoying.

Back then, novels for preteens and teens didn't include characters with my brother's particular developmental disorder, or really, any learning disability at all. Kids who struggled to read and write and do math took the bus to special schools, like my brother, or gathered in classrooms at the far end of my junior high and high school campuses, where they remained all day every day—in stark contrast to the more integrated classrooms we see today.

Now tweens and teens curious about siblings' and classmates' learning challenges—or who are dealing with these issues themselves—have Beth Vrabel's preteen *Pack of Dorks* (and subsequent series), featuring a protagonist who has a sister with Down syndrome. Ann M. Martin gives us Rose Howard, a resilient and candid ten-year-old with autism and a beloved dog, in *Rain Reign*, and Claire LaZebnik's teen novel *Things I Should Have Known* tells of a girl who arranges a date for her older sister on the autism spectrum with a boy from her class.

They can read the 2018 Newbery Medal winner *Hello, Universe*, a preteen novel about how four kids' lives converge unexpectedly on a lazy summer day. One of the children, Valencia, wears hearing aids and lip-reads. She attends a special class at school each week with Virgil, a quiet Filipino American boy who struggles with math and hides from the neighborhood bully, who refers to him as "Retardo."

From the first sentence of Erin Entrada Kelly's novel, readers get a sense of the depression that a kid with a learning disability—one who has to spend Thursday afternoons in the *resource* classroom of all places—might feel.

"Eleven-year-old Virgil Salinas already regretted the rest of middle school, and he'd only just finished sixth grade," Kelly writes. "He imagined all those years stretching ahead of him like a long line of hurdles, each of them getting taller, thicker, and heavier, and him standing in front of them on his weak and skinny legs."

On the first day of summer vacation, Virgil has no friends except for his guinea pig, which suffers from "debilitating depression." He's invisible to everyone except the bully and a local psychic and her younger sister, who describes his face as "Brown. Skinny. Sad."

Virgil is no stranger to depression and anxiety himself—with two perfect older brothers and parents who refer to him as "Turtle," he's got no sense of self-worth. But on one fateful summer day, his peers see him for who he truly is—a kind, gentle boy deserving of friendship who stands up for himself after becoming trapped in a well.

Kids with learning challenges are at greater risk than their nondisabled counterparts for developing clinical depression and/or anxiety. Not all books about disability will resonate positively with all kids, though: I think about Jamie's nine-year-old daughter sobbing and calling herself "dumb" after she got her hands on Patricia Polacco's novel *Thank You, Mr. Falker* about the author's own issues with dyslexia as a child in school.

Still, I'm eternally grateful that contemporary novels include a variety of characters who don't read and write and do math as easily as their peers. Reading about them, seeing these characters reflected in the struggles of the kids around them, may encourage children for whom these academic skills come easily to approach their classmates with compassion and understanding. That's what Anna Monders, booktalk specialist for Jackson County Library Services in Southern Oregon, hopes.

Monders visits fourth- through seventh-grade classes throughout the county to tell students about new books coming out and what makes each one so exciting. On the library's *Booktalk Blog*, she writes, "I want the kids in my audience to go home and beg their parents to take them to the library. I want them to say, 'There was this lady who came to school today and she talked about all these books, and there's this one I've got to read so we need to go to the library *right now*! . . . Please?'"

In a 2018 presentation, she recommended Leslie Connor's preteen novel *The Truth as Told by Mason Buttle* about a twelve-year-old with a learning disability. He's grieving the death of his best friend and dodging a gang of neighborhood bullies. To make matters worse, Mason has a physical condition that makes him sweat profusely—enough that he brings an extra shirt to school and recoils when the bullies call him "Sweat Head."

Originally, Monders would stand in front of a class and describe Mason as sweaty, the biggest kid in his class, a kid with dyslexia. Then a colleague suggested that she skip the labels in favor of describing what happens to Mason when he reads instead.

"So I said that whenever he tries to read, the words slip off the page, and kids around me in the classroom whispered 'dyslexia.' They still made the connection of what was going on for him."

It felt better, she realized, to *describe* a character's experience whenever possible rather than using labels. "I see it as a way to help kids connect with the character and understand what their life is like," she explains. "Many kids may know what dyslexia or autism is, but the word itself may not evoke an experience—or it may evoke something different than the challenges the particular character is actually facing."

Another of the books she discussed was Cammie McGovern's preteen novel *Chester and Gus,* told from the point of view of a dog that fails his service dog test because he's terrified of noise. The dog, Chester, gets adopted into a family with a ten-year-old boy who's living with autism and nonverbal with an aversion to physical touch.

In her booktalk, Monders doesn't say that the boy is living with autism; she tells the students that he doesn't talk, he doesn't like hugs, and he spends a lot of time looking out the window.

Some of the kids understand that Gus is an autistic person, but most of them choose the book simply because they're intrigued by the image of the beautiful brown dog on the cover. "It's brilliant to have that focus," she notes. "The kids are reading it for the dog, but they also get this very important character."

The number of children diagnosed with autism is increasing. It's safe to say that most preteens and teens know several peers on the spectrum, whether or not they identify as such. I did, too, when I was growing up—but my peers and I lacked fiction that included neurodiverse characters.

Not so today. Dozens of novels published in the past decade feature protagonists on the spectrum, and several of them have been written by authors with direct experience.

Author Lyn Miller-Lachmann was diagnosed with Asperger's syndrome, part of the autism spectrum, as an adult. She's the author of the teen novel *Rogue*, about an eighth-grader with Asperger's named Kiara who gets into trouble and has difficulties making friends. After her mother takes off to pursue a career in music, Kiara is asked to leave school for injuring another student. She pursues a friendship with the new boy across the street who is keeping a terrifying secret about his family.

Miller-Lachmann describes her own difficulties fitting in as a teen. The first lines of her novel, narrated by Kiara, offer heartbreaking insight into what it's like to be a kid with learning challenges in a school full of students who don't understand and show little to no compassion.

> It usually took the New Kids two weeks to dump me, three weeks at the most. Melanie Prince-Parker was the quickest. She moved from West Hartford to Willingham when we started eighth grade. I couldn't make her sit across from me for more than five minutes of lunch, and at the end of the first week I spotted her in the middle of the popular girls' table. I wanted to know how she did it.

Kiara identifies with Rogue, a mutant human subspecies from the X-Men comics who is born with superpowers. Rogue can absorb the emotions of anyone she touches, which leaves her feeling cursed and unwilling to make physical contact. Eventually Kiara—like Rogue—learns to use her self-proclaimed "superpower" for good: she helps the boy across the street break free of his abusive parents who force him to participate in making meth, showing that kids with learning and social differences don't have to succumb to a sense of powerlessness. Rather, they can flip their narrative and embrace the abilities they've been given

This idea informs author Brian Tashima's books, which treat kids on the spectrum as having remarkable abilities. In his teen sci-fi/fantasy series, title character Joel Suzuki lives in a world in which autism is a superpower.

Tashima wrote the first book in the series after his twelve-year-old son on the spectrum requested he write a novel just for him. He wanted to give kids like his boy a hero that they could relate to, a character that empowered them. And, he wanted to give all readers—neurotypical and neurodivergent—a great adventure story.

In *Joel Suzuki, Volume One: Secret of the Songshell*, sixteen-year-old Joel contends with poor grades and bullies until he meets a rock star he assumed to be dead and travels with him to Spectraland—a world in which music is magic and autism is a superpower—where he learns to combine his particular brain waves with the music's sound waves to create enchantment.

Tashima sits on the board of directors for the nonprofit Autism Empowerment—an organization that provides community services for people with autism and promotes a mission to accept, enrich, inspire, and empower them. His novels reflect these goals. "It's really important to me to make sure my characters are a respectful and accurate portrayal of people on the spectrum," he says.

Sometimes when Tashima visits classrooms to talk about his books, kids thank him for stories that make them feel better about themselves. Other times, kids who aren't on the spectrum express gratitude for the insight into classmates whose actions and words had previously confused or frightened them.

He loves hearing that. He wants his characters to come out and identify as on the spectrum but then back off and show that they are also just people with individual differences.

This is what Jamie's younger daughter is still learning—that we all have our differences, we all have our challenges. She can find this truth over and over in the preteen and teen fiction published today. Thanks to one conscientious youth services librarian, she's well on her way.

That Saturday in May at the library, when J got down on her knees and told Jamie's daughter that she was dyslexic too, they talked for a few minutes. Afterward, J searched through the stacks to find just the right books.

Jamie just stood there with tears in her eyes. Her daughter was so happy that day. She kept remarking on J's kindness. And then she asked the question that warms the hearts of book-loving parents and caregivers everywhere.

She asked to return to the library.

PRETEEN BOOKS ABOUT LEARNING CHALLENGES

ABSOLUTELY ALMOST by Lisa Graff (Philomel Books, 2014). Fifth-grader Albie has trouble with spelling and math, and he's worried about being the new kid at school. When his babysitter helps him to discover his talents, he gets an opportunity to be one of the popular kids if he abandons his only friend, who has also been the target of bullies.

AL CAPONE DOES MY HOMEWORK by Gennifer Choldenko (Dial Books, 2013). The third novel in the author's Al Capone at Alcatraz series, this is the story of Moose Flanagan and his sister, Natalie, who lives with autism and is gifted at math. Moose and his friends search for a potential arsonist after his sister is blamed for starting a fire and his father's life is threatened.

BLUEFISH by Pat Schmatz (Candlewick Press, 2011). When thirteen-year-old Travis leaves his country home and his dog to move in with his alcoholic grandfather, he must attend a new school, where he tries to hide the fact that he can't read. A spunky girl classmate and a teacher who gives him a book on the natural world inspire him to tackle his learning challenges.

CHESTER AND GUS by Cammie McGovern (HarperCollins Children's Books, 2017). Ten-year-old Gus, who has autism, confuses his new service dog, Chester, who doesn't understand why Gus doesn't want to pet him. Chester must learn new skills and new ways of thinking about his role as a service dog in order to help Gus thrive.

EVER AFTER EVER by Jordan Sonnenblick (Scholastic Press, 2010). Eighth-grade student Jeffrey Alper and his best friend, Tad, are cancer survivors who deal with nerve and brain damage, including difficulty concentrating. In the middle of family troubles and concerns about a cute girl who seems attracted to him, Jeffrey worries that he'll fail a standardized test and get held back a grade.

FISH IN A TREE by Lynda Mullaly Hunt (Nancy Paulsen Books, 2015). Middle school student Ally is an excellent artist who excels in math, but she's unable to read. When a teacher diagnoses her dyslexia and offers to help her, Ally finds a slow but promising escape from her role as a troublemaker, and from the bullies that cause her anxiety and depression.

HELLO, UNIVERSE by Erin Entrada Kelly (Greenwillow Books, 2017). Eleven-year-old Virgil, who has a learning disability, disappears down a well to save the guinea pig that is in a backpack discarded by the neighborhood bully. A deaf girl in his special education class rescues him, along with an adolescent psychic and her little sister.

HOW TO SPEAK DOLPHIN by Ginny Rorby (Scholastic Press, 2015). Middle school student Lily grieves her mother killed in a car accident and worries about her half brother with autism. When her oncologist stepfather helps a dolphin with cancer, her brother bonds with the animal; however, Lily begins to question its potentially lifelong captivity in a marine mammal park.

THE KEY THAT SWALLOWED JOEY PIGZA (and other titles in the series) by Jack Gantos (Farrar, Straus and Giroux, 2014). This final book in a five-part series tells the story of Joey Pigza, who has ADHD, after his father disappears and his mother goes into the hospital due to depression. Joey quits school to care for his baby brother and solve the mystery of his father's disappearance.

THE LIGHTNING THIEF (and other titles in the Percy Jackson and the Olympians series) by Rick Riordan (Hyperion Books for Children, 2005). This first book, as well as its sequels, follows seventeen-year-old Percy Jackson, who has dyslexia and ADHD, as he struggles to stay at boarding school. While at summer camp, he learns that his father is Poseidon, which launches a multi-book conflict involving Greek gods.

LIGHTS, CAMERA, DISASTER by Erin Dionne (Arthur A. Levine Books, 2018). Hester loves filmmaking, but struggles with schoolwork because of executive function disorder. She deals with shame and depression upon learning she may fail the eighth grade. Thanks to teachers, parents, and a classmate newly arrived from the Middle East, she finds hope and support.

MOCKINGBIRD by Kathryn Erskine (Philomel Books, 2010). Eleven-year-old Caitlin is an intelligent and troubled artist with Asperger's syndrome. After her brother is killed in a school shooting, and her widower father retreats into grief, Caitlin works with a school counselor to learn to tolerate the noise and confusion of school and social situations.

NOW IS THE TIME FOR RUNNING by Michael Williams (Little, Brown Books for Young Readers, 2011). Deo protects his disabled older brother after soldiers appear in their Zimbabwe soccer fields. The boys flee their destroyed village and suffer poverty and prejudice before tragedy strikes and Deo must rely on the only thing he has left—his love of soccer.

PACK OF DORKS (and other titles in the series) by Beth Vrabel (Sky Pony Press, 2014). Fourth-grader Lucy has a new little sister with Down syndrome. Learning about the baby's particular needs gives her a welcome break from the agony of going from popular to suddenly very unpopular. She teams up with a quiet boy for a school project on wolves and finds herself making surprising and satisfying new friends.

POSITIVELY IZZY by Terri Libenson (Balzer + Bray, 2018). In this graphic novel, middle school student Brianna is quiet and smart, while Izzy—who loves acting and making up stories—has trouble completing her school work. On the day of the school talent show, the girls' lives intersect unexpectedly in a moment that changes both their lives.

RAIN REIGN by Ann M. Martin (Feiwel and Friends, 2014). Rose, who has been diagnosed with Aspberger's syndrome and is obsessed with homonyms, lives with her father but turns to her uncle for comfort. When her dad lets her beloved new dog out during a storm, Rose and her uncle find the dog and realize it already has an owner. She also learns the truth of her mother's disappearance and confronts a life change.

THINGS I SHOULD HAVE KNOWN by Claire LaZebnik (HMH Books for Young Readers, 2017). Chloe Mitchell sees that Ivy, her older sister with autism, is lonely, and she tries to set her up with her classmate, Ethan. Chloe can't stand Ethan's brother David, but she realizes that he's as devoted to his brother as she is to her sister. The four begin to double date, realizing important truths about each other.

THIS IS NOT THE ABBY SHOW by Debbie Reed Fischer (Delacorte Books for Young Readers, 2016). Twelve-year-old Abby, who has ADHD, fails English but blossoms under the influence of a summer school teacher. She makes new friends and deepens family relationships, learning that while pulling pranks and making people laugh is fun, her careless remarks can hurt others.

THE TRUTH AS TOLD BY MASON BUTTLE by Leslie Connor (Katherine Tegen Books, 2018). After his best friend is discovered dead in his family's orchard, Mason Buttle finds his learning challenges even more pronounced because of grief. He's large and has a physical condition that makes him sweat profusely. He and his friend Calvin form an underground club to hide from bullies, but then Calvin disappears.

UNGIFTED by Gordon Korman (Balzer + Bray, 2012). Donovan Curtis, a middle school student with impulse control issues, is accidentally placed in a school for gifted and talented kids that sacrifices social skills for academic achievement. Donovan helps the smart kids learn to be "normal" in this book about learning to acknowledge your own gifts, whatever they may be.

A WHOLE NEW BALLGAME by Phil Bildner (Farrar, Straus and Giroux, 2015). Fifth-grader Red is on the autism spectrum. He and his best friend, Rip, revere their innovative new teacher, who shares their love of basketball, though Red struggles to adjust to changes in the classroom. Rip befriends an angry girl who uses a wheelchair, and they work on a bizarre science project together.

TEEN BOOKS ABOUT LEARNING CHALLENGES

CARTER FINALLY GETS IT by Brent Crawford (Disney-Hyperion, 2009). High school freshman Will Carter stutters and has ADD, which complicates his obsession with girls. Football players and other peers bully him, but thanks to his sister and a close group of friends, he learns survival skills and self-confidence.

COLIN FISCHER by Ashley Edward Miller (Razorbill, 2012). Fourteen-year-old Colin Fischer has Asperger's syndrome, which complicates his high school life and gets him dunked in the toilet by a boy named Wayne. But when Wayne is accused of bringing the gun that goes off in the cafeteria, Colin solves the mystery that proves him innocent.

THE DISTURBED GIRL'S DICTIONARY by NoNieqa Ramos (Carolrhoda Lab, 2018). Fifteen-year-old Puerto Rican American Macy has ADHD; she'd been labeled both learning disabled and emotionally disturbed. Her father's in prison and can't know about her mother's infidelity; her brother lives in foster care. When her best friend is threatened, Macy comes to her defense with a machete.

DYING TO KNOW YOU by Aidan Chambers (Amulet Books, 2012). Eighteen-year-old Karl is severely dyslexic and asks a famous writer to write a letter to his girlfriend. The author agrees to write it after Karl submits to several interviews to add authenticity, but his girlfriend reacts with fury when she realizes the letter is not actually the work of her boyfriend.

FADE TO US by Julia Day (Wednesday Books, 2018). Seventeen-year-old Brooke Byers's stepsister Natalie, who has Asperger's, moves in for the summer. Natalie needs family near her in case of a meltdown, so Brooke volunteers at her summer drama camp. There they meet Micah—whom Natalie adopts as a mentor, complicating Brooke's romantic attraction to him.

GIRLS LIKE US by Gail Giles (Candlewick Press, 2014). New high school graduates Quincy and Biddie have developmental disabilities, and they become roommates in a house owned by a wealthy widow. The young women share secrets of abandonment and abuse, which includes rape; their friendship and the widow's support give them the strength to succeed out in the world.

THE HALF-LIFE OF PLANETS by Emily Franklin and Brendan Halpin (Disney-Hyperion, 2010). Teenage Hank has Asperger's syndrome and a powerful knowledge of music. He becomes friends with astronomy-obsessed Liana, who swears off kissing after she's called a slut—a vow that complicates their burgeoning romance.

HARMONIC FEEDBACK by Tara Kelly (Henry Holt, 2010). Sixteen-year-old Drea has Asperger's syndrome and a passion for music and sound equipment. After a move to a new town, she overcomes her difficulties with social interactions and forms a band with two teens; one shoplifts and does drugs, while the other appears to be falling in love with Drea.

JOEL SUZUKI, VOLUME ONE: SECRET OF THE SONGSHELL by Brian Tashima (Prism Valley Press, 2017). Sixteen-year-old Joel contends with poor grades and bullies until he meets a rock star he assumed to be dead and travels with him to Spectraland, where he learns to combine his particular brain waves with music sound waves to create magic.

A LIST OF CAGES by Robin Roe (Disney-Hyperion, 2017). Shy high school freshman Julian has undiagnosed dyslexia, and he's being abused at home. He reconnects with his former foster brother, Adam, who has ADHD. Adam tries to figure out a way to help, but suddenly, Julian vanishes.

THE LOVE LETTERS OF ABELARD AND LILY by Laura Creedle (HMH Books for Young Readers, 2017). Tenth-grader Lily lives with ADHD and dyslexia. Her classmate Abelard has Asperger's. When they're sent to the principal together, they begin a texting romance based on twelfth-century love letters, but the relationship is complicated by their neurodifferences and their peers.

MARCELO IN THE REAL WORLD by Francisco X. Stork (Arthur A. Levine Books, 2009). Seventeen-year-old Marcelo Sandoval, who has Asperger's syndrome, gets a summer job at a therapeutic riding stable, but his father asks him to work at his law firm instead. In the mail room, Marcello meets a beautiful coworker and learns to read people's faces to tell whether they're trustworthy or not.

MINDBLIND by Jennifer Roy (Marshall Cavendish, 2010). Fourteen-year-old Nathaniel Clark has Asperger's syndrome and panic attacks when he's forced to interact with people. He also has good friends and a devoted mother and therapist, but when his father forces him to go to a party and "be normal," Nathaniel finds his plans for a girlfriend and graduate school threatened.

MOTORCYCLES, SUSHI, AND ONE STRANGE BOOK by Nancy Rue (Zonderkidz, 2010). Fifteen-year-old Jessie, who has ADHD, moves in with her father after her mother—who has bipolar disorder—attempts suicide. She learns about the life of Jesus, which gives context to her new life as an employee at a sushi bar and as the daughter of an alcoholic father who adores motorcycles.

OKAY FOR NOW by Gary D. Schmidt (Clarion Books, 2011). In New York City in 1968, fourteen-year-old Doug Swieteck has an abusive father and a brother who has returned from Vietnam with post-traumatic stress disorder. Doug hurts his friends and sasses his teachers, but he begins to change when he learns about John James Audubon's birds at the library and develops an interest in drawing.

PINNED by Sharon G. Flake (Scholastic Press, 2012). Teens Autumn and Adonis bond in this story of unexpected connection. Autumn is a popular wrestler; however, she struggles with a learning disability that makes reading a problem. She falls in love with Adonis, who has no legs and adores reading and books; though he pushes her away, he thinks and dreams about her.

PLAYING TYLER by T. L. Costa (Strange Chemistry, 2013). After a businessman hires seventeen-year-old Tyler MacCandless—who has ADHD—to test a flight simulator game, Tyler falls for the simulator's sixteen-year-old designer, Ani. His father is dead, and his mother isn't available, so when his older brother vanishes from a drug rehab program, he risks his own life to bring him back.

ROGUE by Lyn Miller-Lachmann (Nancy Paulsen Books, 2013). Eighth-grader Kiara has Asperger's and gets kicked out of school for violence. She struggles to create a friendship with the new boy across the street and helps him to break free of his abusive parents who enlist him and his younger brother to help with their production of meth.

SAME BUT DIFFERENT by Holly Robinson Peete, Ryan Elizabeth Peete, and RJ Peete (Scholastic Press, 2016). Based on the authors' true story, this narrative follows teen Charlie, who is living with autism, and his twin Callie, who is not. Callie is outgoing and popular; she protects her brother who wants to have a social life but finds friendships difficult. Their mother provides insight and perspective.

SCREAMING QUIETLY by Evan Jacobs (Saddleback Educational Publishing, 2013). Varsity football player Ian Taylor hides the fact that he has a younger brother, who has autism and is prone to public behavior outbursts. But when his brother begins attending the same high school, Ian must confront his internalized rage and humiliation and overcome peer pressure and the fear of his girlfriend's disapproval.

THE STARS AT OKTOBER BEND by Glenda Millard (Candlewick Press, 2018). Fifteen-year-old Alice has a traumatic past and a brain injury that causes her to have difficulty speaking, but she writes poems and puts them in public places. Sixteen-year-old Manny, former child soldier and refugee from Sierra Leone, finds one of her poems, and they become friends.

A STEP TOWARD FALLING by Cammie McGovern (HarperTeen, 2015). When Emily sees Belinda—who has a developmental disability—assaulted, she neglects to intervene and must do community service at a center that serves people with disabilities. Meanwhile, Belinda—having rescued herself from her pursuers—must figure out how to move on with her life.

THE WAY THE LIGHT BENDS by Cordelia Jensen (Philomel Books, 2018). In this novel in verse, Linc struggles in school, watching as her sister Holly—adopted from Ghana—pleases their surgeon mother with her academic success. Linc finds new purpose and self-worth when she immerses herself in a photography project based on Seneca Village which is now Central Park.

WHAT TO SAY NEXT by Julie Buxbaum (Delacorte Press, 2017). Socially isolated David, who has Asperger's syndrome, trusts only a few people, including a popular classmate named Kit, who is grieving her father's death. When she asks him to help her figure out the details of her father's accident, they find that they're both harboring secrets and falling in love.

WHEN MY HEART JOINS THE THOUSAND by A. J. Steiger (HarperTeen, 2018). Seventeen-year-old Alvie, who has Asperger's syndrome, runs away from foster care and works at a zoo with a one-winged hawk. When a boy falls in love with her, she loses her job and ends up homeless.

5

BOOKS ABOUT
LGBTQIA+ YOUTH

M y friend Marcia, realizing she couldn't be present for every moment of screen time, taught her transgender ten-year-old daughter to watch movies with the TV remote in hand. Confronted with examples of gender policing—a girl being encouraged not to be successful or boys won't like her; a group of boys concluding that the most important thing in a girl's life is shopping—my friend's daughter learned to hit the pause button and say out loud, "Well, that's a load of crap!"

She found herself hitting the pause button a lot.

My friend's daughter also reads a novel every couple of days—books less concerned with chasing laughs for outdated clichés and more representative of the nuanced characters that populate her real world. Thankfully in books for her age group, some protagonists do identify as heterosexual, gay, lesbian, transsexual, pansexual, gender fluid, genderqueer—and have friends and family members who do as well.

But such models weren't always so available. When my mother's life partner came of age and came out in the 1960s, lesbian protagonists in novels had two choices: they could convert magically to heterosexuality, or they could commit suicide.

Imagine being the recipient of this message presented to fragile teens at that time—you either sublimate your desires and pretend to be someone you're not, or you off yourself.

Well, that's a load of crap.

Flash forward twenty years. Gay and lesbian and trans kids—and kids like me who had two moms (or two dads)—still lacked literature reflecting our life experiences. We did have Rosa Guy's 1976 teen novel *Ruby* and Nancy Garden's teen novel *Annie on My Mind*, published in 1982, about two high school girls who fall in love against a backdrop of homophobia that causes their lesbian teachers to lose their jobs.

But there wasn't a single book that reflected how a homophobic court system separated me and my younger siblings from our newly out mother and forced us to live with our volatile father instead. I didn't see my story anywhere until Cristina Salat's preteen novel *Living in Secret* was published in 1993. It's about a girl who runs away from her father to live with her mother and her mother's girlfriend. By the time *Living in Secret* appeared on shelves, I'd been out of my father's house for five years and dealt with my sorrow alone.

There were also no notable books reflecting the experiences of gay boys, or kids like myself with a gay brother or other family member.

Except for *Weetzie Bat*.

Teen novel *Weetzie Bat* is author Francesca Lia Block's homage to Los Angeles and the kids who live and play there. Yes, there's gay bashing. But also, there's a playful celebration of gay culture and same-sex relationships that previously eluded novels written for and about young people. The book preceded hundreds of teen stories with gay and lesbian protagonists who may struggle significantly with homophobia, but they certainly aren't resigned to either converting to heterosexuality or killing themselves.

In spite of their popularity with young readers, *Weetzie Bat* and *Ruby* and *Annie on My Mind* were banned from schools around the country because of content some adults found to be offensive or inappropriate for young people. That censorship sent readers a powerful message about our society at the time; many of my friends and family members regarded their identity with shame and remained in the closet or crept back inside.

"You used to put a gay character in a book and you were banned from all of Kansas," says author Chris Crutcher. "But now, it's trans kids. When you ban books about them, it says to every trans kid, 'You don't matter. I hate you, and I want other people to hate you too. Your existence stinks.' That's criminal."

Whenever Crutcher learns that a school has banned one of the teen novels he's written, he orders five copies delivered to the region's public library. He recognizes how easy it is to stand up for a controversial book you like but believes you also have to be willing to stand up for a controversial book you hate. "When you ban a book, you ban a group, and then everyone becomes a possible target," he says.

One commonly banned book is Alex Gino's preteen novel *George*. After it was published, *George* rocked the worlds of young transgender readers and their allies. Gino, who identifies as genderqueer (neither male nor female), worked for ten years on the story of a transgender fourth-grader assigned male at birth who can no longer stay silent about being a girl.

The novel demonstrates how adults impose gender restrictions on every aspect of a child's life, creating inner turmoil for a trans kid. "You will always be my little boy, and that will never change," George's mother tells her. "Even when you grow up to be an old man, I will still love you as my son."

George's teacher lines up students into rows of boys and girls. There are boys' bathrooms and girls' bathrooms at school, and boys' roles and girls' roles in the fourth-grade play. When George tries out for the part of the spider in *Charlotte's Web*, her teacher is both angry and terrified.

Sadly, this reaction is not uncommon. Anger and fear compelled some parents and school districts to pull out of Oregon Battle of the Books (OBOB) for the 2018–2019 competition year rather than ask students to read and report on *George*. Some cited the theme of a transgender child as too mature for young readers. Others simply said, "God doesn't make mistakes," negating the 150,000 teens in the US who identify as trans, as well as the thousands of younger children yet unstudied who know without a doubt they've been assigned the wrong gender at birth.

Like other book battles across the country, OBOB consumes young bibliophiles for much of each school year. Students across districts—broken up into grammar, middle, and high school teams—read sixteen books, then vie to win the state's title. There are YouTube videos of kids huddling in quartets during classroom trivia competitions in customized T-shirts and funny hats and wigs. The kids consult minuscule details in the books they've studied: In which book does a character root for the Los Angeles Dodgers? What was the name of a character's horse?

Book battles are supposed to be fun—joyful celebrations of reading. But when *George* made the Oregon list for grades 3 to 5, the fur began to fly. Two districts pulled their youngest teams from OBOB. Outraged parents took to social media, saying their kids had never met a trans child and didn't need to know about them.

Inspired by Chris Crutcher's approach, when those districts pulled their teams from the book battle, I sent several copies of *George* to their local public library. I got a few friends to send copies too.

But my friend Marcia, who taught her ten-year-old daughter to watch television with the remote in her hand, became despondent. "Those parents want my child to just go be invisible, please," she told me. "It would be so much easier for them if they could deny her very existence."

Nearly half of transgender youth attempt suicide. They're bullied or ashamed, or their parents reject them, or their friends reject them, or they just don't see how life is ever going to change. After discovering that stark statistic, author Donna Gephart wrote the preteen novel *Lily and Dunkin*.

Lily is a trans girl with an incredibly supportive mother and sister, and a father who evolves from frustrated and worried to accepting. She knows exactly who she is, and so does her best friend, Dare. It's a heartwarming story that shows, as so many preteen novels do, the power of friends and family to smooth out the rough patches in an adolescent's life.

After its publication, a Georgia parent reported to Gephart that students weren't allowed to read *Lily and Dunkin* in a "book bowl" competition, though it appeared on the list of librarian-selected novels. The irate parent complained to the school district superintendent, who, in response, worked to ensure access to every book on the list for every student in the competition.

"Not all school boards respond in that way," Gephart explains. "One school board in a tiny district in Florida moved to ban a large number of books. The school librarian fought the sweeping ban, speaking at board meetings with some of her students who knew they needed access to all the books to be academically competitive and more fully human. The books remained on the shelves."

More fully human. That's what we want for our children at every age, right?

When they find themselves, their friends, and their class-mates reflected positively in the pages of a novel, they see their humanity affirmed and enhanced.

But what if they're not allowed to read these novels?

As I followed the Oregon Battle of the Books controversy surrounding Alex Gino's *George*, I found myself thinking a great deal about the comments from parents who lamented the lack of "sweet and innocent" novels on the booklist.

As a preteen, I read *Little Women* and *Anne of Green Gables* until the covers frayed and fell off. I still adore E. B. White's *The Trumpet of the Swan* and pretty much everything by Madeleine L'Engle. I'm not advocating that we do away with these less controversial classics. But we need novels that reflect real kids' lives and challenges today. What better way to delve into the social and political issues affecting young people than through a competition that asks them to memorize characters and actions and motivations cover to cover? That sort of in-depth study can't help but build compassion for people whose lives look vastly different from their own.

Knowing this, Gephart is disappointed that there's so much pushback against many books with LGBTQIA+ content, such as *George* and *The Best Man*, Richard Peck's preteen novel about a boy whose beloved uncle marries his equally revered male teacher. "When we remove these books, we tell kids that their identities aren't valid, that they don't matter and shouldn't see themselves portrayed in literature," she says. "And we tell other students that it's okay to treat these students differently—as 'less than'—which creates toxic environments that can lead to violence and tragic consequences."

In *George,* as in *Lily and Dunkin,* the protagonists' best friends show readers how to greet the revelation of a trans peer with grace and encouragement. George's friend Kelly organizes a zoo excursion and loans her clothes and makeup so that for one glorious day, George can walk among strangers as Melissa.

At the end of *Lily and Dunkin,* Lily wears a dress and makeup to a school dance and her new boyfriend, Dunkin, dances with her to Donna Summer's "Last Dance" before Lily's father cuts in and hugs his daughter close.

Gephart recalls a trans woman who once shared how stories in her adolescence depicted trans characters as having horrible lives: "She assumed this was the only story her life could take and considered suicide. She marveled at how her life would have been different if she'd had access to stories and books with trans characters who lived typical lives and ones that had hopeful endings."

If only she'd had Benjamin Alire Sáenz's teen novel *Aristotle and Dante Discover the Secrets of the Universe* about two Mexican American high school boys in El Paso who meet and become best friends. Their relationship is challenged by guilt and fear and horrific gay bashing before a resolution that defies readers not to press the book against their heart with appreciation for a realistic and gratifying love story.

Sáenz, a university creative writing teacher in El Paso, came out as gay in his fifties. Molested as a child, he didn't fully come to terms with his sexuality until he began to write gay characters. Fear almost kept him from completing *Aristotle and Dante,* which went on to win a Lambda Literary Award and a Stonewall Book Award and was named a Michael L. Printz honor book.

Aristotle and Dante are fearful as well. But they also find support where they least expect it—from their parents.

The mothers and fathers in the book make this just as compelling a story for adults as it is for teens. The parents are complex, flawed, and troubled by what they know is a difficult path for their sons. But they're courageous enough to recognize love for what it is and to help their boys to see it as something to be revered.

Intersectionality—how gender, race, and class connect and overlap—informs every page of the book. Aristotle and Dante defy stereotypes of Mexican American males (or embrace them with a winking sense of irony) and dispute preconceived notions of homosexual young men. Readers who make the journey with Aristotle from angry and taciturn to exuberant and empowered may just move from a similar emotional paralysis to triumphant acceptance of their own sexual identity.

We cannot deny them that journey from bewilderment and shame to revelation and celebration.

"That novel was incredibly important to me," says the fourteen-year-old daughter of my friend Beth. "It's a deeply intimate, important book dealing with queer characters—but at its heart, it's not a coming out story. It made me realize that my sexuality was my own and that it was okay to take my time understanding it. It was a book I needed to feel comfortable in my own skin."

Books that represent LGBTQIA+ characters in a positive light are life-affirming, even lifesaving. They expand minds and hearts; they build bridges of empathy and understanding.

In 2017 author Donna Gephart spoke at a librarian conference in Florida. After her talk, a librarian from a small, conservative district came up to tell her how the administration either didn't purchase LGBTQIA+ books or kept them behind the desk.

However, the librarian told Gephart about how she created a safe space for the LGBTQIA+ students by personally purchasing these books with her own money so she could put them into the hands of the kids who needed them. "They'd come into her library to chat with her, hang out, and read," Gephart says.

If these teens seem unusual, spend half an hour in the teen section of your local public library. What you witness in terms of rapport between devoted staff and vulnerable young adults might just bring tears to your eyes.

The librarian went on to describe a trans student who had an unsupportive family and a hostile town environment; she'd given her a copy of Gephart's *Lily and Dunkin*. "With permission, the librarian later sent me a photo of this girl hugging her copy of the book," she says. "The student then sent me an eloquent, heartbreaking letter about how much she loved it and wished that she could have the support and hopeful ending that Lily does in the novel."

What a joy to connect a frightened trans kid with books like *Lily and Dunkin* and *George*. What a pleasure to learn of a teen's coming out and give him *Aristotle and Dante Discover the Secrets of the Universe*. These novels and their counterparts mostly end on a happy note. While these books don't reflect the experiences of all LGBTQIA+ youth, they're a lot more encouraging and realistic than those in which the protagonist has faked being heterosexual, or died by suicide.

Because, hey, even ten-year-olds know that's a load of crap.

PRETEEN BOOKS ABOUT LGBTQIA+ YOUTH

ASHES TO ASHEVILLE by Sarah Dooley (G. P. Putnam's Sons, 2017). After one of her mothers dies, twelve-year-old Fella is forced to leave her remaining mother and her sixteen-year old sister, Zany, to live with her grandmother. Zany retrieves Fella, and they journey with a charismatic poodle on a disaster-filled road trip to scatter their mother's ashes in North Carolina.

THE BEST MAN by Richard Peck (Dial Books for Young Readers, 2016). Fifth-grade student Archer Magill admires his teacher, Mr. McLeod—who outs himself as gay in response to school bullying—then finds that his beloved uncle might just marry Mr. McLeod.

BETTER NATE THAN EVER by Tim Federle (Simon & Schuster Books for Young Readers, 2013). Thirteen-year-old Nate Foster sneaks away from his small town and leaves his religious father and depressed mother. With his best friend, he heads for New York City to audition for *E.T.: The Musical*, where he discovers his estranged aunt along with a sense of belonging and an emerging sexuality.

THE BOY IN THE DRESS by David Walliams (Razorbill, 2009). Twelve-year-old Dennis loves soccer and fashionable dresses in *Vogue* magazine. After a friend persuades him to wear a sequined dress and wig to school and portray a French female exchange student, the headmaster expels Dennis and forbids him from playing in the soccer Final Cup.

DRAMA by Raina Telgemeier (Graphix, 2012). In this graphic novel, twelve-year-old musical theater set designer Callie becomes friends with two twin boys, and all three find themselves preoccupied by sexual identity and crushes and dates while working to put on a show with little money and low ticket sales.

DRUM ROLL, PLEASE by Lisa Jenn Bigelow (HarperCollins, 2018). Thirteen-year-old Melly spends two weeks at summer camp after her parents announce their impending divorce. There, she watches her best friend become preoccupied with boys, while she learns to play drums in a band and finds herself attracted to a girl musician.

GEORGE by Alex Gino (Scholastic Press, 2015). Fourth-grader George knows she's a girl; she just has to prove it to her mother, her brother, her teacher, and her best friend. She's not allowed to play Charlotte in the school play, and she becomes the target of two bullies, but her best friend recognizes the truth about her identity and helps her to come out in public as female.

GRACEFULLY GRAYSON by Ami Polonsky (Disney-Hyperion, 2014). Transgender sixth-grade girl Grayson Sender is a loner terrified of rejection and ridicule. In the midst of being bullied, she finds support and courage thanks to a caring teacher, a surprising friendship, and the coveted role of Persephone in the school play.

HURRICANE CHILD by Kheryn Callender (Scholastic Press, 2018). Twelve-year-old Caroline's mother has left her, and the kids on Saint Thomas of the US Virgin Islands won't stop bullying her, but she finds herself distracted by a new girl from Barbados on whom she's developed a crush.

IVY ABERDEEN'S LETTER TO THE WORLD by Ashley Herring Blake (Little, Brown Books for Young Readers, 2018). After twelve-year-old Ivy Aberdeen and her multiple siblings lose their house in a tornado and have to share a tiny hotel room, she struggles with feeling invisible as a middle child and with her attraction to another girl at school until she finds an adult in whom she can confide.

LILY AND DUNKIN by Donna Gephart (Delacorte Books for Young Readers, 2016). On a summer morning, an eighth-grade transgender girl meets the new kid in town—a boy with bipolar disorder. Both kids struggle with parental and peer expectations and with being ridiculed as they come to terms with their particular challenges and find comfort and joy in friendship with each other.

MARCO IMPOSSIBLE by Hannah Moskowitz (Roaring Brook Press, 2013). Gay eighth-graders Stephen and Marco find their friendship with its history of pranks challenged by a school bully and by Marco's plan to sneak into the high school prom and confess his love on stage for a bass-playing exchange student who's heading back to London.

THE MISADVENTURES OF THE FAMILY FLETCHER by Dana Alison Levy (Delacorte Press, 2014). Two dads and their four adopted kids navigate the school year and friends and extended family while trying to dodge the wrath of their resentful elderly neighbor.

MY MIXED-UP BERRY BLUE SUMMER by Jennifer Gennari (HMH Books for Young Readers, 2012). In Vermont in the year 2000, twelve-year-old June Farrell lives with her mother and her mother's partner, Eva, who plan a civil union ceremony. June becomes increasingly worried when an anti-gay campaign threatens her friendships but inspires her to stand up for her family's rights.

MY SEVENTH-GRADE LIFE IN TIGHTS by Brooks Benjamin (Delacorte Press, 2016). In this book with LGBTQIA+ characters, seventh-grader All Dillon's goal to win a scholarship at a dance studio is threatened by his father's plan for him to play football. Meanwhile, his freestyle friends want him to ace his dance audition so that he can tell the studio that their rules kill the creative process.

THE OTHER BOY by M. G. Hennessey (HarperCollins, 2016). Twelve-year-old Shane Woods has a best friend and a passion for graphic novels and baseball, but all are threatened when a classmate threatens to tell everyone that he's a trans boy.

THE PRINCE AND THE DRESSMAKER by Jen Wang (First Second, 2018). In this graphic novel set in Paris, Prince Sebastian's parents search for a bride for their son who secretly becomes fashion icon Lady Crystallia. His dressmaker, Frances, has big dreams herself—dreams she finds threatened by keeping the Prince's secret from the world.

PRINCELESS: RAVEN, THE PIRATE PRINCESS BOOK 1: CAPTAIN RAVEN AND THE ALL-GIRL PIRATE CREW by Jeremy Whitley (Action Lab Entertainment, 2016). In this first volume of a series, Raven, a young queer girl of color, steals a ship and assembles an all-girl crew of pirates to get revenge on the thieving brothers who caused her to be imprisoned in a tower.

P.S. I MISS YOU by Jen Petro-Roy (Feiwel and Friends, 2018). Evie confesses her crush on a new female classmate to her pregnant sister who's been sent away by their strict Catholic parents to live with distant relatives. In letters, Evie questions their religion and worries about what she views as a dysfunctional family.

SAVING MONTGOMERY SOLE by Mariko Tamaki (Roaring Brook Press, 2016). Young high school student Montgomery Sole hopes the crystal amulet she purchased will help her fight the bullies who disparage her lesbian mothers and gay best friend.

STAR-CROSSED by Barbara Dee (Aladdin, 2017). Twelve-year-old Mattie has a crush on her classmate Elijah. But during rehearsals for a school production of *Romeo and Juliet*, she develops an attraction to smart and beautiful Gemma Braithwaite—a crush observed by her friends when Mattie herself is asked to step in at the last minute and play the part of Romeo.

TEEN BOOKS ABOUT LGBTQIA+ YOUTH

ARISTOTLE AND DANTE DISCOVER THE SECRETS OF THE UNIVERSE by Benjamin Alire Sáenz (Simon & Schuster Books for Young Readers, 2012). Two Mexican American boys, Aristotle and Dante, meet and become close friends. Aristotle is angry; his brother is in prison, and his father is taciturn. He must come to grips with his feelings and with his sexuality when he realizes he's in love with Dante, who is the victim of a hate crime.

BEAST by Brie Spangler (Knopf Books for Young Readers, 2016). Tragically hairy fifteen-year-old Dylan is forced to attend therapy sessions for self-harmers and finds himself enamored of an intelligent and gorgeous transsexual girl.

BEING JAZZ: MY LIFE AS A (TRANSGENDER) TEEN by Jazz Jennings (Crown Books for Young Readers, 2016). Jazz Jennings wrote this memoir about transitioning to a girl at age five and coming of age as a celebrity figure while navigating discrimination, bullying, and high school.

THE DANGEROUS ART OF BLENDING IN by Angelo Surmelis (Balzer + Bray, 2018). Seventeen-year-old Evan Panos has an abusive mother and a father who works all the time. He's also beginning to realize he's gay. He hides in an abandoned monastery and draws. When he and his friend Henry begin a romantic relationship, Evan realizes he must pull away from his family in order to survive.

DEAR RACHEL MADDOW by Adrienne Kisner (Feiwel and Friends, 2018). After Brynn Harper writes to Rachel Maddow and receives a response, she drafts emails to the TV host about breaking up with her girlfriend, how her brother died, and how she takes remedial classes. Inspired by Maddow, she fights for a chance to weigh in on the selection of a new school superintendent.

EVERYTHING LEADS TO YOU by Nina LaCour (Dutton Books for Young Readers, 2014). The summer before her freshman year at college, eighteen-year-old Los Angeles set designer Ami finds a letter from a Hollywood film legend that leads her to a beautiful homeless teen named Ava.

THE FIVE STAGES OF ANDREW BRAWLEY by Shaun David Hutchinson (Simon Pulse, 2015). Seventeen-year-old Andrew Brawley falls in love with Rusty, a teen burn victim he meets in the hospital, where he's living after a car accident that kills his family. He reads Rusty parts of the superhero comic he's created, and realizes that he has to stop feeling guilty about being a survivor and allow himself to be loved.

GEORGIA PEACHES AND OTHER FORBIDDEN FRUIT by Jaye Robin Brown (HarperTeen, 2016). When high school senior Joanna Gordon's father relocates the family to a conservative town in Georgia, he makes her promise to keep her homosexuality a secret because of his work as a radio evangelist. She agrees, but then she finds herself falling for the sister of a new classmate.

GIRL MANS UP by M-E Girard (HarperCollins, 2016). Sixteen-year-old Penelope Oliveira overcomes cultural expectations and a friend's bullying to come to terms with her physical appearance and her attraction to other girls.

HISTORY IS ALL YOU LEFT ME by Adam Silvera (Soho Teen, 2017). After the love of his life, Theo, dies in a drowning accident, Griffin's obsessive-compulsive disorder worsens, and he confides in the only person who understands him—Theo's boyfriend.

I AM J by Cris Beam (Little, Brown Books for Young Readers, 2011). J, identified as female at birth, binds his breasts to the despair of his Puerto Rican mother and Jewish father. He runs away and starts classes at a school for LGBTQIA+ teens. After his best friend abandons him, he decides to pursue testosterone injections and attends college as a transgender man studying photography.

I HAVE LOST MY WAY by Gayle Forman (Viking, 2018). Harun, who is gay with traditional Muslim parents, sees a girl named Freya plummet off a pedestrian bridge onto a boy named Nathaniel. He accompanies both teens to the hospital, where he learns that Nathaniel has just arrived in town with desperate plans. Freya, scheduled to record her debut album, reveals that she can no longer sing.

IF I WAS YOUR GIRL by Meredith Russo (Flatiron Books, 2016). Transsexual teen Amanda Hardy is the new girl at school. When she finds herself falling in love with Grant, she's tempted to confess both her suicide attempt and her former life in her old school as a male.

IF YOU COULD BE MINE by Sara Farizan (Algonquin Young Readers, 2013). It's illegal to be a lesbian in Iran, and seventeen-year-old Sahar hides the fact that she and her best friend are in love. Though she doesn't want to become a man, it's legal to be transsexual in her society, and so Sahar contemplates sex reassignment—with the support of a trans friend—so that she can marry her beloved.

THE INEXPLICABLE LOGIC OF MY LIFE by Benjamin Alire Sáenz (Clarion Books, 2017). High school senior Sal is adopted into a Mexican American family with a gay father. After his best friend, Samantha, moves in with him, they befriend a teen living on the streets, and Sal gradually makes peace with his feelings of loss and grief about his birth family.

THE INSIDE OF OUT by Jenn Marie Thorne (Dial Books, 2016). When high school junior Daisy learns that her best friend, Hannah, is a lesbian, she petitions for same-sex dates at school dances and gains the attention of an attractive college journalist. After the story goes viral, protesters begin to gather, and Daisy finds herself taking on both the school board and the entire country.

LEAH ON THE OFFBEAT by Becky Albertalli (Balzer + Bray, 2018). Teen drummer Leah keeps her art and her bisexuality from her friends, including her gay friend Simon. But when her friends start to disband, reacting to tensions about college and prom, Leah is forced to confront her unexpected feelings for a girl.

LET'S TALK ABOUT LOVE by Claire Kann (Swoon Reads, 2018). Black asexual teen Alice finds her plans for a fun summer confounded by an unexpected crush on Takumi—a fellow employee at the library where she works. Alice must decide whether to risk this new friendship for a romance that could prove potentially bewildering to both of them.

LITTLE AND LION by Brandy Colbert (Little, Brown, 2017). Black teen Suzette finds herself attracted to a girl that her white brother likes in the midst of dealing with a crush on her childhood friend and a secret relationship with her boarding school roommate. Her feelings are further complicated by the fact that her brother is mentally ill.

LOVE IN THE TIME OF GLOBAL WARMING by Francesca Lia Block (Henry Holt, 2013). Seventeen-year-old Penelope loses her family and her home after a Los Angeles earthquake and flood. She goes in search of her parents and younger brother, picking up travelers on the way, and reflects on her love for her girlfriend in this nod to Homer's *The Odyssey*.

THE MISEDUCATION OF CAMERON POST by Emily M. Danforth (Balzer + Bray, 2012). Cameron Post, who has lost her parents, falls in love with a beautiful bisexual cowgirl, and her conservative aunt sends her to a religious conversion therapy camp in order to "cure" her of homosexuality.

MORE HAPPY THAN NOT by Adam Silvera (Soho Teen, 2015). After sixteen-year-old Aaron Soto's father commits suicide, he leans on his mother and his girlfriend for comfort. When his girlfriend leaves for a few weeks, he finds himself attracted to Thomas, but the fall-out from his friends inspires him to consider a cutting-edge procedure that will alter his memories and his identity.

MY CRUNCHY LIFE by Mia Kerick (Harmony Ink Press, 2018). Sixteen-year-old Kale Oswald joins a human rights organization, hoping to become a hippie. There, he meets Julian Mendez, who's taking puberty blockers and wants to transition to female. Through their friendship, Kale learns about his own sexuality, and Julian learns to defy bullies and be honest about who she really is.

NOTEWORTHY by Riley Redgate (Harry N. Abrams, 2017). Chinese American high school junior Jordan Sun sings second alto at a boarding school for the performing arts and can't land a part in the fall musical. When an elite all-male a cappella octet announces a vacant spot, Jordan dresses in drag and lands a spot, making her question femininity and masculinity.

ODD ONE OUT by Nic Stone (Crown Books for Young Readers, 2018). Three high school friends with nontraditional families navigate sexual fluidity told from multiple perspectives. New girl Rae Evelyn Chin meets and becomes attracted to best friends Jupiter and Courtney, launching a love triangle and challenges to their identity.

OPENLY STRAIGHT by Bill Konigsberg (Arthur A. Levine Books, 2013). When Rafe—who has been publicly out in Colorado—transfers to an all-boys high school in New England, he finds himself trying to blend in with straight jocks. Then he falls in love with one of them and has to come out of the closet for the second time, costing him important friendships.

PICTURE US IN THE LIGHT by Kelly Loy Gilbert (Disney-Hyperion, 2018). High school student Danny Cheng, son of Chinese American parents, gets into his dream college but panics at the thought of leaving his best friend Harry, and then discovers a shocking secret about his family history.

RUNNING WITH LIONS by Julian Winters (Duet Books, 2018). High school senior and star goalie Sebastian Hughes is open about his sexuality. Then his ex–best friend Emir Shah appears at summer training camp, and Sebastian attempts to befriend him again despite their difficult past, for the good of the team. Unexpectedly, they rekindle a friendship that turns romantic.

SHIP IT by Britta Lundin (Freeform, 2018). Sixteen-year-old Claire is dismayed when an actor in her beloved show *Demon Heart* assures her on a video gone viral that his character isn't gay as she'd assumed. The show's producers hire Claire to help win back the LGBTQIA+ community on a Comic-Con tour, where she develops a crush on a cute fan artist named Tess.

SIMON VS. THE HOMO SAPIENS AGENDA by Becky Albertalli (Balzer + Bray, 2015). A witty story about sixteen-year-old Simon Spier, a high school musical theater actor who is forced to confront his friends and his feelings about a handsome and confusing boy when an email meant for someone else goes astray.

SOCIAL INTERCOURSE by Greg Howard (Simon & Schuster, 2018). Gay South Carolina teen Beck rebels when his father begins to date the mother of a former bully named Jax, who's also star quarterback. Jax hopes his mother will get back together with her girlfriend, and the boys band together and attempt to ruin the romance at their conservative town's inaugural Rainbow Prom.

THE SUMMER OF JORDI PEREZ (AND THE BEST BURGER IN LOS ANGELES) by Amy Spalding (Sky Pony Press, 2018). Gay seventeen-year-old Abby Ives adores fashion and writes a plus-size style blog. After she gets an internship at her favorite boutique, she finds herself competing with the girl she's fallen in love with for a paid position at the internship's end.

UNBECOMING by Jenny Downham (Scholastic, 2016). After seventeen-year-old Katie's grandmother shows up at the door suffering from dementia, Katie discovers the truth about her mother and grandmother and comes to terms with her own powerful feelings for girls.

WHAT IF IT'S US by Becky Albertalli and Adam Silvera (HarperTeen, 2018). Ben carries a box of his ex-boyfriend's belongings to a post office in New York and meets teen actor Arthur who's in the city for the summer. After a series of separations that complicate plans for a first date, they wonder whether they're destined for romance, or not.

6

BOOKS ABOUT
MENTAL HEALTH

A nxiety just about destroyed my second-grader. At 2:45 p.m. Monday through Friday, she staggered into her school's corridor with enormous holes chewed into the neck of her T-shirt and her curls twisted into impenetrable knots. At home, she closed herself in her bedroom, where she sat for hours playing silently with her stuffed animals, recovering from the demands of the day.

My husband and I adopted our child from the foster care system when she was a toddler. Six years later, she still suffered from separation anxiety that sent her into a heart-pounding, gut-writhing panic each morning when we left her in the classroom.

When she began to retreat under a table at the back of the room and scream all day, we rearranged our work schedules so we could teach her at home for two years. With therapy and dance lessons and our constant support, she learned to trust her environment—even when it didn't include her parents. These days, she skips home from sixth grade with her shirt and her curls intact, laughing and chattering about her day.

But what about children with similar anxiety who can't—because of financial and/or time constraints—be homeschooled or participate in therapy or take part in extracurricular activities? What about parents privileged enough to provide their children and young adults with everything they need ostensibly, yet they still find themselves grappling with angst on a clinical scale?

The American Psychological Association estimates that fifteen million young people in the US suffer from a mental health disorder at any given time, and anxiety occupies the number-one spot. This might look like restlessness and irritability, or insomnia and fatigue, or difficultly concentrating, or emotional outbursts, or withdrawal from family and friends—the list goes on. Anxiety and depression often walk hand in hand, triggered by bullying, racism, homo- and transphobia, overscheduling, academic pressure, and a crippling fear of everything from climate change to the threat of terrorist attacks.

These mental issues may manifest as alcohol or drug addictions. They may be by-products of bipolar disorder or schizophrenia. Here's the really scary part: more than half of kids with clinical anxiety and depression don't receive any sort of treatment. Way back in the 1980s, after my parents' ugly and violent divorce, I was one of them.

At fourteen years old, I woke up at dawn and stood in the shower battling a crippling depression as I pictured the day's honors classes and yearbook meetings and play rehearsals and track practices and hours of homework each night. I coped with my father's volatile household and the enforced separation from my mother by becoming a straight A student who slept four hours a night. My parents and new stepparents, busy with their own lives, had no idea how I struggled, and I didn't tell them. I believed I was too weak, too sensitive to handle the obligations that my peers seemed to manage with grace.

If anxiety appeared in my shelf of teen novels, it looked like Madeleine L'Engle's bookish heroines gently worrying about parents and boys, or Holden Caulfield wandering around Central Park obsessing over ducks on the lagoon and the carousel's brass ring. Later I discovered Paul Zindel's *The Pigman* and Paula Danziger's *The Cat Ate My Gymsuit*—darker fictional treatments of adolescent unrest—and they became friends I turned to by flashlight when insomnia struck in the middle of the night.

It's easy for adults to say that every generation is anxious—there's always been something to worry about. As a teen, I lay awake at night terrified of AIDS and Iranian air strikes and catastrophic earthquakes (growing up in Los Angeles, this—at least—was a valid concern). But the internet and smartphones have raised the stakes. Every moment of every day, technology launches threats to young people's well-being from all sides. Hazards run the gamut from not getting invited to a party publicized all over social media to cyberbullying to potential missile attacks by countries at odds with the US.

All of these dangers, and so many more, appear in the pages of contemporary literature for tweens and teens—often as the motivation for character actions that complicate their young lives further. Protagonists struggle with a variety of mental health issues—everything from panic attacks and eating disorders to binge-drinking and suicidal ideation. As a high school insomniac, I read until 3 a.m., studying anxious narrators like Holden Caulfield in *Catcher in the Rye* and Vicky Austin in Madeleine L'Engle's *A Ring of Endless Light* for tips on how to survive.

Newer middle-grade and young adult novels are even more instructive and inspiring. Got a preteen with obsessive compulsive disorder? Give him Wesley King's *OCDaniel*— about a boy on a high school football team who struggles with mental illness until he's distracted by an eccentric girl and a life-changing mystery. Have a teen with attention deficit disorder? Give her Anna Priemaza's *Kat and Meg Conquer the World* about two girls—one with clinical anxiety and one with ADHD—who form an unexpected bond over video games and a school science project, but who find their friendship complicated by boys and sex and new online relationships with other gamers.

Jason Reynolds, author of the National Book Award finalist *Ghost*, got the idea for his preteen novel from a friend who—as a child—fled from his mother's gun-toting lover. The boy and his mom hid in a convenience store just like *Ghost*'s eleven-year-old Castle Cranshaw, whose father threatens to shoot them.

Three years after the incident, a sympathetic coach for the local track team recruits Castle, self-nicknamed "Ghost." Despite the boy's passion for competitive running, he's stricken with sudden panic attacks and fits of rage. In his words: "I got a lot of scream inside."

A lot of kids got a lot of scream inside. *Ghost* demonstrates how to navigate feelings of fear and anger safely by showing how the protagonist acts out at school until he begins to run track and finds adult mentors—his coach and a convenience store owner—to offer him guidance.

Ghost's house, with its memories of parental battles, terrifies him. Getting stuck accidentally in the stockroom of the neighborhood market terrifies him. But he survives thanks to his mentors . . . and exercise.

The benefits of an endorphin rush aren't news. Those "feel-good" chemicals released into the body when we exercise can fight pain and enhance our sense of well-being. Young adults benefit from an hour of exercise daily. Ghost, who runs at least that much to fulfill the demands of his track team, becomes fast and strong and confident as a result—and newly resilient to challenges at school and at home. Even if readers finish the novel and don't go out for the track team, they'll see the advantage of physical activity on the character's mental health.

Reynolds followed the publication of *Ghost* with three other books in his Track series: *Patina, Sunny,* and *Lu.* They each feature one of Castle Cranshaw's teammates and their own particular issues, which range from biracial adoption to parental neglect to friendlessness. In these novels, too, running is salvation. It's not a cure-all, but it's one heck of a survival strategy to combat anxiety and depression.

Another strategy is reading.

Cognitive neuropsychologists at the University of Sussex in the United Kingdom found that reading can reduce stress levels by almost 70 percent. Compare that to the study's 42 percent reduction after taking a walk. (The implications for reading to yourself while walking have not yet been studied.)

Participants in the study demonstrated reduced muscle tension and slower heart rate after just six minutes of silent reading. It doesn't even matter what you read, doctors tell us—just the act of slowing down and immersing ourselves in words is enough. Imagine the implications for teens, one in eight of which struggle with anxiety. Feeling tense? Crack open your favorite novel.

Still, sometimes even the rereading of a beloved Harry Potter book isn't going to soothe teens who battle clinical depression and anxiety as the result of feeling physically and emotionally unsafe on a daily basis.

Kerry Sutherland works as a youth services librarian in Ohio. She also volunteers for In the Margins, a committee formed through Library Services for Youth in Custody, to identify books that appeal to multicultural and LGBTQIA+ youth, as well as those in restrictive custody or living on the streets. Many of the books she suggests involve teens in marginalized situations—foster care, prison, homelessness, poverty, or a cycle of any or all—and who find themselves in these situations because of mental illness.

Sutherland spends a lot of time deciding on the titles she'll recommend to the kids she serves. One such book is Tom Rogers's preteen novel *Eleven*, about a New York City boy turning eleven on September 11, 2001, the day after a horrible fight with his father, who drives a commuter train to the Twin Towers. The boy, Alex, goes through almost the entire day before he realizes there's been a terrorist attack, and then he's overcome with anxiety about his father's well-being.

She's also on the lookout for novels that give readers the tools they need to make sense of what the *New York Times* refers to as "the deadliest drug epidemic in American history." Ohio ranks in the top five states for deaths due to opioid-related overdose. For kids affected by the drug crisis, Sutherland recommends Robin Bridges's teen novel *Dreaming of Antigone*, about a high school student with epilepsy whose soccer-star twin sister overdoses on heroin—a story far too common in the US, she tells me.

"When a child loses someone to overdose, it's a completely different animal than losing someone to terminal illness," she says. "There is anger, and then guilt at being angry. Sadly a lot of kids are reading novels about heroin addiction and overdose because that's their experience."

Can a novel nudge us toward empathy for a family member or friend who falls apart—who dies—because of drugs?

It can, insists Sutherland. "Kids get a lot of information thrown at them and it's very impersonal, but when they get it in a story—if it's really well written with believable characters—they fall into it. They're able to put themselves in someone else's shoes."

In her teen novel *10 Things I Can See from Here*, Carrie Mac puts readers in the shoes of sixteen-year-old Maeve, the clinically anxious daughter of an alcoholic father and an absentee mother. She begins with a chapter titled "Stupid Things People Say":

> You are not your anxiety.
> Don't worry your pretty little head.
> It doesn't matter.
> Don't exaggerate.
> Why get upset about something so small?

10 Things I Can See from Here illustrates the ineffectiveness of well-meaning, but ultimately ignorant, platitudes from friends and family and therapists and teachers. It shows how neglect can exacerbate a young adult's mental illness. Maeve's mother takes off for Haiti with her new boyfriend, and her father struggles with addiction; both refuse to put their teen on antianxiety medication.

"If they actually realized how bad it was—if they truly understood—they'd let me have pills," Maeve says. "If a leg is broken, put a cast on it. If you have cancer, do the chemo. If your head is messed up, take the pills."

But her parents are too self-involved to understand how anxiety ruins her life. Only her new girlfriend, Salix, comprehends the seriousness of Maeve's disorder and sets about helping her to deal with it. She teaches her distraction techniques and encourages her sketching—as lifesaving for

Maeve as competitive running is for Ghost. Teen readers who have never met someone suffering from clinical anxiety can gain a great deal of insight from novels such as Mac's.

"If a teen's life is void of individuals with the experiences and relationships they need to see, they can find those in books. And thank goodness," Mac adds. "So many people talk about 'escaping' into books, because that's what so many readers do. They're leaping out of their life and into a world where they are seen, and where they see characters thriving—or coping—with the things the reader might struggle with."

The benefits extend to adult readers as well. Parents, teachers, and other caregivers who read *10 Things I Can See from Here* or *Ghost*, or the hundreds of other novels featuring anxious and/or depressed kids, get a crash course in what symptoms to look for in a struggling young person, along with an idea of just how serious an undiagnosed mental illness can be.

In 2017 the *New York Times* reported that young people admitted to children's hospitals for suicidal ideation or self-harm more than doubled over the last ten years. Teens across the country admitted that academic pressure—both from parents and from themselves—accounts for a tremendous amount of stress. So does social media.

Kids with constant access to smartphone apps like Snapchat and Instagram receive a never-ending assessment of their own worth. Cyberbullying is omnipresent, along with the internal pressure to be as perfect as a painstakingly styled soft-focus selfie.

Most young adults won't overcome their anxiety and depression by staring into screens, and the protagonists they read about don't either. The message in novels like *Ghost* and *10 Things I Can See from Here* suggests that kids struggling with mental illness find a mentor or peer confidante and develop a passion. Running, sketching, slam poetry, basketball—these endorphin-producing activities offer something to distract from sleepless nights and downward spiraling thoughts, and help build a sense of self-worth.

Dancing, reading, and wildlife biology saved my daughter. Running, reading, and writing saved me. Exercise and a good book can't cure a child's anxiety and depression, but they sure can help.

Kerry Sutherland, the teen services librarian, shared a final story about an eleven-year-old girl at a shelter where she volunteers. The girl was physically mature with lots of makeup and bites on her neck, and she was suffering from delusion. The girl volunteered the information that her nineteen-year-old boyfriend was in jail, and that he was a vampire. Sutherland listened without judgment.

"She was proud of the marks on her neck and showed them to me," Sutherland says. "She wanted vampire books, but all I had was Sarah Dessen's *Just Listen*, which was as far from a supernatural book as it could be. It's about a relationship between a girl and her boyfriend who have communication issues."

The girl balked at the pink cover—at the image of a blond girl in skinny jeans and a lacy top lying on a pink bedspread listening to music on stylish pink headphones—the antithesis of vampire goth. Still, she ended up reading the entire book.

Afterward, she was more accepting of the fact that she wasn't allowed to see her boyfriend. Sutherland liked to think that the book gave her a more realistic perspective on how relationships are supposed to work. "You never know. You give them books, and you do the best you can."

Sometimes, kids discard the books she's given them, abandoning them at the shelter. The eleven-year-old girl took hers home.

These days, knowing a thing or two about middle-grade and young adult literature, I love offering carefully chosen books to my sixth-grader's classmates and my friends' children as gifts. Even more, I love being able to suggest books to kids who might be struggling with a particular issue, and then pointing them in the direction of the local library.

It doesn't take much effort to tune in to what's being published right now. Type "young adult novel" and a subject or theme into your favorite search engine, set it to look for books published in the last ten years, and prepare to be amazed at the wealth of literature out there. You don't have to be an author, a teacher, a librarian, or even a parent to give a tween or teen a book.

Be bold. You never know when the book you offer could save a young person's life.

PRETEEN BOOKS ABOUT MENTAL HEALTH

ALL THE THINGS THAT COULD GO WRONG by Stewart Foster (Little, Brown Books for Young Readers, 2018). Alex suffers multiple phobias, which make him the target of a bully named Sophie. Her friend Dan finds himself thrown together with Alex on a project, and he has to hide their growing friendship from Sophie, as Alex struggles to deal with his obsessive-compulsive disorder.

BOOKED by Kwame Alexander (HMH Books for Young Readers, 2016). In this novel in verse, bullies cause anxiety and fear for twelve-year-old Nick, who just wants to win a youth soccer tournament. Nick finds new hope and encouragement thanks to a rapping librarian who offers him inspiring books.

CHECKED by Cynthia Kadohata (Atheneum/Caitlyn Dlouhy Books, 2018). Eleven-year-old hockey player Conor McRae must give up the sport when his beloved dog gets cancer so that his single father can pay for chemotherapy. Without constant practices and games, Conor realizes the magnitude of his father's depression and wonders who he is himself without hockey.

COURAGE FOR BEGINNERS by Karen Harrington (Little, Brown Books for Young Readers, 2014). When twelve-year-old Mysti Murphy's father is hospitalized in a coma, she overcomes the challenges presented by her agoraphobic mother and her best friend who abandons her.

THE CROSSOVER by Kwame Alexander (HMH Books for Young Readers, 2014). In this novel in verse, twelve-year-old basketball star Josh struggles with anger and abandonment issues when his twin brother Jordan gets a girlfriend and their father's health begins to decline.

DARIUS THE GREAT IS NOT OKAY by Adib Khorram (Dial Books, 2018). Teen Iranian American pop culture expert Darius Kellner suffers from clinical depression and anxiety about taking his first trip to Iran. There he meets a neighbor boy named Sohrab, and they develop a bond based on soccer and endless conversations that help Darius to discover and celebrate his identity.

THE EDUCATION OF IVY BLAKE by Ellen Airgood (Nancy Paulsen Books, 2015). Eleven-year-old Ivy loves living with her best friend's family, but she returns home at her mentally ill mother's request. Art and movies offer comfort and distraction from the stress of attending a new school combined with her mother's neglect and volatile public temper tantrums.

ELEVEN by Tom Rogers (Alto Nido Press, 2014). Alex Douglas turns eleven years old on September 11, 2001, the day after a fight with his father, who drives a commuter train to the Twin Towers. That day, a bully crushes his cupcakes, and school lets out early for no apparent reason. Alex rescues a dog and babysits his sister, then hears that terrorists have attacked the World Trade Center.

FINDING LANGSTON by Lesa Cline-Ransome (Holiday House, 2018). It's 1946, and when eleven-year-old Langston's mother dies, he and his father move to from highly segregated Alabama to a lonely apartment in Chicago. There, he takes refuge from bullies in a library where he discovers the work of Langston Hughes and learns how much his mother admired the poet.

FINDING PERFECT by Elly Swartz (Farrar, Straus and Giroux, 2016). Twelve-year-old Molly Nathans develops obsessive-compulsive disorder after her mother leaves to take a yearlong job and may or may not show up at the slam poetry competition that Molly plans to win.

FLORA AND ULYSSES: THE ILLUMINATED ADVENTURES by Kate DiCamillo (Candlewick Press, 2013). When ten-year-old Flora, sorrowful over her parents' divorce and her mother's distance, meets a squirrel with superpowers in this illustrated novel, she begins to heal with the help of a neighbor and a strange boy. She defies her self-absorbed mother, who offers a surprising revelation of her own.

FORGET ME NOT by Ellie Terry (Feiwel and Friends, 2017). After her father dies in this novel told in free verse, middle school student Calliope June struggles with Tourette's syndrome and bullying in a new school in Utah. She finds both confusion and comfort in her new friendship with her neighbor, baseball pitcher and student body president, Jinsong.

FRAZZLED: EVERYDAY DISASTERS AND IMPENDING DOOM by Booki Vivat (HarperCollins, 2016). In this illustrated story, sixth-grader Abbie Wu struggles with fear and anxiety as the middle child between perfect siblings. When her school forbids junk food, Abbie organizes an underground lunch exchange and finds both self-confidence and a passion for effecting social change.

FROM YOU TO ME by K. A. Holt (Scholastic Press, 2018). When eighth-grader Amelia finds a to-do list created by her deceased older sister, she decides to complete it. In the process, she befriends a sad boy who knew her sister, and realizes she has to put a unique spin on the list in order to overcome her grief.

GHOST by Jason Reynolds (Atheneum/Caitlyn Dlouhy Books, 2016). Eleven-year-old Castle Cranshaw suffers from post-traumatic stress disorder after his father threatens to shoot him and his mother. Three years after the incident, with his father in jail, a kindhearted track coach invites Castle (aka "Ghost") to join the team and teaches him about trust and honesty.

THE GIRL WITH MORE THAN ONE HEART by Laura Geringer Bass (Harry N. Abrams, 2018). After Briana's beloved father dies, she feels like a new heart is growing inside her and telling her to find herself. But how can she, when she doesn't have time to write for the school magazine or pursue her crush because her grief-stricken mother asks her to take care of her little brother?

IN YOUR SHOES by Donna Gephart (Delacorte Books for Young Readers, 2018). Miles suffers from anxiety, though he'll brave his fears in order to visit his family's bowling center. There he meets Amy, a new girl with a passion for writing who dislikes living above her uncle's funeral home. Together they imagine a new way of being in the world.

THE LAND OF NEVERENDINGS by Kate Saunders (Delacorte Press, 2018). Emily, grieving the death of her older sister, shares an imaginary world created by her neighbor who has lost her son. When Emily dreams of toys that tell her she can find the beloved teddy bear that was buried with her sister, she embarks on a magical and dangerous journey.

THE MISCALCULATIONS OF LIGHTNING GIRL by Stacy McAnulty (Random House, 2018). Twelve-year-old Lucy is a homeschooled genius who survived being struck by lightning and has obsessive-compulsive disorder. Her grandmother insists that she attend middle school for a year where she must read one book that isn't about math, try one new activity, and make a new friend.

NINE, TEN: A SEPTEMBER 11 STORY by Nora Raleigh Baskin (Atheneum Books for Young Readers, 2016). Will struggles to make sense of his father's accidental death, while Sergio deals with hatred for his absent father. Aimee starts at a new school and misses her mother; Naheed is Muslim and getting strange looks for her head scarf. The stories of four preteens intersect before and during the 9/11 terrorist attacks.

OCDANIEL by Wesley King (Paula Wiseman Books, 2016). Thirteen-year-old Daniel struggles to hide his obsessive-compulsive disorder until he's enlisted to help a selectively mute classmate to uncover the mystery of her father's disappearance.

RAYMIE NIGHTINGALE by Kate DiCamillo (Candlewick Press, 2016). After Raymie's father leaves the family for a dental hygienist, she enters the Little Miss Florida Tire contest, where she meets an angry and abused girl with an absent father, and a poverty-stricken girl with an eccentric grandmother. The three form a powerful friendship and help each other cope with anxiety.

THE SEVENTH WISH by Kate Messner (Bloomsbury USA Childrens, 2016). Twelve-year-old Charlie catches a magical fish that grants her several imprudently phrased wishes. When Charlie discovers her older sister's addiction to heroin and watches her go into treatment, she resents her family's preoccupation with her sister and realizes wishing can be foolish.

SMALL AS AN ELEPHANT by Jennifer Richard Jacobson (Candlewick Press, 2011). Eleven-year-old Jack finds that his mentally ill mother has abandoned him in a national park, and he must find his way from Maine to his home in Boston while avoiding child welfare and his grandmother.

SOME KIND OF HAPPINESS by Claire Legrand (Simon & Schuster Books for Young Readers, 2016). Eleven-year-old Finley, sent to stay with her grandparents during her parents' impending divorce, finds solace from depression in her writing and in a forest full of fantastical creatures.

SPARROW by Sarah Moon (Arthur A. Levine Books, 2017). Eighth-grader Sparrow deals with profound social anxiety by climbing up on her Brooklyn school roof and pretending to fly. She's sent to a therapist who helps her deal with the death of a beloved librarian. When Sparrow attends a month-long girls' rock music camp, she begins to overcome her fears.

A STITCH IN TIME by Daphne Kalmar (Feiwel and Friends, 2018). Eleven-year-old Donut loves geography and taxidermy in this story set in 1927. Her mother is dead; when her father dies as well, Aunt Agnes moves in to escort Donut to Boston. Grieving, she and her best friend create a plan so Donut can stay in her home in the village near the forest with memories of her father.

SWING IT, SUNNY by Jennifer L. Holm (Graphix, 2017). Set in 1976, this is a graphic novel about tween Sunny who mourns the loss of her older brother, Dale, after he is sent to boarding school because of drug addiction. She finds comfort in friendship and music and television shows, but grows increasingly concerned when Dale returns home for Thanksgiving resentful and angry.

WHERE THE MOUNTAIN MEETS THE MOON by Grace Lin (Little, Brown and Company, 2009). Minli and her parents work the rice fields in China, sad and hungry, until she sets off on a journey to meet the Old Man of the Moon and ask him the secret to good fortune. She meets an orphan, a dragon without flight, and a talking fish in this coming-of-age novel based on Chinese folklore.

YOU GO FIRST by Erin Entrada Kelly (Greenwillow Books, 2018). Eleven-year-old Ben Boxer lives in Louisiana and twelve-year-old Charlotte Lockard lives in Pennsylvania, but they both struggle with bullying and family dysfunction and seek solace in outside interests like geology and history. When they meet in an online word game, they find their lives connected in mysterious ways.

TEEN BOOKS ABOUT MENTAL HEALTH

ALL THE BRIGHT PLACES by Jennifer Niven (Knopf, 2015). Teens Violet Markey and Theodore Finch meet on the ledge of their school's bell tower. He lets people think he's talked her out of committing suicide while his own anxiety continues to haunt him. They collaborate on a contest that requires them to explore Indiana, challenging stereotypes and finding unity.

ANGER IS A GIFT by Mark Oshiro (Tor Teen, 2018). High school sophomore Moss Jeffries suffers from panic attacks at his West Oakland High School after his father is killed by a police officer and denigrated by the media. Moss and classmates organize to protest random locker searches and intimidation by police officers stationed in the corridors, and he finds courage and purpose.

THE ASTONISHING COLOR OF AFTER by Emily X. R. Pan (Little, Brown Books for Young Readers, 2018). After Leigh's mother commits suicide, she and her father go to Taiwan to meet her mother's family. In her grief, Leigh is convinced that her mother has turned into a bird; she stays in Taiwan with her grandparents to uncover the reasons her mother never told Leigh about her childhood.

THE BATTLE OF JERICHO (and other titles in the Jericho Trilogy) by Sharon M. Draper (Atheneum Books for Young Readers, 2003). In this three-novel series, teen Jericho Prescott struggles with depression and anxiety after his cousin's accidental death, and he seeks solace in football while trying to help his cousin's pregnant girlfriend. The final book deals with prescription drug addiction, online bullying, and how three teens prevent a schoolwide tragedy.

BEAUTIFUL MESS by Claire Christian (Text Publishing, 2018). Grieving Ava meets anxious teen Gideon; they bond as coworkers and exchange letters. Poetric Gideon falls in love with Ava, but she is involved with her deceased best friend's brother. They deal with suicide, anger, cutting, and depression before realizing that they can help each other to heal.

THE BEAUTY THAT REMAINS by Ashley Woodfolk (Delacorte Press, 2018). Three former teen bandmates cope with depression and anxiety after each suffers a powerful loss. This novel explores issues surrounding suicide and fatal illness, anger and fear, and the power of love and friendship to provide solace in the midst of devastating grief.

BENEATH A METH MOON by Jacqueline Woodson (Nancy Paulsen Books, 2012). Fifteen-year-old Laurel has lost her mother and grandmother in Hurricane Katrina. She moves to Mississippi and becomes a high school cheerleader; however, when her athlete boyfriend introduces her to meth, she becomes addicted and homeless.

CHALLENGER DEEP by Neal Shusterman (HarperTeen, 2015). Caden Bosch is obsessive-compulsive and has paranoia. When he begins to believe that he's crewing for a pirate captain on a journey to an ocean trench and certain that people are trying to kill him, his parents have to take action. The author's son, diagnosed with schizoaffective disorder, provided input.

CLEAN by Amy Reed (Simon Pulse, 2011). Set in a drug and alcohol rehabilitation center for young adults, and told through journal entries and medical forms and notes from group therapy sessions, this is the story of five teens dealing with addiction and mandatory residence at the center as they reflect on dysfunctional families, rape, and other life challenges.

DOPE SICK by Walter Dean Myers (Amistad, 2009). Seventeen-year-old heroin addict Lil J hides from police in an abandoned crack house after a botched drug deal, and meets a man who is watching scenes from Lil J's past and potential future on a television. The man inspires Lil J to reflect on his life and his experiences with grief, regret, jail time, and addiction.

DR. BIRD'S ADVICE FOR SAD POETS by Evan Roskos (Houghton Mifflin, 2013). Sixteen-year-old James Whitman struggles with anxiety and guilt after his sister is kicked out of school and their house. He turns to poet Walt Whitman for solace and has imaginary conversations with an avian therapist, hoping he can heal himself along with his family.

DREAMING OF ANTIGONE by Robin Bridges (Kensington Books, 2016). Sixteen-year-old Andria, born with epilepsy, loses her father to suicide and her twin to heroin. Overcome with guilt at failing to recognize her sister's drug problem, she becomes romantically involved with her twin's ex-boyfriend while trying to stay seizure-free so that she can get her driver's license.

EVERYTHING ALL AT ONCE by Katrina Leno (HarperTeen, 2017). Lottie Reaves's beloved aunt—a bestselling author—dies of cancer and leaves her niece several letters with mysterious instructions that ask her quiet, cautious niece to start taking risks. When she realizes a secret about her aunt's past, Lottie finds herself dealing with her most powerful fears.

THE FALL OF INNOCENCE by Jenny Torres Sanchez (Philomel Books, 2018). Sixteen-year-old Emilia DeJesus stifles the memory of being attacked behind her elementary school, and she tries to forget the boy who hurt her. She's supported by her family and boyfriend, and by the crows in the forest that helped her survive. But a new truth surfaces about her attacker's identity.

FINDING AUDREY by Sophie Kinsella (Delacorte Books for Young Readers, 2015). Fourteen-year-old Audrey has just been released from the hospital for an anxiety disorder. She almost never leaves the house, and she doesn't attend school. But when Audrey connects with her brother's gaming teammate, she begins to recover with the help of a therapist who teaches her to work through her fears.

FORGIVE ME, LEONARD PEACOCK by Matthew Quick (Little, Brown Books for Young Readers, 2013). Loner Leonard Peacock plans to shoot his best friend-turned-bully after school on his eighteenth birthday and then kill himself. But first, he gives presents to a neighbor, a classmate, a teen evangelist, and a teacher; the latter helps Leonard to disclose the sexual and emotional trauma that plagued his adolescence.

GIRL IN PIECES by Kathleen Glasgow (Delacorte Press, 2016). When her insurance runs out, seventeen-year-old Charlotte Davis— an artist and a scammer—is released too soon from a mental health facility for treatment of girls with self-injury disorders. She's lost her parents and best friend, and she cuts herself to cope with anxiety in this story about learning to survive.

HEY, KIDDO by Jarrett J. Krosoczka (Graphix, 2018). This author's memoir—in graphic novel form—tells the story of living with his grandparents while his mother battles addiction and moves in and out of rehab. As a teenager, he struggles to understand his mother's mental illness and tracks down his absentee father.

I HAVE LOST MY WAY by Gayle Forman (Viking, 2018). When Freya falls off a pedestrian bridge onto Nathaniel, and Harun sees the accident, the teens bond over confessions about their anxiety. Harun is gay, with traditional Muslim parents. Nathaniel has just arrived in town with desperate plans. And Freya, scheduled to record her debut album, can no longer sing.

I'M WITH STUPID by Geoff Herbach (Sourcebooks Fire, 2013). High school football star Felton Reinsten finds himself overcome with stress when he's asked to reveal his college choice on television. Then his girlfriend breaks up with him, and the brother of the freshman he's mentoring commits suicide. In the midst of depression, Felton realizes what truly matters in life.

KAT AND MEG CONQUER THE WORLD by Anna Priemaza (HarperTeen, 2017). Two teens—one with clinical anxiety and one with ADHD—form an unexpected bond over their shared love for a video star and a yearlong school science project. Meg's decision to have sex with her boyfriend threatens her relationship with him, and her friendship with Kat.

THE LOCAL NEWS by Miriam Gershow (Spiegel & Grau, 2009). Fifteen-year-old Lydia struggles with anxiety about her undesired celebrity after her cruel older brother is murdered and her parents are overcome by grief.

THE LOOKING GLASS by Janet McNally (HarperTeen, 2018). Sixteen-year-old ballerina Sylvie goes on a road trip armed with a mysterious list of names discovered in a family storybook. She is searching for her older sister, who suffered an injury that ended her own dance career and caused her to overdose on pain medication.

THE MEMORY OF LIGHT by Francisco X. Stork (Arthur A. Levine Books, 2016). After Vicki Cruz attempts suicide, she meets other people with mental illness in the psychiatric wing of the hospital and begins to heal. But when she returns to her home and to the forces that drove her to depression, she must attempt to find courage without the support of her new friends.

THE PLACE BETWEEN BREATHS by An Na (Atheneum/ Caitlyn Dlouhy Books, 2018). Sixteen-year-old Grace interns in the gene-sequencing department of her father's lab, studying the schizophrenia that made her mother disappear. Just when researchers at the lab make a breakthrough, Grace begins to show symptoms of the disease, challenging her thoughts about religion and science.

THE REST OF US JUST LIVE HERE by Patrick Ness (HarperTeen, 2015). Senior high school student Mikey has obsessive-compulsive disorder. His older sister Mel struggles with anorexia. Three other friends deal with dysfunctional families and issues of envy, while a group of their more exceptional peers battle zombies and find themselves smitten with vampires.

ROGUE by Lyn Miller-Lachmann (Nancy Paulsen Books, 2013). Eighth-grader Kiara overcomes her depression and anxiety to help the new boy across the street get free of his abusive parents who enlist him and his younger brother to help with their production of meth.

SAY WHAT YOU WILL by Cammie McGovern (HarperTeen, 2014). Seventeen-year-old Amy has cerebral palsy and uses a walker and voice augmentation device. She asks her parents to pay for peer companions in her last year of school and falls in love with one of them—Matthew, who struggles with obsessive-compulsive disorder and devastating fears.

THE SHARK CURTAIN by Chris Scofield (Black Sheep, 2015). Fourteen-year-old Lily Asher struggles with schizophrenia—Jesus speaks to her in witticisms, and she frequently sees her dead dog. Her parents attempt to help her, but her mother struggles with alcoholism and drug abuse—and then begins an affair—in this book set in 1960s Portland, Oregon.

THE SKY IS EVERYWHERE by Jandy Nelson (Dial Books, 2010). Seventeen-year-old Lennie has an absentee mother and an older sister who dies suddenly. In the midst of her grief, she experiences moments of happiness and guilt as she navigates romantic relationships with her sister's grieving boyfriend and a new boy who's a vibrant and gifted musician.

THE SMALLER EVIL by Stephanie Kuehn (Dutton Books for Young Readers, 2016). In this psychological thriller, high school senior Arman Dukoff attends a pricey and secluded self-help retreat hoping to overcome anxiety and chronic illness. When the retreat leader who has championed him mysteriously disappears, Arman must figure out who he can trust, and whether he can even trust himself.

STARFISH by Akemi Dawn Bowman (Simon Pulse, 2017). When teenage Kiko Himura is rejected by an art school in New York, she overcomes crippling anxiety and leaves her narcissistic mother and abusive uncle to tour art schools with a friend on the West Coast.

THE STRANGE FASCINATIONS OF NOAH HYPNOTIK by David Arnold (Viking, 2018). Noah Oakman suffers from feelings of dread after he gets drunk at a party and spends time with the son of a deceased inventor. Suddenly, he notices strange things happening all around him and has to delve into the mysteries of his own mind to figure out truth and delusion.

TELL ME NO LIES by Adele Griffin (Algonquin Young Readers, 2018). High school senior Lizzy Swift befriends a transfer student, Claire, and they explore the 1980s art scene and dance clubs of Philadelphia. Lizzy's dating Matt, but he's holding something back. Meanwhile, Claire keeps a secret about a breakup that—when revealed—proves both shocking and threatening to Lizzy's relationships.

---

10 THINGS I CAN SEE FROM HERE by Carrie Mac (Alfred A. Knopf, 2017). Sixteen-year-old Maeve is the clinically anxious daughter of an alcoholic father and an absentee mother. She begins to cope with her disorder after she meets and falls in love with an independent girl musician named Salix, who builds up her confidence and encourages her love of sketching.

---

32 CANDLES by Ernessa T. Carter (Amistad, 2010). Fifteen-year-old Davidia Jones leaves her small Mississippi town and her alcoholic mother and moves to Los Angeles, where she becomes a nightclub singer. Her perfect life is disrupted when her crush from back home reappears in her life.

THIS ONE SUMMER by Mariko Tamaki and Jillian Tamaki (First Second, 2014). In this graphic novel, Rose and her friend Windy—who meet each summer at a lake house—begin to leave behind their childhood preoccupations with swimming and games. Rose, troubled by her parents' constant arguments, becomes fascinated with a group of drinking and smoking teens.

WE ARE OKAY by Nina LaCour (Dutton Books for Young Readers, 2017). College freshman Marin flees her secretive grandfather's house in San Francisco and heads for upstate New York, where her best friend agrees to spend winter break with her. Marin must confess the events of the previous spring and summer and address her complicated relationship with her friend at the same time.

WE REGRET TO INFORM YOU by Ariel Kaplan (Knopf Books for Young Readers, 2018). Prep school over-achiever Mischa Abramavicius finds her college applications rejected by all of the Ivy League schools, as well as her safety schools. Suspecting her computer has been hacked, she and her best friend Nate enlist the help of tech-savvy classmates to uncover the truth.

WE WERE LIARS by E. Lockhart (Delacorte Press, 2014). Wealthy Cadence Sinclair Easton and her cousins and friend gather together each summer on a private island off of Cape Cod. But after Cadence, at fifteen, suffers a confusing accident, she deals with amnesia and chronic pain as well as a dysfunctional family and a heartbreaking romance.

WHAT I LEAVE BEHIND by Alison McGhee (Atheneum/Caitlyn Dlouhy Books, 2018). Sixteen-year-old Will walks the Los Angeles streets depressed about his father's suicide and the rape of his friend Playa at a party from which he left early. He gives cornbread to a homeless man and leaves gifts for a child and for Playa, finding that these acts of kindness help him to heal.

WINTERGIRLS by Laurie Halse Anderson (Viking, 2009). Eighteen-year-old Lia, with a severe eating disorder, struggles with crippling self-doubt after her best friend Cassie dies. Lia must navigate therapy and treatment centers, while deceiving her parents about her mental health.

7

BOOKS ABOUT
NATURE AND
ENVIRONMENTALISM

When I worked as a high school literature teacher, I met freshman Celina Matthews, who stood out among hundreds of my students for two reasons: One, her parents had just divorced and she lived with her father instead of her mother as I had as a teen.

Two, she adored nature.

When I say adored, I mean she immersed herself in the natural world with a single-minded passion. She nurtured an avocado tree, amending the Virginia clay soil in her backyard with compost from her homemade pile. She grew potatoes and mashed them into cookie dough. She staffed an apple stand at the local farmers' market every week, absorbing the importance of sustainable organic produce on the health of our planet. And she read lots and lots of eco-fiction. Like me at her age, she realized that if she was going to find—and save—herself in the midst of domestic disturbance, she had to look deeply outside.

Reading nature-themed novels was a welcome distraction from the craziness of the divorce, Celina, now a college graduate, recalls. "Grief shrinks certain areas of the brain, which makes absorbing new information hard. Because I liked and was already familiar with the subject matter, my brain had an easier time engaging with these stories."

She began to learn about birds. She observed them in the wild and learned their species names; it made her world feel a little less out of control. "I found a lot of stability being able to list facts about bird/plant/natural phenomenons around me."

She also found herself thinking about the middle-grade fiction she'd read about the natural world and humans' effects on it, including the Magic Tree House and Boxcar Children series, as well as *Judy Moody Saves the World!*, about a third-grader with a passion for saving the rain forest.

Judy Moody reinforced for Celina that one person *can* make a difference. Unlike the parents in that book, though, her parents supported her eco-consciousness by gifting her with three recycling bins for her birthday—the household has been recycling ever since.

My sixth-grader wails about how hard it is to be a kid when it comes to environmental causes. She reads about endangered animals and threatened wetlands and beaches polluted with interminable, infinitesimal bits of plastic and wonders how on earth she's going to save it all. "Adults have all the power," she grumbles.

But that's not entirely true. And we have the literature to prove it.

Preteen eco-fiction—novels about the environment and our effect on it—sprout from publishers' catalogs annually, regular as daffodils. The stories most often feature a young person who feels just a little different from his or her peers—a kid who spots an environmental issue and figures out a way to help.

In S. Terrell French's *Operation Redwood*, twelve-year-old Julian Carter-Li protects a redwood forest from being chopped down. In *The True Blue Scouts of Sugar Man Swamp* by Kathi Appelt, Chap Brayburn—also twelve—saves ecologically rich swampland from an amusement park developer. In *Hoot*, the new kid in town bands together with a mysterious barefoot boy and a tough girl, toppling plans to erect a pancake house over a colony of burrowing owls.

Author and conservationist Carl Hiaasen wrote *Hoot* in 2002, followed by four more preteen novels: *Chomp, Flush, Scat,* and *Squirm*. He knows just how to entice young readers to consider and defend the natural world, with rollicking plot lines rich in mystery and absurdity and always with a conservationist theme.

The books in his series have bright and whimsical animal-themed covers. Each story boasts his signature sense of comic adventure along with the message that even kids—heck, *especially* kids—can fight back against greedy and unethical adults to protect their land and air and water.

Hiaasen grew up in Florida watching bulldozers destroy wilderness every day. He and his friends rearranged or pulled up survey stakes to disrupt development—mischievous acts replicated by his characters who sink pollution-dumping boats, surreptitiously film human threats to black panthers, and tuck themselves into owl burrows to halt bulldozers.

"Just because something was legal didn't automatically make it right," the new kid, Roy, in *Hoot* observes about developers while pondering how best to preserve the owl habitat without ending up in jail.

Three years after *Hoot*'s publication, journalist Richard Louv released his blockbuster parenting book *Last Child in the Woods: Saving Our Children from Nature-Deficit Disorder.* In it, he laments our decreased exposure to nature, and our kids' fondness for staying indoors "where the outlets are." He explains that in a world threatened by climate change, it's critical for adults to get outside into forests and mountains and beaches and backyard gardens—and to bring our children with us. We love what we understand, he observes, and we fight to protect what we love.

"More than ever," he writes, "building a future generation of conservationists will depend on helping children and adults fall in love with the natural world."

Hiking and kayaking and mountain biking and surfing all help us to fall head over heels for the land and water around us. But even kids growing up surrounded by skyscrapers can develop a devotion to animals and trees and plants by visiting their local parks—and through the pages of a novel.

In my own childhood, there was a scraggly willow under which I did homework every afternoon while observing starlings in the gutter—this was the flora and fauna of my home a mile from LAX. I grew carrots and lettuce in my father's tiny backyard, training sweet peas on strings up the pink stucco wall. My dresser was covered with houseplants and endless experiments involving potato peels and avocado pits. All that green stuff in the middle of my cement world kept me sane.

The dolphins in Madeline L'Engle's teen novel *A Ring of Endless Light* inspired me. Ditto, Louis, the mute trumpeter swan in E. B. White's *The Trumpet of the Swan.* I learned to look and listen closely to any nature I discovered under the often-smoggy skies.

Another E. B. White novel profoundly affected my colleague Kelly Milner Halls as a child. She was so captivated by the animals in *Charlotte's Web*, and the eight-year-old protagonist's habit of quietly observing them, that she devotes her life to writing children's fiction and nonfiction books about the natural world.

Halls notices how a lot of parents are so busy that they're not teaching their children how to turn over rocks and look at the animals, or how to respect creatures and how delicate they are. She is a firm believer—as I am—that it's critical to get kids outside.

In her preteen novel *Blazing Courage*, Halls gives voice to fourteen-year-old Annie, who mucks stalls until she's earned enough money to save a wild horse from becoming dog food. In the midst of training it, she deals with false accusations from a wealthy girl who boards her horse at the same stable.

"Books are safe," Halls says, "because even though you can recognize the pain that someone else is going through, it's not you. As a reader, you can think about what a character should do but still maintain your anonymity."

This is true of a novel whether the story is set in an old barn in eastern Washington or at Central Park's Turtle Pond. Through eco-fiction, readers see how a fish out of water can fight to ensure that the water remains habitable for all. It's a bonus when a character in a book also inspires young readers to take action.

Eighth-grader Avery McCrae is one of twenty-one kids suing the US government for failure to protect the Earth against the ravages of climate change through the nonprofit

Our Children's Trust. She became an environmental activist at age five, raising $200 to help snow leopards after she read about their endangered status in a book.

Library and bookstore shelves are packed with preteen novels that illustrate how kids can fight developers, polluters, and poachers while falling in love with redwood forests and burrowing owls and wild mustangs. But what about similar books for teens?

When teen novels start to grapple with such themes, the results are often dark and dystopian. While preteen novels present readers with a world that can still be saved, in novels for teens, the message is often that we're too late. What this tells me is that teens are aware of how dire the situation is for our planet, that they aren't as hopeful as their tween counterparts. In dystopian teen eco-fiction, water, land, and air are prohibitively toxic. Common animals have vanished. People in North America are parched, starving, dying off. Teen protagonists struggle to survive with varying degrees of success.

While it might seem hard to fall in love with a dying planet, especially if you've been raised to play where the outlets are, I find that these dystopian novels serve an important purpose in getting a conversation started. For example, by way of teens like Annie, who blogs at *Blossoms and Bullet Journals*. She published a post about Cindy Pon's teen novel *Want*, which is set in futuristic smog-suffocated Taipei and full of impoverished characters who can't afford protection from pollution.

Annie was not defeated but instead driven to action. "*Want* was a great reminder to me about why I need to do everything in my power to protect the planet," she writes, and then goes on to list action items she and her readers can put into practice, like taking shorter showers, turning off the water when brushing teeth, and walking or biking instead of driving.

She notes that the reason the book struck her so powerfully was because it felt so imminent. "Most dystopian novels—the kinds with invading aliens, or a bunch of kids running around murdering each other—aren't anything close to realistic, but a world where pollution is killing people and big corporations are taking advantage of it? That's believable."

Annie immediately brainstormed actions she could take to prevent the sort of environmental devastation she'd read about, and she hopes that enough people will realize that we need to start being more environmentally conscious so that such a ravaged world will never come to fruition. She also believes that books can be an avenue for change.

I come from a different generation; at Annie's age, I learned to conserve water and pick up trash on my Southern California beaches, but I rambled happily through the outdoors without the knowledge that my beloved ocean and forests were under deadly siege.

Decades ago, my friend Merie and I walked along Goleta Beach and dissected dead seagulls on the sand before sitting in our college classes on environmental literature and nature poetry. Now a literature professor and the mother of a daughter in junior high, Merie suggests that teen booklovers are drawn more to novels about social conflict and identity than stories about threatened animals and forests.

She wonders if the age when avid readers hit young adult fiction is also the age at which we realize the real wilderness we have to deal with might be peers, family, and school environment. "Nature recedes—sometimes becoming more of an intermittent refuge, or a refuge that isn't so much engaged in," she explains. For example, Katniss from the Hunger Games series may live in the forest, but she's nature-allied, Merie says, rather than nature-centered. She may appreciate the trees and hills of Appalachia, but she's not going to dedicate her life to saving them; she's too busy trying to save herself.

For teen readers who enjoy dystopian novels—who are perhaps, like Katniss, "nature-allied" but not "nature-centered"— try suggesting one of the more optimistic novels listed here to broaden their outlook. At the very least, it could spur a thoughtful conversation. Read the books yourself, and you just might find your family engaged in a lively dinner table discussion about how best to shrink your ecological footprint while making plans to visit a favorite state or national park.

Among the dystopia, fourteen-year-old Dave, in Brian Doyle's teen crossover novel *Martin Marten*, may strike readers as an anomaly, even as Doyle insists early on that he's a "regular guy" who's "not particularly strong or athletic or brilliant in school or handsome or talented in music."

Martin Marten follows two years in the parallel lives of Dave and a pine marten living in Oregon's Mount Hood wilderness. It's about as far from dystopian dread as a story can get. The setting is a small, diverse community of eccentric kids and adults, and of elk and weasels and pine martens.

"You've gotta be kidding?" I imagine most teens are saying about now. "You want me to read what?"

As a counterpoint to dystopia, they'll find in this novel a winking wit and profound commentary on what it means to be a teenager, regardless of where you grow up and whether you have two legs ... or four.

While *Martin Marten*'s plot has fewer hijinks than the eco-fiction kids might be used to, its meditative storytelling reminds kids of who they are in the natural world, how it provides refuge, and what it offers to those willing to pay attention—resilience, self-confidence, a grounding on the forest floor or sandy beach or mountain hiking trail.

There's a glamour, too, in simply surviving the natural world. As Dave's father tells him at twelve years old: "Of all the places on this green earth where weather can hurt or kill you right quick, this is the king of those places, more than a desert or ocean. Snow comes fast, temperature drops fast, rain turns to ice fast, rivers burst their banks fast. Know where you are, and be wary of the weather."

In an essay for the *Oregonian*, Doyle explains that he wanted to write a book in which the child and animal protagonists carried equal weight. "There are so many books in which human beings are stars and other species are sidekicks and props, and this seems arrogant and willfully blind to me, because there are millions of species of beings, and why not try to imagine what some of their wild lives are like?"

He also wanted to explore the difficulties of growing up—a process he described as "hard and humiliating and thrilling." Both boy and pine marten love their families, and they each feel the pain of impending separation. They're restless—sometimes hostile. They fight. They court females. They maintain a quiet, watchful regard that sustains them through their more angst-ridden times. But this is not some sleepy poetic tribute to the woods. *Martin Marten* has the same sly wit that makes *Hoot* and the rest so much fun. Nature bats last, after all, and the joke's on us.

In *Martin Marten*, Doyle tells of a cougar that appropriates the exit ramp of a freeway. He describes mysterious evidence of thirty bobcats gathered in the forest. He narrates the story of a young skier who gets stuck upside down in a fir tree after trying to do flips, concluding: "It took hours to bring him down safely, during which his friends stood under him and threw peanut-butter sandwiches up to keep him *fortificated*, as one of the brothers said to a television news reporter."

This type of teen eco-fiction gives kids an antidote to the turbulence they feel inside of themselves as they grow up, as well as the chaos they see outside of themselves as temperatures rise and glaciers melt and species disappear. Still, as long as kids are reading, they're cultivating a place of stillness and sustenance—a place that inspires many of them, like teen blogger Annie, and the twenty-one kids from Our Children's Trust, and my former student Celina.

Books such as *Hoot* and *Martin Marten* give readers role models—like-minded protagonists who've found solace and purpose and wisdom and hilarity in defending the natural world.

Celina graduated from college with honors in 2017 after defending her thesis—a book of eco-poems about insects. "The thesis defense was fantastic and unusual," she tells me. "I found a giant click beetle before the meeting, and my supervisor gave me a hornet to identify, so for the first few minutes of the meeting we discussed these bugs and swapped random bug stories."

She sent me her thesis manuscript, and I spent a morning poring over poems as delicate and subtle as the cricket antennae and beetle carapaces she described. Beneath the surface of the verses, there's the story of a bewildered teen navigating her parents' divorce, taking comfort in growing a cantaloupe plant in a cookie dough tub and sprouting potatoes whose vines covered the counters of her home.

For Celina, learning facts about nature gave her a sense of control because she could label specifics in the world around her. "The labeling made me feel like I understood something at a time when I didn't understand anything about all the changes going on," she says.

These days, she volunteers at her local children's nature museum and works to finalize an anthology of eco-poetry on animals and plants in the Appalachians. She's waiting to see where her love of science and literature takes her next.

I'm also waiting eagerly. Celina represents a cadre of young people who care passionately about the natural world—young people like Mercy and Shetuuka, who work as environmentally friendly farmers in Nambia, with a focus on eliminating hunger and creating jobs in their community. Young people like Dariya and Max, who created a clean energy plan adopted by their school that—in its first year alone—saved 30 percent in heating and electricity bills and sidestepped 103.8 tons of greenhouse gas emissions.

Looking to all of them, to their commitment and their innovations, I'm full of hope for what the world's future leaders will accomplish.

PRETEEN BOOKS ABOUT NATURE AND ENVIRONMENTALISM

AVENGING THE OWL by Melissa Hart (Sky Pony Press, 2016). Fourteen-year-old surfer Solo Hahn has to move with his family from Southern California to a trailer in Oregon after his father tries to commit suicide. When Solo accidentally injures a neighbor with Down syndrome, he must care for injured and orphaned birds of prey, and begins to develop a passion for the natural world.

BE PREPARED by Vera Brosgol (First Second, 2018). In this graphic novel, Russian American tween Vera watches her friends go off to fancy summer camps, but all her mother can afford is Russian summer camp. It's a humorous debacle full of terrifying outhouses, Russian history lessons, and girl-dramas that complicate Vera's desire to simply blend in.

BLAZING COURAGE by Kelly Milner Halls (Darby Creek Publishing, 2015). Fourteen-year-old Annie gets a job at a stable in Colorado to earn enough money to buy a wild mustang and then learns to train her. When a wealthy girl's thoroughbred goes missing at the stable and later a fire breaks out, Annie discovers new reserves of passion and bravery as she risks her life to save the horses.

COSMIC by Frank Cottrell Boyce (Walden Pond Press, 2010). Twelve-year-old Liam has a condition that makes him look like he's thirty. This has always gotten him into trouble, until the day he cons his way into being the adult chaperone on the first flight to take a group of kids into space and finds himself in a father role as they explore their new surroundings.

ELSIE MAE HAS SOMETHING TO SAY by Nancy J. Cavanaugh (Sourcebooks Jabberwocky, 2017). Elsie Mae adores the swamp around her grandfather's house and spends the summer exploring and attempting to save both the land and swamper families who are being robbed. When her religious cousin shows up and thwarts her investigation into the thefts, she proves herself a hero.

ENDANGERED by Eliot Schrefer (Scholastic Press, 2012). In this first book of the Ape Quartet series, fourteen-year-old Sophia spends the summer at her mother's bonobo sanctuary in the Democratic Republic of Congo, where she bonds with an infant bonobo named Otto. After the president is assassinated and armed revolution threatens the sanctuary, Sophie and Otto escape into the jungle.

ENDLING #1: THE LAST by Katherine Applegate (HarperCollins, 2018). Byx is the youngest of a pack of a mythical doglike species hunted to near extinction. When her pack is killed, she goes in search of safety, meeting friends who join her adventures with their own unique motivations for seeking safety and survival.

FINDING ESME by Suzanne Crowley (Greenwillow Books, 2018). When twelve-year-old Esme finds dinosaur bones on her family's Texas peach farm, she decides they are a message from her recently deceased grandfather. When the media learns about the discovery, they and scientists crowd the family farm, teaching Esme valuable lessons about life and loss.

FOREST WORLD by Margarita Engle (Atheneum Books for Young Readers, 2017). In this novel in verse, eleven-year-old Edver travels from the United States to meet his twelve-year-old sister, Luza, who lives in the Cuban jungle with their father. After the siblings post the discovery of a new butterfly on the internet with the hope that their cryptozoologist mother will see it, a poacher threatens their finding.

HALF A CHANCE by Cynthia Lord (Scholastic Press, 2014). Lucy's family moves to a house on a lake in New Hampshire, and she gets to know the boy next door whose grandmother suffers from dementia. Lucy learns to photograph her surroundings and anonymously enters a photo contest judged by her famous father, who's away on a shoot.

ME AND MARVIN GARDENS by Amy Sarig King (Arthur A. Levine Books, 2017). Eleven-year-old Obe Devlin watches as developers build on his family's farmland around their hundred-year-old Pennsylvania farmhouse. Then he discovers a mysterious plastic-eating creature at the creek and keeps the animal and its toxic feces a secret from everyone included his former best friend.

NATURE GIRL by Jane Kelley (Random House, 2010). Eleven-year-old Megan gets lost on the Appalachian Trail without her television and cell phone, and decides to hike all the way from Vermont to her best friend in Massachusetts.

THE ONE AND ONLY IVAN by Katherine Applegate (HarperCollins, 2012). A gorilla held captive in a mall loses an elephant friend but gains the friendship of another elephant, a dog, and a little girl. Authorities discover the gorilla's predicament and transfer him from his tiny enclosure to a zoo where he can live with other gorillas.

THE ONE SAFE PLACE by Tania Unsworth (Algonquin Young Readers, 2014). After twelve-year-old Devin's grandfather dies, he finds himself struggling to take care of their farm—one of the few left in the world because of climate change. He ends up at the Gabriel H. Penn Home for Childhood with gorgeous surroundings, and an administrator tells him that he has amazing sensory gifts.

OPERATION REDWOOD by S. Terrell French (Amulet Books, 2009). Twelve-year-old Julian Carter-Li meets Robin Elder, a homeschooled girl devoted to protecting a grove of redwood trees that his greedy and callous uncle wants to harvest through his company. Julian and Robin team up with his friend Danny to confront his uncle and save the trees.

PAX by Sara Pennypacker (Balzer + Bray, 2016). When Peter is forced to abandon his pet fox at the side of the road and move in with his grandmother, he swiftly runs away and heads for home three hundred miles away. Pax learns to survive thanks to other foxes that teach him to hunt, but the war-torn world is dangerous for animals threatened by land mines.

POACHED by Stuart Gibbs (Simon & Schuster Books for Young Readers, 2014). Teddy Fitzroy lives in a zoo and theme park called FunJungle. He hides from a troublemaking classmate in the koala exhibit, but then the koala goes missing. He didn't steal the koala, but he's the only one the camera has caught going into and out of the exhibit, and so he must set out to find the real kidnapper.

REFUGEE by Alan Gratz (Scholastic Press, 2017). An intertwining story of three children: Josef and his family flee Nazi-controlled Germany for Cuba on a ship. Isabel escapes Cuba and Fidel Castro's rule on a boat with her family. Syrian Mahmoud and his family cross the Aegean Sea to Greece. In parallel tales, the children survive shipwrecks and shark attacks, discovering the power of family and friends to help them persevere.

THE SKELETON TREE by Iain Lawrence (Delacorte Press, 2016). Twelve-year-old Chris and his uncle take a sailing trip down the Alaska coast, but their boat sinks. Chris and a boy named Frank are the only survivors. The boys take an instant disliking to each other, but they realize they must work together to find food and shelter and help in the wilderness if they hope to survive.

SQUIRM by Carl Hiaasen (Knopf Books for Young Readers, 2018). Billy Dickens has lived in six different Florida towns with his mother—who insists on residing next to a bald eagle nest—and he hasn't seen his father since he was four. When he finds his father's Montana address, he travels across the country to find him, dodging grizzly bears and saving endangered panthers along the way.

STEERING TOWARD NORMAL by Rebecca Petruck (Harry N. Abrams, 2014). Eighth-grade 4-H member Diggy Lawson is excited to enter a calf in the Minnesota State Fair. But suddenly, his classmate Wayne's mother dies, and Diggy finds out that they have the same father, which threatens his plans to win big with both the cow and the girl in 4-H he likes.

STORM-WAKE by Lucy Christopher (Chicken House, 2018). Moss loves her father and the flower-filled island she's grown up on, despite the intense storms that threaten the shore. She loves her friend, Cal, as well, but when a boy from the outside world washes up on the beach, she finds herself questioning her love for Cal, her father, and her island home.

THE THING ABOUT JELLYFISH by Ali Benjamin (Little, Brown Books for Young Readers, 2015). Convinced that her ex-best friend Franny died by jellyfish sting instead of drowning, Suzi stops talking and delves deeply into research to prove her theory. In the process, she relives Franny's unkindness to her and befriends a boy with ADHD.

THE TRUE BLUE SCOUTS OF SUGAR MAN SWAMP by Kathi Appelt (Atheneum Books for Young Readers, 2013). Twelve-year-old Chap Brayburn and two raccoons band together to save a beloved swamp from development into a wrestling arena and theme park.

WHERE THE WATERMELONS GROW by Cindy Baldwin (HarperCollins, 2018). Twelve-year-old Della Kelly watches her father try to save their farm; her mother is delusional and in danger of being hospitalized again. Della turns to the Bee Lady of Maryville, North Carolina, for a jar of her magic honey, hoping to cure her mother, and learns instead to accept her the way she is.

THE WILD ROBOT by Peter Brown (Little, Brown Books for Young Readers, 2016). Robot Roz learns to survive on a remote island by adapting to her environment, but her friendship with the animal inhabitants is threatened by the robot's past.

WILLA OF THE WOOD by Robert Beatty (Disney-Hyperion, 2018). Set in the Great Smoky Mountains, this fantasy story follows an orphaned girl named Willa who has been taught by her clan to loathe humans as murderers of the trees. But when her forest home is under attack and she is stranded among them, she learns shocking truths about her own Faeran people.

TEEN BOOKS ABOUT NATURE AND ENVIRONMENTALISM

ADRIFT by Paul Griffin (Scholastic Press, 2015). Teen Matt has plans to major in forestry at Yale. He and his best friend John spend the summer working in Montauk and discussing their plans for the future. They meet three teens in a Hamptons mansion, and all five steal a boat and head out at midnight into the Atlantic, where they become stranded in a disastrous five-day journey.

AFTER THE SNOW by S. D. Crockett (Feiwel and Friends, 2012). When Willo's family disappears from their wilderness home in a world made of ice and snow, he must venture into the terrifying city with a mysterious girl in order to find them.

BALANCE OF FRAGILE THINGS by Olivia Chadha (Ashland Creek Press, 2012). High school student Vic Singh barely notices the strange new environmental oddities around his home in upstate New York because of bullying and parental pressures. Then his grandparents move in with his family, and three generations learn to survive in a world devastated by climate change.

BETWEEN TWO SKIES by Joanne O'Sullivan (Candlewick Press, 2017). Sixteen-year-old Evangeline Riley lives in a Louisiana fishing town, where she loves to fish and sail her skiff. When Hurricane Katrina wrecks her world, she turns for comfort to a boy she once rescued—a blues musician who struggles alongside her to make sense of the devastation and loss of home.

BREATHE by Sarah Crossan (Greenwillow Books, 2012). Teens Bea and Quinn live in a world in which oxygen is rare and afforded mainly to the privileged, and they meet Alina, a girl who risks her life to plant trees and save the planet. When the government comes after Alina, she, Bea, and Quinn seek refuge in a rebel stronghold.

COPYBOY by Vince Vawter (Capstone Editions, 2018). This sequel to *Paperboy* tells the story of seventeen-year-old Victor, who takes a road trip from Tennessee to Louisiana to scatter the ashes of his deceased teacher at the treacherous mouth of the Mississippi River. Victor meets a beautiful young Cajun woman and deals with a drug dealer and a dangerous hurricane.

THE DISTANCE BETWEEN LOST AND FOUND by Kathryn Holmes (HarperTeen, 2015). Sophomore Hallie Calhoun and two other teens must survive in the Smoky Mountains wilderness, learning to trust themselves and each other despite the vicious rumors surrounding Hallie.

THE DISTANCE FROM ME TO YOU by Marina Gessner (G. P. Putnam's Sons Books for Young Readers, 2015). McKenna Berney defers her college acceptance and hikes the Appalachian Trail, where she falls in love with Sam and becomes lost in the wilderness, fighting for survival.

THE FALL OF INNOCENCE by Jenny Torres Sanchez (Philomel Books, 2018). Crows in the forest around her help sixteen-year-old Emilia DeJesus survive after she's attacked behind her elementary school. But when new information comes to light about her attacker's identity, she finds herself struggling to overcome anxiety and depression again.

GIRL UNDERWATER by Claire Kells (Dutton Books, 2015). After an airline crash in the Rocky Mountains, nineteen-year-old Avery Delacorte must survive freezing temperatures in the wilderness with her college swim teammate and three little boys.

I AM STILL ALIVE by Kate Alice Marshall (Viking, 2018). After a car crash kills her mother, Jess must move into her survivalist father's cabin in the Canadian wilderness. When he's murdered and the cabin burns to the ground, she has only her father's dog for companionship as she forages for food and builds a shelter, all the while plotting revenge on the killer.

THE ISLANDS AT THE END OF THE WORLD by Austin Aslan (Wendy Lamb Books, 2014). Leilani, a teen with epilepsy, must get home to Hawaii's Big Island with her father after technology fails and the islands are cut off from the rest of civilization.

THE LUCKIEST SCAR ON EARTH by Ana Maria Spagna (Torrey House Press, 2017). Fourteen-year-old Charlotte moves with her mother from Colorado to the mountains of Washington State, where she plans to train for a snowboarding championship. When her father petitions against land development, Charlotte loses access to the local ski resort and learns to ski in the backcountry.

MARTIN MARTEN by Brian Doyle (Thomas Dunne Books, 2015). Fourteen-year-old Dave lives in a community that borders the Oregon wilderness. His journey through adolescence parallels that of a young pine marten. Dave navigates high school and friendships, a first job, and a first love in a world populated by charismatic people and animals.

MEET THE SKY by McCall Hoyle (Blink, 2018). After a brutal accident that injures her older sister, Sophie just wants to get accepted to veterinary school and protect her family. But when a hurricane heads for their home, she's separated from her mother and sister and trapped on an island with a reckless boy who once broke her heart and now offers her his wild friendship.

MIDNIGHT AT THE ELECTRIC by Jodi Lynn Anderson (HarperCollins, 2017). In the year 2065, Adri is chosen to relocate to Mars. She discovers the journal of Catherine, alive during the Dust Bowl, whose family is suffering. As Adri tries to solve the mystery of Catherine's fate, their story is intertwined with that of British Lenore, who grieves her brother killed in World War I and attempts to travel to the US.

MY REAL NAME IS HANNA by Tara Lynn Masih (Mandel Vilar Press, 2018). Teen Hanna Silva escapes with her family and her friend Leon to the forest outside their Ukranian *shtetele* after Hitler's army crosses the border. When they are forced into caves, sickly and starving, Hanna's father disappears. She must find him while keeping hope alive for the rest of her family.

THE OTHER SIDE OF LOST by Jessi Kirby (HarperTeen, 2018). After eighteen-year-old internet star Mari Turner confesses her true self in an online video, she decides to hike the John Muir Trail in honor of her late cousin. She struggles with challenging terrain, both external and internal, as she tries to remember who she was before she became obsessed with her online world.

SAFEKEEPING by Karen Hesse (Feiwel and Friends, 2012). When Radley Parker-Hughes returns to the United States after volunteering in Haiti to find her parents gone and her country in chaos, she must escape through the woods to Canada, and then back to Haiti.

A SERIES OF SMALL MANEUVERS by Eliot Treichel (Ooligan Press, 2015). Fifteen-year-old Emma struggles at home and school. Her father, who has become distant, hopes to bond with her on a canoe trip. After Emma accidentally causes an incident that kills him, she's overcome by grief, but recovers thanks to a bond with her horse and the support of those who work on the river and her ranch.

STRANDED by Melinda Braun (Simon Pulse, 2015). Emma struggles with guilt after she survives a car accident that killed her sister, and sets off with a group to camp in the Minnesota wilderness. When their guide is killed, Emma and the others struggle to find food and shelter—battling wild animals and a potentially sociopathic teen as they attempt to find Lake Superior and home.

TORCHED by April Henry (G. P. Putnam's Sons, 2009). The FBI won't throw Ellie's parents in jail for marijuana possession as long as she agrees to infiltrate a radical environmental organization—an arrangement complicated by first love and potential murder on behalf of the planet.

WANT by Cindy Pon (Simon Pulse, 2017). Jason Zhou lives in the futuristic smoggy city of Taipei, where only wealthy people can afford special suits to protect them from the toxic air. When Jason and his friends discover foul play by the manufacturer of the suits, they set out to destroy the corporation—a plan complicated by Jason's feelings for the manufacturer's daughter.

WILDLIFE by Fiona Wood (Poppy, 2014). Introspective sixteen-year-old Sib and her best friend, Holly, spend a semester with other private school classmates in a challenging outdoor education program in the wilderness. There they meet a new girl named Lou, who's struggling with the death of her boyfriend, and who steps in to help Sib when Holly betrays her.

8

BOOKS ABOUT
PHYSICAL DISABILITY

As a new mother, children's author Beth Vrabel stood in the middle of a bookstore swaying with fatigue, her daughter asleep in a stroller beside her. She scanned the rows of books, then suddenly swept up her sleeping infant and pressed her against her chest.

Doctors had just diagnosed the baby, Emma, with a severe visual impairment. "I didn't know much of anything," Beth tells me, "but I was certain I'd be fine—*we'd* be fine—if I could just find a book to help me, a guide of some sort on being the mom of a visually impaired child."

That day, she couldn't find such a book to address her daughter's diagnosis, but as it turned out, doctors had over-estimated its severity. Emma has a mild form of albinism and vision impairment that hasn't inhibited her love of reading for an instant. When she turned ten years old, she asked her mother to help her find a book with a character who shares her disability.

The results discouraged them both. When they did a search, Vrabel recalls that the only books they could find featured characters who were villains or mystical—they either had otherworldly powers or were pure evil. "There wasn't a single story about a regular kid, with regular hopes and dreams, who just happened to also have albinism. Every single character was defined by their difference. It broke my heart."

This absence of positive models inspired Vrabel to write *A Blind Guide to Stinkville*, a preteen novel about twelve-year-old Alice, a girl with albinism and vision impairment. After Alice's parents relocate the family across the country and begin exploring schools for the blind, she proves how capable she is in the sighted world by entering an essay contest that asks her to explore her new town on foot with her dog.

Approximately 8 percent of people under the age of seventeen in the US live with a disability. That's almost three million kids with physical and/or cognitive challenges—kids at risk of being bullied and ostracized, who deal daily with stares and stereotypes when they just want to fit in.

"Everyone faces challenges. Everyone has a story," Beth notes. The trick, she says, is to figure out how you see yourself as a kid with a disability. "How you view yourself changes how others view you."

R. J. Palacio's preteen novel *Wonder* changed forever the way readers think about kids with severe facial differences—the story delves deep into the apprehension Auggie Pullman feels about his physical appearance when attending public school for the first time.

In 2015, Louisiana-based English teacher Martha Guarisco teamed up with guidance counselor Alicia Kelly and psychology professor Louise Freeman to teach *Wonder* to eighty sixth-grade students from the Episcopal School of Baton Rouge. They found that after the preteens completed an academic unit on the novel, they showed improved scores on a psychological empathy assessment.

Multiple characters take turns narrating in *Wonder*, so readers can feel Auggie's determination to succeed at school as well as sense his older sister's concern for him. They experience a classmate's hesitation when the boy first sees Auggie's face, then witness his gradual transformation into a loyal ally and friend.

All through my childhood, peers gawked and pointed at my younger brother with Down syndrome. He remained happily unaware of their discomfort. Despite my own adolescent irritation at the unwanted attention, I understood. Children stare at what's different. Sometimes those differences provoke fear. *Reading* about characters with disabilities lets a kid explore potentially frightening situations in a safe manner, especially if guided in conversation by a skilled adult.

Beth Vrabel notes that reading allows us to envision what we would do in the same circumstances presented in books. Then, if we find ourselves meeting someone who shares experiences with the character, we already have a well of understanding and compassion from which to draw.

I wish that as a young reader, I'd known Auggie. I also wish I'd known Melody, the eleven-year-old protagonist in Sharon M. Draper's preteen novel *Out of My Mind*. Melody is a girl with cerebral palsy who describes herself as "ridiculously smart." She's unable to feed or dress herself or communicate until her parents give her a computer affixed to her wheelchair. Then she becomes unstoppable.

"I don't set out to change readers' minds or their lives, but I do set out to give them something to think about couched in a cool character and a good story," Draper explains. In the case of *Out of My Mind*, "something to think about" means contemplating what life would be like for an intelligent and witty preteen stuck in a body that doesn't function like everyone else's, and who lacks a voice of her own.

Readers of all ages have emailed Draper to let her know how the novel changed their thinking and their way of looking at people with disabilities. Children come up to her and say about kids like Melody, "I didn't know they had thoughts in their heads."

Teachers report back to Draper about the book too. They've said to her, "I've worked with these kids for years, and I had no idea there could be that much hidden behind a wall of a body that doesn't work." Draper finds it both gratifying and sad. "But at least their eyes are open," she says. "People who work with similar groups of young people will say, 'Wow, we have conversations now. I found out that this particular person likes to crack jokes!'"

Out of My Mind spent two years on the *New York Times* best seller list. The story of Melody's quick and witty mind trapped in a body that allows her to control only her thumbs has captivated readers. Using those thumbs and a computer pro-grammed with thousands of words and phrases, Melody shows off her photographic memory and genius-level intelligence—traits that land her a spot on the school's quiz team made up otherwise of able-bodied children in mainstream classes.

Melody is an ideal protagonist to inspire kids' empathy for anyone with a physical disability. Her sassy candor defies pity and commands respect . . . and maybe just a little guilt from able-bodied people who walk by those who use wheel-chairs pretending they don't exist.

Consider the chapter in which Melody reflects on what it's like to sit immobile beside others from her special education room while kids from the mainstream classes play four-square at recess.

"They ask one another to play, but no one's ever asked any of us," she observes. "Not that we could, anyway, but it would be nice if someone would say 'Hi.' I guess the four-square players must think we're all so backward that we don't care that we get treated like we're invisible."

Books like *Out of My Mind* are expanding minds, inspiring young adults to embrace peers with disabilities as part of their classrooms and scouting troops and sports teams. A Nebraska high school basketball team includes a player with Down syn-drome. A junior high engineering class in Minnesota creates accessible products for preschool kids who use wheelchairs or walkers. In Oregon, a boy with autism about to be placed in a third-grade classroom without any other disabled students brings home a laminated book of drawings they've made for him along with a note from his teacher that reads, "We are so thankful that you are coming to our class! We love the same things you love, and we will love you!"

What a difference such acceptance would have meant to my younger brother, who—later in his adolescence—went to the local Boys and Girls Club after school and fielded insults such as "retard" from nondisabled peers. He attended only special education classes in the 1990s, and while he had dozens of buddies with disabilities, he had not a single non-disabled friend.

I witnessed the positive social effects of integration when I spent a year as a third-grade teacher at a school that served students with moderate to severe physical and/or cognitive disabilities. A mainstream elementary school sat next to ours; we used the same peer buddy system that Sharon M. Draper describes in *Out of My Mind*.

The premise is simple: a child with a disability in a special ed class is matched with a child or two in a mainstream class, and they travel back and forth between rooms a few hours each week. Children with disabilities gain greater access to rich and varied curriculum and friends. Kids from mainstream classes practice compassion and kindness while gaining insight from schoolmates who may look and act very differently from them.

The children from the mainstream school flocked to sit with my students in the cafeteria, happily feeding those who couldn't feed themselves, pushing their wheelchairs or guiding their walkers, and chatting with them constantly. They weren't "on the clock" at lunch, but they developed friendships and genuine affection for my students, and they wanted to help them as much as they possibly could.

In *Out of My Mind*, Melody's peer buddy Rose is kind-hearted but conflicted about becoming friends with someone who drools and flails. Though Rose goes to the local aquarium with Melody, she's embarrassed when her able-bodied peers see them together. These types of ethical scenarios make the novel a powerful conversation-starter about privilege and inclusion. Young readers will undoubtedly find themselves rooting for Melody after an unexpected and unsettling conclusion that they just might remember for a lifetime.

Over the past thirty years, technology has allowed mute children to voice their thoughts and feelings. Children who don't have the use of a single body part can get eye-tracking computers that allow for articulation. These advances are incredibly beneficial in aiding communication—it's easier than ever to reach out and say hello.

Other contemporary novels share the perspectives of kids with a variety of disabilities and needs. Sherman Alexie introduces us to fourteen-year-old Arnold Spirit Jr., an ambitious cartoonist who speaks with a lisp and a stutter, in *The Absolutely True Diary of a Part-Time Indian*. And Josh Sundquist offers up *Love and First Sight* about sixteen-year-old Will Porter—born blind and attending mainstream classes for the first time. Like Melody in *Out of My Mind*, Will develops friendships and wins a spot on his high school's quiz team.

Sundquist lost a leg to bone cancer when he was nine years old. He took up ski racing and competed on the US Paralympic team in 2006. He relied on his experiences as a disabled young adult when he wrote *Love and First Sight*. The novel illuminates the stigmas that complicate life for teens with a disability. As Will gets to know his classmate Cecily, with whom he eventually falls in love, he defies her pitying comments to him at the local art museum.

"You think my experience of the world is less rich because I'm blind?" he demands. "That's sightist. Assuming that blind people can't have a full life because they don't have eyesight. My sensory experience isn't *less* than yours. It's just different."

Teens who read *Love and First Sight* will come away with a new understanding of their peers with vision impairment. Will's voice is brutally honest, smart, and often hilarious. He accidentally gropes a female student on his first day of school. He sits on another in the cafeteria. And then Sundquist throws readers a curve ball. Right when Will has a surgery that gains him some sight, he (and we) learn that his girlfriend has a disability herself—a facial difference that has caused her to be ostracized from her peer group.

Meeting someone with a disability can be frightening even for older teens. Humor provides a way to understand and talk about it—to acknowledge difference as just that, and move on. Will joins a collection of witty teen narrators with disabilities, including Robyn Schneider's varsity tennis captain, Ezra, who suffers a shattered leg in *The Beginning of Everything*, and seventeen-year-old Piper, who's deaf and manages her school's rock band, in Antony John's *Five Flavors of Dumb*.

It's critical for kids with disabilities to see themselves represented in literature. At the same time, books with able-bodied characters speak to readers like author Beth Vrabel's daughter. Emma—now a teenager—found herself particularly drawn to *The Hate U Give*—Angie Thomas's novel inspired by the Black Lives Matter movement about a black teen whose mother drives her to a predominantly white school across town every day.

Though the struggles they face are vastly different, Emma felt a deep affinity for the novel's protagonist, Starr. "We both experience feelings of isolation—her as a black girl from a rough neighborhood in a school comprised mostly of privileged white kids, and me as a person living with a disability in a school of mostly abled students. This is not to say I understand the experiences Starr goes through, but I felt a strong connection to her emotional state."

How you view yourself affects how others view you. This is the message Beth Vrabel instilled in her daughter through the books she wrote with Emma in mind, and it's the theme of so many contemporary tween and teen novels, regardless of whether the protagonist is able-bodied or living with a physical disability.

As Vrabel points out, children living with challenges are just children. "Your story is so much more than just your challenges, and it's up to each of us to decide how our story is written," she says. "Sometimes you have to write your own guidebook when you're lost."

And sometimes, if you're lucky, someone like Beth Vrabel writes it for you.

174

PRETEEN BOOKS ABOUT PHYSICAL DISABILITY

ALL BETTER NOW by Emily Wing Smith (Dutton Books for Young Readers, 2016). A memoir about being diagnosed, after a near-fatal accident at age twelve, with a large benign brain tumor that caused the author to grapple with mental and physical disabilities, including dizziness, depression, anger, and chronic headaches. A loner and introvert, she describes how writing saved her life.

AS BRAVE AS YOU by Jason Reynolds (Atheneum/Caitlyn Dlouhy Books, 2016). Black eleven-year-old Genie Harris learns to love his blind but pistol-packing and irascible Grandpop when he and his older brother leave Brooklyn to spend a month with their grandparents in rural Virginia. They also learn about how their uncle died during Desert Storm.

THE BAKING LIFE OF AMELIE DAY by Vanessa Curtis (Stone Arch Books, 2015). Thirteen-year-old Amelie adores baking and has cystic fibrosis, which can make breathing difficult. When she gets an opportunity to compete in the Best Teen Baker of the Year contest, she has to convince her worried mother that she's healthy enough to participate.

A BLIND GUIDE TO STINKVILLE by Beth Vrabel (Sky Pony Press, 2015). Middle school student Alice never had issues with her albinism and near-blindness until her parents move her to Stinkville, where she decides to enter a community writing contest to prove her worth and finds herself exploring her new city with her dog.

BRACED by Alyson Gerber (Arthur A. Levine Books, 2017). Twelve-year-old Rachel Brooks, who has scoliosis, finds both her coveted spot on the soccer team and a relationship with a boy she likes threatened after doctors tell her she must wear a bulky back brace. Rachel overcomes issues with body image and self-confidence to triumph.

EL DEAFO by Cece Bell (Amulet Books, 2014). In this graphic novel, preteen Cece is deaf and struggles with the expectations of her mother, along with the insensitivities of teachers and peers. She deals with a series of failed friendships and battles misconceptions about being deaf before finding a girl who becomes her lifelong friend.

EVERYTHING ELSE IN THE UNIVERSE by Tracy Holczer (G. P. Putnam's Sons Books for Young Readers, 2018). After twelve-year-old Lucy's father is sent to Vietnam as an Army doctor, she and her mother move close to their eccentric Italian American relatives. Her father comes back an amputee, and she comprehends his changed behavior with help from a new friend and the discovery of another soldier's photos.

HALFWAY NORMAL by Barbara Dee (Aladdin Books, 2017). Seventh-grader Norah Levy has been away from school for two years battling cancer. When she returns, fragile and with a reputation, she struggles to maintain friendships, and meets a boy who shares her interest in Greek myths—a boy who has no idea that she's had leukemia until she has to figure out a way to tell him.

HELLO, UNIVERSE by Erin Entrada Kelly (Greenwillow Books, 2107). Deaf preteen Valencia teams up with a self-proclaimed adolescent psychic and her younger sister to rescue eleven-year-old Virgil who's trapped in a well after a neighborhood bully throws away a backpack containing Virgil's beloved guinea pig.

I FUNNY by James Patterson and Chris Grabenstein (Little, Brown and Company, 2012). In this illustrated novel, middle-grade standup comedian Jamie Grimm uses a wheelchair and deals with a cruel adoptive brother. Humor prevails, and Jamie—supported by two good friends and his uncle—enters a talent show and delivers a comedy routine to child patients in a rehab center.

THE LAND OF NEVERENDINGS by Kate Saunders (Delacorte Press, 2018). After her severely disabled sister dies, Emily shares an imaginary world created by a neighbor who has lost her son. When Emily dreams of toys that tell her she can find the beloved teddy bear that was buried with her sister, she embarks on a magical and dangerous journey.

LUCKY BROKEN GIRL by Ruth Behar (Nancy Paulsen Books, 2017). Set in 1960s New York City, this is the story of fifth-grader Ruthie Mizrahi, who emigrates with her family from Cuba and becomes a hopscotch champion. After a car accident leaves her in a body cast at home for an extended recovery, she learns to rely on friends and neighbors and develops a passion for the arts.

MAXI'S SECRETS (OR, WHAT YOU CAN LEARN FROM A DOG) by Lynn Plourde (Nancy Paulsen Books, 2016). When petite Timminy starts a new middle school, his fears are confirmed: he's constantly bullied. He takes comfort in his deaf Great Pyrenees and forms a friendship with his blind classmate, Abby, who gets lost in a snowstorm and rescued by Timminy and his dog.

MAYDAY by Karen Harrington (Little, Brown Books for Young Readers, 2016). Wayne Kovok is obsessed with unusual facts to distract from the facts of his absentee father and a baffling potential romance. After he and his mother survive a plane crash, Wayne loses his voice; when he eventually finds it again, he discovers that he has a lot more on his mind than simply reciting encyclopedia trivia.

MIA LEE IS WHEELING THROUGH MIDDLE SCHOOL by Melissa Shang and Eva Shang (Woodgate Publishing, 2016). Written by a teen with muscular dystrophy, this is the story of sixth-grade Mia who uses a wheelchair and has a talent for stop-motion filmmaking. When a mean girl threatens her plans to become Video Production Club President, she and her friends set out to reveal the girl's dishonesty.

NOT AS WE KNOW IT by Tom Avery (Schwartz & Wade Books, 2016). Ned, who has cystic fibrosis, and his brother, Jamie, find a strange creature caught in a net in their English fishing village. Their grandfather tells them stories of mermaids with the power to heal, and Jamie becomes certain that the creature will save his brother, whose condition is getting worse.

OUT OF MY MIND by Sharon M. Draper (Atheneum Books for Young Readers, 2010). Eleven-year-old Melody has cerebral palsy, which leaves her unable to walk or talk or move except for her thumbs. When her parents give her a computer with speech capability, Melody is at last able to convey the incredible intelligence and photographic memory that earn her a coveted spot on the school's trivia team.

PAPERBOY by Vince Vawter (Delacorte Books for Young Readers, 2013). Set in 1959 Memphis, eleven-year-old baseball star Victor Vollmer has always been withdrawn because of a stutter, but when he takes over a paper route for an injured friend, he finds himself interacting with people and developing a community—all of which are threatened when he's targeted by a "junk man" who's both bully and thief.

RED BUTTERFLY by A. L. Sonnichsen (Simon & Schuster Books for Young Readers, 2015). In this story told in verse, Kara—a child with a malformed hand—is abandoned as an infant in China and informally adopted by American parents living in the country. When police discover Kara, they deport her mother and send her to an orphanage for disabled children, where a new family hopes to adopt her.

SOAR by Joan Bauer (Viking, 2016). After Jeremiah learns that he has a severe heart condition and can no longer play baseball, he moves with his father to a new town, where the community is still reeling from the death of a school baseball player. With optimism and determination, Jeremiah becomes a coach and brings the sport back to the town's middle school.

SOUNDS OF SILENCE by Phillip Tomasso (Barking Rain Press, 2013). Twelve-year-old star pitcher Marco Lippa wakes up from hospitalization for meningococcal disease to find that he's deaf. His parents send him to a boarding school for the deaf, and he learns to communicate again, but he finds himself grappling with grief and bullies and how to talk with girls.

THIS KID CAN FLY by Aaron Philip (Balzer + Bray, 2016). This memoir is about the author moving with his family from St. John's in Antigua to the United States, where he was diagnosed with cerebral palsy. Despite poverty and difficulty maintaining friendships, Aaron creates a successful blog that gives readers insight into his condition as well as the discrimination faced by people with disabilities.

UGLY by Robert Hoge (Viking, 2016). This illustrated memoir by an Australian author describes life as a child born with deformed legs and a tumor in the middle of his face; in the midst of several surgeries, he deals with bullies and finds friends, attends summer camp, and participates in a school talent show. He eventually decides not to have any more operations.

THE WAR THAT SAVED MY LIFE by Kimberly Brubaker Bradley (Dial Books for Young Readers, 2015). Ten-year-old Ada has a clubfoot, and she's forbidden to leave her abusive mother's one-room apartment. When she sneaks out to join her brother and escape London during World War II, both kids end up in the care of a reclusive woman who nurtures them and teaches Ada to read and ride a pony.

WILD BLUES by Beth Kephart (Atheneum/Caitlyn Dlouhy Books, 2018). Thirteen-year-old Lizzie spends the summer in a renovated schoolhouse cabin with her uncle and El Salvadorian painter friend Matias, who has dwarfism. When two escaped convicts kidnap Lizzie's uncle and friend, she sets out alone in the Adirondacks with her guidebook to rescue them.

WONDER by R. J. Palacio (Alfred A. Knopf, 2012). Fifth-grader August Pullman, born with a facial difference, attends school for the first time. There he contends with a bully and finds true friendship. The story is told from multiple perspectives, which include August's older sister and the boy who becomes his best friend.

WONDERSTRUCK by Brian Selznick (Scholastic Press, 2011). Rose, who is deaf, lives in 1927 and is captivated by silent movies. Motherless Ben, in 1977, loses his hearing after being struck by lightning. He runs away from his aunt's house to live in the American Museum of Natural History, where his life—told in words, while Rose's is portrayed in pictures—begins to intersect with hers in mysterious ways.

THE ZOO AT THE EDGE OF THE WORLD by Eric Kahn Gale (Balzer + Bray, 2014). Marlin has a stutter, and people treat him poorly despite his position as the son of a famous explorer and owner of a Guyana zoo, where wealthy people can come to witness all the wilderness that remains. Life changes when a mysterious jaguar gives Marlin the power to talks to, and understand, animals.

TEEN BOOKS ABOUT PHYSICAL DISABILITY

THE ABLES by Jeremy Scott (Clovercroft Publishing, 2015). When Phillip Sallinger, who is blind, learns that he'll begin superhero high school, he finds himself assigned to a class for disabled kids. He's bullied and betrayed until he and his friends learn to escalate their powers and overcome their disabilities to battle the evil that threatens all of humanity.

ALTHEA AND OLIVER by Cristina Moracho (Viking, 2014). North Carolina 1990s teen Althea adores her best friend, Oliver, who has developed a mysterious disorder that causes him to fall asleep suddenly and stay asleep for months. When he leaves to participate in a study at a New York City hospital, Althea goes to find him but ends up living in a collective house of Brooklyn punks.

BECAUSE YOU'LL NEVER MEET ME by Leah Thomas (Bloomsbury Children's Books, 2015). Two teens who live in isolation with debilitating disabilities become best friends through a letter-writing correspondence in which they confess to loneliness and depression from being bullied, along with first love. Then they discover a disturbing connection with origins in a German laboratory.

THE BEGINNING OF EVERYTHING by Robyn Schneider (Katherine Tegen Books, 2013). Seventeen-year-old Ezra Faulkner suffers a car accident that shatters his leg and terminates his tennis career. His friends ignore him, and he reconnects with the best friend he'd rejected after a bizarre tragedy in middle school. He also develops a relationship with an intriguing new girl who's full of secrets.

BEHIND THESE HANDS by Linda Vigen Phillips (Light Messages, 2018). When elite musician Claire discovers that her younger brothers are diagnosed with an incurable illness that causes them to deteriorate physically and mentally before an early death, she sets aside her preparations for an important competition and uses her music instead to enrich their lives.

THE FAULT IN OUR STARS by John Green (Dutton Books, 2012). Sixteen-year-old Hazel Grace Lancaster has survived stage IV cancer over three years, and she meets fellow survivor Augustus Waters at a support group. Hazel is obsessed with a novel about cancer, and Augustus helps her to travel to Amsterdam, where they meet the author with unexpected consequences.

FIVE FLAVORS OF DUMB by Antony John (Dial Books, 2010). Shy chess-playing eighteen-year-old Piper, who is deaf, agrees on a whim to manage a popular school rock band in the Pacific Northwest. When her parents spend her college money on cochlear implants for her deaf baby sister, she's determined to get the band a paying gig despite its difficult and eccentric members.

GIRL, STOLEN by April Henry (Henry Holt, 2010). Blind teen Cheyenne Wilder, dealing with pneumonia, is accidentally kidnapped when Griffin steals her mother's car. His friends, learning that her father is the president of Nike, hold her captive, and Cheyenne must depend on her other senses and break free with unexpected help from Griffin, who becomes injured helping her escape.

LAUGHING AT MY NIGHTMARE by Shane Burcaw (Roaring Brook Press, 2014). This humorous memoir by the author at twenty-one describes his life using a wheelchair because of spinal muscular atrophy, which causes him to shrink and become weaker. He depends on close friends and family members for assistance, and he navigates romantic relationships with several girlfriends.

LOVE AND FIRST SIGHT by Josh Sundquist (Little, Brown Books for Young Readers, 2017). Sixteen-year-old Will Porter, born blind and attending mainstream classes for the first time, wins a spot on his high school's quiz team as well as a mysterious and troubled girlfriend. But when an operation allows Will partial sight, he discovers the truth about Cecily's physical appearance and the source of her anxiety.

LOVELY, DARK, AND DEEP by Justina Chen (Arthur A. Levine Books, 2018). Eighteen-year-old Viola wants to be a journalist and travel the world, but she develops an extreme case of photosensitivity and must stay away from all light sources. As she struggles to accept her chronic illness and her exciting new boyfriend, her parents grow more and more overprotective.

PUSH GIRL by Chelsie Hill and Jessica Love (St. Martin's Griffin, 2014). Cowritten by the star of Sundance Channel's *Push Girls*, this is the story of popular high school junior Kara, who is paralyzed in a car accident and has to adjust to her new life without her boyfriend and girls from the in-crowd. With the help of a longtime friend and a devoted ex-boyfriend, she triumphs.

THE RUNNING DREAM by Wendelin Van Draanen (Knopf Books for Young Readers, 2011). After sixteen-year-old star sprinter Jessica has to have her right leg amputated, she gets a prosthetic leg and returns to school. She becomes friends with a girl with cerebral palsy and a handsome, supportive boy. Because of insurance issues, the community raises money to buy her a $20,000 running leg.

SAY WHAT YOU WILL by Cammie McGovern (HarperTeen, 2014). Seventeen-year-old Amy has cerebral palsy and uses a walker and voice augmentation device. She asks her parents to pay for peer companions in her last year of school and falls in love with one of them—Matthew, who struggles with obsessive-compulsive disorder and devastating fears.

THE THING WITH FEATHERS by McCall Hoyle (Blink, 2017). Emilie has epilepsy; she's got a seizure dog and she's been homeschooled. When her mother enrolls her at public school, Emilie is partnered with a basketball player who develops a romantic interest in her as they work on a project about Emily Dickinson, and she must decide whether to tell him about her seizures.

TONE DEAF by Olivia Rivers (Sky Pony Press, 2016). Seventeen-year-old gifted musician Ali is deaf because of a brain tumor, and she's physically abused by her father. When she meets the guitarist for a boy band during a concert, he recognizes her bruises for what they are and helps her hide out with the band in their RV on a cross-country tour.

UNBROKEN: 13 STORIES STARRING DISABLED TEENS edited by Marieke Nijkamp (Farrar, Straus and Giroux, 2018). These fictional stories include protagonists with various physical disabilities, as well as intellectual disabilities and mental illnesses. One girl has a gastrointestinal disease and writes an advice column. A boy who uses a cane and suffers chronic pain accidentally wakes up the spirit of Richard III.

WE SHOULD HANG OUT SOMETIME by Josh Sundquist (Little, Brown Books for Young Readers, 2014). This memoir tells of the author losing his left leg to cancer at age nine and becoming a Paralympic ski racer who can't keep a girlfriend throughout high school. He interviews the women he's dated to examine the embarrassing and often hilarious reasons his adolescent relationships failed.

WHEN MY HEART JOINS THE THOUSAND by A. J. Steiger (HarperTeen, 2018). Seventeen-year-old Alvie, who has Asperger's syndrome, escapes foster care and works at a zoo with a one-winged hawk. She meets Stanley, who walks with a cane and falls in love with her; this terrifies Alvie so deeply that she loses her job and ends up homeless.

9

BOOKS ABOUT
POVERTY AND
HOMELESSNESS

A round the December holidays, stacks of mailing envelopes and packages in brown paper crowd Seattle children's author Martha Brockenbrough's hallway. Every year, she collects new books for young readers who might otherwise not have access to them. The idea grew from a 2017 report that estimated more than 3,600 homeless students were attending Seattle Public Schools. Her own kids are at schools where concentrations are the highest. Brockenbrough wanted to give something to these kids struggling with poverty and daily insecurity.

What she gave these students—after taking up a collection from author friends around the country—was two brand-new books apiece. They could keep one, and give one as a gift. This second copy was particularly important to her because homeless kids aren't often able to give presents.

The next year, friends asked if they could help wrap the stacks of more than six hundred books. "And then people started showing up," she says. "They brought wrapping paper. They brought friends. They brought their children to help—we even had some tiny ones going at it. I was astonished and so grateful."

In the end, they had enough books to give two to every homeless child at the nearby middle school, as well as extra books to take to the YWCA, which coordinates holiday gifts for hundreds of homeless Seattle families.

Inspired by Martha's social media post about the project, I took up a collection in my own city and ended up with hundreds of new books for kids between the ages of five and eighteen—books I wrapped in colorful paper and distributed to homeless and low-income kids at local schools and shelters.

The National Center for Children in Poverty estimates that, as of 2018, approximately fifteen million kids in the

United States live below the federal poverty line. Their parents struggle to keep a roof overhead and put food on the table as a result of low wages, unpredictable jobs, and the rising cost of housing. Going to school hungry and cold makes it difficult for a child to sit still and learn. Many schools provide free breakfast and lunch to students from low-income households, but that doesn't cover the long hours between noon and 8 a.m. the next morning. Poor nutrition, combined with poor sleep, only adds to the problem. Impoverished kids struggle with physical and mental health issues, behavioral concerns, and low self-esteem as they perceive all the privileges their classmates can afford.

It's hard for my twelve-year-old daughter and me to imagine a house without a bookshelf in every room, without books piled on end tables and dressers and under the cat. But sixteen-year-old Eleanor, in Rainbow Rowell's teen novel *Eleanor & Park*, doesn't even have money for a toothbrush, let alone a novel. She lives with her abusive, alcoholic stepfather, her cowed mother, and a horde of brothers and sisters in a tiny house in Omaha.

"There were only five rooms in the house, and the bathroom just barely counted. It was attached to the kitchen—like literally attached, without a door," Eleanor narrates.

Poverty informs every detail of her life. She shows up on the bus to her new school in oversize men's clothes and ragged blue jeans with curtain tassels tied in her hair, which she washes with whatever soap happens to be available. Her personal space at home is the top of a bunk bed and a cardboard box of art supplies and an old Walkman—a device she can't even use until a boy she meets on the bus offers her a couple of batteries.

The best preteen and teen contemporary novels, I think, offer powerful and relevant stories that show kids how to be friends and allies to one another despite their differences. We've all known (or been) kids who looked like Eleanor—scrappy, unkempt children and young adults slightly disturbing in their weirdness and their need. I think of Alora, a grammar school classmate of mine, who lurked near my family's picnic blanket at the local park one summer afternoon until my stepmother invited her over to eat. Still, I didn't befriend her—I lacked the courage and confidence.

But Park, a sixteen-year-old Korean American boy, braves the condemnation of the popular kids at school and befriends Eleanor, then begins to date her. He finds beauty in her original appearance and intrigue in their shared love of 1980s music and the comic books he gives her. The book shows readers how an open mind and a warm heart—plus a powerful chemistry—can transcend narrow-minded gossip and give way to an intimate and surprising connection.

Fictional stories can challenge the stigma of poverty for readers. They provide kids with insight into classmates who might not be able to afford the newest sneakers or the latest mobile device, but who are absolutely worthy of friendship and romance.

There's a message in *Eleanor & Park* for parents as well. Initially, Park's elegant and proper Korean mother rejects Eleanor because of her bizarre clothing and wild hair. But after she observes her and her multiple siblings in the grocery store, Park's mother softens. She buys Eleanor a Christmas present and tells her son what it was like to grow up in a large family.

"In big family, everything... everybody spread so thin," she says. "Nobody gets enough. Nobody gets what they need. When you always hungry, you get hungry in your head."

Hungry in your head. That's how Lewis Blake feels growing up in the 1970s on the Tuscarora Indian Reservation in Eric Gansworth's preteen novel *If I Ever Get Out of Here*. Lewis is poor—really poor, with a mother who works hard but can't afford a car or home repairs. He stuffs his clothes into a plastic bag instead of a duffel for sleepovers, wears dingy cotton briefs instead of pajamas, and gets his hair cut with a pair of deafening garage sale clippers that give off a burning odor.

And still, it's a story full of humor. Gansworth feels there's a tremendous courage in being funny. "Reading isn't encouraged for a large demographic—it's considered not cool. But if you can find a source of humor in reading, it's a way to cultivate a new possible allegiance. Books are a window that allow much greater empathy than when you're casually walking by somebody." Once you've spent time immersed in a narrative, he says, it's harder to unsee the real-life representations of those characters.

Novels increase awareness of marginalized communities. But publishers have to take a chance on publishing a variety of voices like Gansworth's, even if it threatens their bottom line. According to the excellent blog by multicultural children's publisher Lee & Low Books, black, Latinx, and Native authors combined wrote just 6 percent of children's books published in 2016. The majority of authors are still white and middle or upper class, though some of them are writing protagonists of different races and ethnicities and abilities. In response, young adult author Corinne Duyvis created the hashtag #ownvoices to refer to novels about marginalized people written by authors who share their same marginalization, whether it relates to race, disability, or poverty.

"If you're in the business of shaping young minds," Gansworth says, "you have a responsibility to do it in a way that broadens young adult novels. And if you're solely acquiring books from people who aren't #ownvoices, you're still part of the problem. I don't know where the overconfidence comes from that you could write outside your community about a siege and feel you've gotten it right."

Many Native American children are among the poorest in the nation. Geographically isolated reservations lack economic opportunity, and Native Americans have a particularly low full-time employment rate. Lewis's troubles in *If I Ever Get Out of Here* stem from embarrassment about his rundown house and lack of pocket money. They're confounded by racist comments and attitudes from classmates and adults who live off the reservation.

Shopkeepers regard him with suspicion. Pizza restaurants won't deliver to homes on the reservation, afraid they'll get jumped and robbed. Kids tell each other to stay away from Lewis because he's an "Indian." When Lewis bonds with the new kid, George, over a shared love of The Beatles and visits his middle-class home in local Air Force base housing, he begins to lie about his living situation. He's terrified that he'll lose a friendship that means everything to him.

"Friends are always worth the moments of joy you share, even if they don't last," Lewis narrates.

Stories like his show readers that despite a difference in socioeconomic level, they can form deep friendships based on a shared love of music and comic books and pizza . . . all the things that *really* matter. Gansworth explains how his novel resonated with one young reader in an unusual way.

"A number of years ago, a young downstate guy in late middle school from a more privileged background than my characters sought me out," he says. "He collected high-end sneakers—a pricey hobby. Because of the ways in which limited resources are portrayed in the novel, he wanted to know if I thought my community would be receptive to a sneaker drive."

The teen ended up joining the student council and soliciting hundreds of pairs of new and lightly used sneakers, which he and his family arranged to ship and then Gansworth distributed through a social worker on his reservation. The recipients were delighted.

"This fourteen-year-old kid married his passion for sneakers with this idea of generosity and benefiting the lives of others," Gansworth recounts. "If I have any evidence that my work has changed someone's opinion, here's this sustained effort to change a community of people you don't know at all—a concrete action that goes beyond, 'Can I write you a check?' or 'Here's twenty bucks.'"

When adults read books like his to and with their kids, they may just be inspired to lend a hand as well. In *Eleanor & Park*, Park's parents welcome Eleanor into their home and help her escape her stepfather's wrath. In *If I Ever Get Out of Here*, George's father lends Lewis his treasured Beatles albums, feeds him pizza, and takes him on an epic journey to see the band Wings in concert.

Knowing that I'm a role model to my daughter, I wonder how best to support the kids in our community who may long for more opportunities than their parents can afford to give them, whether for lack of time or money. I think back on my grammar school classmate Alora lurking around my family's picnic blanket, and how my stepmother shared our sandwiches without question. I think of the books I collected and wrapped and donated to homeless kids and young adults in December.

It's a start, but it's not enough.

There's so much we can do, in our busy world, to make a difference in the lives of vulnerable young people. We can share our picnics, our music, our circles of friends. And we can share stories.

Thank goodness for books, and for public libraries, which author Chris Crutcher describes as sanctuaries for kids. "If you're being bullied, it's a good place to run. There's solitude, it's warm, and there's always a teen section with beanbag chairs."

Crutcher, a trained therapist, has often told kids that they can always find a place to get a little foothold. "You don't get a happy ending very often, but if you can keep yourself alive, you can get a foothold to get to the next place."

I think of the teens who flock to my public library after school each day for art projects and movies and book clubs—the kids in ragged clothing, the blond cursing tween who totes a backpack and sleeping pad. I see them finding footholds among the stacks.

It's not so hard to get good books into the hands of kids who need them. My neighbor, a teacher, has slipped paperbacks for my daughter into our Little Free Library for years—novels about former foster kids, about biracial kids, about kids who love nature and dogs.

Dismayed by all the children on screens in the lobby at my daughter's dance studio, I put out a big box of books and rotated them with novels and nonfiction from the Little Free Library at her school. Many public libraries hand free books to kids who sign up to read a certain number of pages each summer. Various nonprofits distribute complimentary books to underserved communities. Dolly Parton, bless her, launched the Imagination Library in 1995, which has delivered over a million books specially selected for kids birth to five years old across the United States, personalized with their name and delivered to their home.

Kids care about books. In Monroe, Washington, a fifth-grader who learned that his elementary school might lose its librarian gathered a group of students and picketed outside the school with signs that read "Save Our Library." He spoke to the teachers' union, and wrote to a congresswoman about the importance of librarians to young people. When I read the boy's story, I sent him a signed copy of my preteen novel, *Avenging the Owl*. The letter he sent back knocked my socks off.

"I have been so grateful that this has brought attention to two things: kids can do more if we try, and literacy is important to people," he wrote.

In December from now on, I'll spend a little less time shopping and baking so I can pick up books and wrap them and deliver them to my local schools and homeless shelters. Last year, I lugged a laundry basket full of wrapped packages into a support center for low-income families with children a mile from my house.

"New picture books for little kids," I told the two women behind the counter.

"Oh!" They leaped up to help me with the basket, smiling broadly. "You brought books? Our children *love* books."

We don't know where the gift of a single story may lead children. At minimum, it offers a blissful few hours of distraction from trouble at home or at school. But perhaps it will give young readers a foothold—just the barest outcropping of optimism upon which they can climb high enough to see a new possibility, a new life.

PRETEEN BOOKS ABOUT POVERTY AND HOMELESSNESS

AFTER THE SHOT DROPS by Randy Ribay (HMH Books for Young Readers, 2018). Teens Bunny and Nasir find their friendship threatened when Bunny takes an athletic scholarship at an upscale school, and Nasir hangs out with his gambling cousin who's being evicted from his home.

ALMOST HOME by Joan Bauer (Viking, 2012). After twelve-year-old Sugar's father takes off to gamble and her grandfather dies, she and her mother lose their Missouri home. They move to Chicago and become homeless until Sugar moves in with a foster family where she discovers a love of poetry.

AMAL UNBOUND by Aisha Saeed (Nancy Paulsen Books, 2018). Pakistani girl Amal, who hopes to become a teacher, has to stay home to take care of her siblings, and then work as a servant to her village's corrupt landlord. When she realizes how corrupt his family is, she must figure out a way to work with the villagers to overcome the landlord and pursue her career dreams.

BINNY BEWITCHED by Hilary McKay (Margaret K. McElderry Books, 2017). When Binny finds cash next to an ATM, she takes it to buy a gift for her mother's birthday. But when the money disappears from her family's rundown English beach cottage, she must turn detective and solve clues to figure out which family member or neighbor has taken the cash.

BODY OF WATER by Sarah Dooley (Feiwel and Friends, 2011). After twelve-year-old Ember loses her trailer home in a fire set by a friend who thinks her parents are witches, she finds herself homeless and living with her family in a campground. She can't find her dog, and she struggles with how to navigate school with no clean clothes and not even enough money for a notebook.

THE BOY WHO LIED by Kim Slater (Pan Macmillan, 2019). After fourteen-year-old Ed Clayton's father goes to prison, he begins to lie compulsively. His mother loses her job, and they rely on a food bank in order to survive. When his younger brother disappears, a new neighbor tries to help find him; the two discover a secret that Ed longs to tell, but he worries that no one will believe him.

CRENSHAW by Katherine Applegate (Feiwel and Friends, 2015). Ten-year-old Jackson and his little sister and parents are about to get evicted from yet another home. Then, a seven-foot talking cat named Crenshaw appears—the same cat he met years before when his father was diagnosed with multiple sclerosis and the family lived out of their car.

THE DOLLAR KIDS by Jennifer Richard Jacobson (Candlewick Press, 2018). Middle school artist Lowen Grover and his family purchase a rundown home in a former mill town for a dollar. Lowen grieves the death of his friend, detailed in graphic novel panels. Some neighbors refer to his family as impoverished opportunists, but Lowen eventually develops friendships with his peers.

FAST BREAK by Mike Lupica (Philomel Books, 2015). After twelve-year-old Jason's mother dies, he tries to remain near the old basketball court behind the projects in North Carolina. But when authorities catch him stealing a pair of shoes, he moves in with a foster family that can help him on his path toward playing college basketball.

FLOR AND MIRANDA STEAL THE SHOW by Jennifer Torres (Little, Brown Books for Young Readers, 2018). Eleven-year-old friends Flor and Miranda have families who work at a traveling carnival; Miranda is in a band, and Flor's father runs a petting zoo. When Flor hears the owner talking about eradicating the zoo to pay the band more, she becomes friends with Miranda to keep her from performing.

HOLD FAST by Blue Balliett (Scholastic Press, 2013). When Early's poetry-loving father disappears from their one-room apartment in South Side Chicago, she and her brother and mother have to move into a city shelter. Early walks the winter streets and haunts the public library, looking for the truth of her father's disappearance as she starts a campaign for housing for the homeless.

HOPE IN THE HOLLER by Lisa Lewis Tyre (Nancy Paulsen Books, 2018). After Wavie B. Conley's mother dies, the teen must move in with her aunt, who only wants the money from her deceased mother's social security check. Wavie makes new friends in the poor Kentucky neighborhood and defies her aunt's attempts to become her legal guardian.

HOW TO STEAL A DOG by Barbara O'Connor (Square Fish, 2009). Georgina Hayes steals a dog for the potential reward money, hoping to help her family who have been living in their car since her father left. But the dog's owner can't afford a reward. After Georgina makes friends with Mookie—a squatter in an abandoned house—she decides to make amends.

IF I EVER GET OUT OF HERE by Eric Gansworth (Arthur A. Levine Books, 2013). Junior high student Lewis Black lives on the Tuscarora Indian Reservation in upstate New York in 1975, and goes to school with bigoted white classmates. He bonds over a shared love of music with new kid George Haddonfield, and struggles to keep the fact of his poverty a secret.

INVISIBLE GIRL by Kate Maryon (HarperCollins, 2013). Twelve-year-old Gabriella Midwinter once had a home, but when her father and his new girlfriend begin to argue and treat her as if she's invisible, she finds herself living on the city streets. Struggling to survive and surrounded by other homeless kids, she looks for her older brother with the hope that he'll provide a home.

JUST UNDER THE CLOUDS by Melissa Sarno (Knopf Books for Young Readers, 2018). Cora is homeless and living in a shelter with her mother and eccentric sister after her father dies. Her sister almost never speaks and hates wearing shoes. She's fine at the shelter, but after their room is raided, Cora's mother appeals to a friend for assistance—a friend that tells Cora about the resilient "tree of heaven."

LOUISIANA'S WAY HOME by Kate DiCamillo (Candlewick Press, 2018). Louisiana Elefante must leave her best friends when her grandmother—who says they're both cursed—drives away with her to a small town in Georgia. There, Louisiana meets a minister, a motel owner, and a strange boy with a crow, and begins to worry that she'll have to say goodbye to them as well.

MIDNIGHT WITHOUT A MOON by Linda Williams Jackson (HMH, 2017). Thirteen-year-old Rose Lee Carter lives with her grandmother in poverty on a Mississippi cotton plantation in 1955. After a boy named Emmett Till is murdered in the next town, Rose decides not to go to her mother and stepfather in Chicago, but to join the civil rights movement in Mississippi.

THE MIGHTY MISS MALONE by Christopher Paul Curtis (Wendy Lamb Books, 2012). Twelve-year-old Deza Malone and her brother and parents rely on each other's love and support as a poverty-stricken black family in a racist part of the country in 1936. When her father, out of work, suffers a debilitating accident, even Deza's beloved family is in danger of falling apart.

NOW IS THE TIME FOR RUNNING by Michael Williams (Little, Brown Books for Young Readers, 2011). When soldiers appear in the Zimbabwe soccer fields, Deo and his disabled older brother must flee their destroyed village. The boys experience poverty and prejudice, along with the kindness of strangers before tragedy strikes, and Deo must rely on the only thing he has left—his love of soccer.

PAPER THINGS by Jennifer Richard Jacobson (Candlewick Press, 2015). Fifth-grader Arianna Hazard hides her homelessness from her classmates, couch surfing and staying in a shelter with her older brother. As she struggles with personal hygiene and difficult friendships, her slipping grades threaten her plans to go to the middle school her mother picked out for her.

RED LEAVES by Sita Brahmachari (Pan MacMillan, 2014). When thirteen-year-old Somalian refugee Aisha is forced to leave her foster mother, she runs away and lives in an old air-raid shelter in the woods. There she meets twelve-year-old Zak, who is depressed by his parents' divorce, and together they form a bond with a homeless woman who also lives in the trees.

THE SEVENTH MOST IMPORTANT THING by Shelley Pearsall (Knopf Books for Young Readers, 2015). In 1963 Arthur Owens's father dies, and he throws a brick at the neighborhood "junk man," who's wearing his dad's hat. The junk man persuades the judge to let Arthur work 120 hours of community service, collecting seven important things from people's trash cans in order to create an artistic masterwork.

SO DONE by Paula Chase (Greenwillow Books, 2018). Jamila Phillips and Tai Johnson are best friends living in a low-income housing project. But after Mila returns from a month in the affluent suburbs, she and Tai begin keeping secrets from one another, even as they audition for the same gifted arts program that will give them purpose as dancers and keep them from danger on the streets.

THIS KID CAN FLY by Aaron Philip (Balzer + Bray, 2016). This memoir is about the author moving with his family from St. John's in Antigua to the United States, where he was diagnosed with cerebral palsy. Despite poverty and difficulty maintaining friendships, Aaron creates a successful blog that gives readers insight into his condition as well as the discrimination faced by people with disabilities.

TRASH by Andy Mulligan (David Fickling Books, 2010). Orphans Raphael, Gardo, and Rat live in poverty, combing through piles of trash in order to eke out a living. When Raphael decides to keep a mysterious item he's found instead of handing it over to the police for a large reward, the three boys find themselves in the midst of a dangerous conspiracy, afraid for their lives.

THE TRUTH ABOUT TWINKIE PIE by Kat Yeh (Little, Brown and Company, 2015). When school dropout hairstylist DiDi wins a million dollars in a cooking show contest, she moves her little sister GiGi from their deceased mother's trailer park to New York and an expensive private school. A mean girl named Mace becomes close with DiDi, and GiGi becomes friends with a popular boy.

TURTLE IN PARADISE by Jennifer L. Holm (Random House Children's Books, 2011). In the midst of the Great Depression, eleven-year-old Turtle finds herself shipped off to Florida to live with her scrappy boy cousins in her aunt's dilapidated house. There they find buried treasure, and Turtle begins to feel happy until her mother shows up with a new husband who steals Turtle's money and vanishes.

UPSIDE DOWN IN THE MIDDLE OF NOWHERE by Julie T. Lamana (Chronicle Books, 2014). When Hurricane Katrina hits, ten-year-old Armani gets separated from her parents and must flee with her younger sisters to the Superdome, and then a shelter. In the midst of death and destruction in the Lower Ninth Ward, she finds courage and resilience.

TEEN BOOKS ABOUT POVERTY AND HOMELESSNESS

CHERRY MONEY BABY by John M. Cusick (Candlewick Press, 2013). After seventeen-year-old Cherry Kerrigan and her family lose everything in a trailer park fire, she considers earning $250,000 as a surrogate mother for a British movie star's child. When she sees the star's English mansion, however, she sees her hardworking family and devoted boyfriend in a new light.

COMPROMISED by Heidi Ayarbe (HarperTeen, 2010). After fifteen-year-old Maya's con-man father gets thrown in prison, she runs away from a foster placement and heads for a long-lost aunt's house in Idaho. When she meets up with two other runaways, she finds herself questioning both her passion for scientific laws and her ability to live on her own.

ELEANOR & PARK by Rainbow Rowell (St. Martin's Griffin, 2013). Eleanor moves home from foster care to live with her abusive stepfather and cowed mother and siblings in a tiny, rundown house, and falls in love with Park—a Korean American boy who defies his classmates' prejudice against poverty-stricken Eleanor and helps her to find a safe place to live.

THE FIVE STAGES OF ANDREW BRAWLEY by Shaun David Hutchinson (Simon Pulse, 2015). Seventeen-year-old Andrew Brawley survives a car accident that kills his family and hides out in the hospital where they died. He falls in love with Rusty, a teen burn victim, and makes friends with other patients and the nurses, then gets a job in the hospital cafeteria.

GEM AND DIXIE by Sara Zarr (Balzer + Bray, 2017). In the midst of parental neglect and drug addiction, anxious Gem protects her outgoing sister, Dixie, who distances herself. When their father shows up after a long absence, the sisters find themselves alone in Seattle for three days, where Gem gains unexpected clarity about her broken home and her relationship with Dixie.

GIRL IN PIECES by Kathleen Glasgow (Delacorte Press, 2016). When her insurance runs out, seventeen-year-old Charlotte Davis— an artist and a scammer—is released too soon from a mental health facility for treatment of girls with self-injury disorders. She's lost her parents and best friend, and she struggles with cutting herself as a result of profound anxiety.

GIRL IN TRANSLATION by Jean Kwok (Riverhead Books, 2010). Kimberly Chang and her mother live a life of poverty in Brooklyn after emigrating from Hong Kong. Kimberly must juggle her ambitions as a student with her work in a Chinatown sweatshop at night, while struggling to learn a new language and a new culture.

IF ONLY by Richard Paul Evans (Simon Pulse, 2015). When Eric moves with his family from California to Utah, he meets a runaway girl scavenging for food behind a fast food restaurant. While his parents are preoccupied with the Cuban Missile Crisis, Eric hides the girl—his classmate—in his tree house and discovers unexpected truths about her situation.

IN REAL LIFE by Cory Doctorow and Jen Wang (First Second, 2014). Anda must confront her feelings about poverty and privilege in this graphic novel when—while playing an online game—she meets a cheating Chinese teen who has no health coverage and works excruciating hours.

THE INEXPLICABLE LOGIC OF MY LIFE by Benjamin Alire Sáenz (Clarion Books, 2017). High school senior Sal and his best friend Samantha befriend a teen living on the streets, offering him a new sense of hope. Sal, adopted into a Mexican American family with a gay father, finds himself grappling with his own powerful emotions.

LEAH ON THE OFFBEAT by Becky Albertalli (Balzer + Bray, 2018). Teen drummer Leah loves drawing, but hides her interest from her friends. She has a young, single mom, and money is scarce. While her more privileged friends succumb to worries about college and prom, Leah must confront her bisexuality and her romantic feelings for a girl.

NO PARKING AT THE END TIMES by Bryan Bliss (Greenwillow Books, 2015). After Abigail's parents sell their house and give the money to a faux preacher, they move into their van and travel to San Francisco to his so-called church, where they anticipate the end of the world. Abigail attempts to protect her angry brother, who falls in with a group of homeless teens and their street drama.

NO PLACE by Todd Strasser (Simon & Schuster Books for Young Readers, 2014). When star baseball pitcher Dan Halprin moves into a tent community with his middle-class family after his parents lose their jobs, he gains insight into fellow residents and their fight for more humane living conditions. A local real estate magnate wants to destroy the community, and Dan finds himself fighting to help them.

ON THE COME UP by Angie Thomas (Balzer + Bray, 2019). Sixteen-year-old Bri's plan to become a famous rapper intensifies after her mother loses her job and relies on food banks; they are under the constant threat of becoming homeless.

PANIC by Lauren Oliver (HarperCollins, 2014). Teens Heather and Dodge grow up in a small, impoverished town, and each hopes to win $67,000 in a life-threatening game called Panic. When they band together to compete, each discovers a secret, along with first love and unexpected courage to fight for what they care about the most.

PERFECTLY GOOD WHITE BOY by Carrie Mesrobian (Carolrodha Books, 2014). When Sean Norwhalt's alcoholic father leaves, and he and his mother move to a decrepit apartment, he falls in love with a girl from the thrift shop where they both work and contemplates whether to join the US Marine Corps—a decision he keeps secret from his mother.

PIG PARK by Claudia Guadalupe Martinez (Cinco Puntos Press, 2014). After businesses and schools close in her Chicago neighborhood during an economic downturn, and her mother disappears, fifteen-year-old Masi Burciaga must help her father run their Mexican bakery while community members sell their cars to fund a giant tourist-attracting pyramid.

PUNKZILLA by Adam Rapp (Candlewick Press, 2009). Fourteen-year-old street kid Punkzilla from Portland, Oregon, overcomes meth addiction with the hope of getting to Tennessee before his older brother dies of cancer. He hitchhikes, interacts with eccentric—and often dangerous—people, and navigates unsettling bus stations and motels in his trip across the country.

SORTA LIKE A ROCKSTAR by Matthew Quick (Little, Brown and Company, 2010). Seventeen-year-old practicing Catholic Amber Appleton and her alcoholic mother live in a school bus with a rescued dog. She teaches English to Catholic Korean women and volunteers at a retirement home until a fatal tragedy involving her mother threatens her optimism and her faith.

SPEED OF LIFE by J. M. Kelly (HMH Books for Young Readers, 2016). Twin sisters Crystal and Amber hope to be the first in their impoverished family to graduate high school, then Amber gets pregnant, and Crystal gets accepted at her dream college.

TAP OUT by Eric Devine (Running Press, 2012). Seventeen-year-old Tony Antioch lives in a trailer park and takes martial arts classes hoping to free his mother of her meth-addicted boyfriend. But when a drug-dealing biker gang attempts to recruit him, Tony must rely on the confidence and hope he's learned from martial arts in order to stay true to himself and his goals.

A TINFOIL SKY by Cyndi Sand-Eveland (Tundra Books, 2012). Twelve-year-old Mel has alternately lived under bridges with her mother, singing on the streets for spare change, and shacked up with her and the abusive men she chooses. When her mother goes to jail for shoplifting, Mel finds herself forced to live with her cold and bitter grandmother.

UNDER THE MESQUITE by Guadalupe Garcia McCall (Lee & Low Books, 2011). In this novel in free verse, Mexican American teen Lupita struggles to provide food and care for her seven younger siblings after her mother gets cancer and her father takes her to a faraway clinic. Lupita relies on her passions for acting and poetry during hardship and the fear that she'll lose her beloved mother.

WE ARE THE ANTS by Shaun David Hutchinson (Simon Pulse, 2016). Henry Denton's mother struggles to make ends meet, and his brother is an unemployed dropout. In the midst of Henry's own grief about his boyfriend who committed suicide, he finds himself with an ultimatum from the aliens who have periodically abducted him—let the world end, or push a button to stop it.

WE'LL FLY AWAY by Bryan Bliss (Greenwillow Books, 2018). Best friends Luke and Toby have absent mothers, abusive fathers, and a desire to escape poverty and their dead-end town. After Luke—a champion wrestler—lands on death row, he writes letters to Toby charting family abuse and first love and the events that led him to be imprisoned for life.

WHERE I LIVE by Brenda Rufener (HarperTeen, 2018). High school blog editor Linden Rose keeps the fact of her homelessness a secret. But when a popular girl shows up with a bloody lip, she recognizes the abuse for what it is and comes forward to report the violence at the risk of jeopardizing her own future.

10

BOOKS ABOUT RACE
AND ETHNICITY

Last year, the diversity and inclusion committee at my daughter's middle school sponsored a showing of Shakti Butler's documentary *Cracking the Codes: The System of Racial Inequality*. Parents, teachers, and others from around the community gathered to watch and discuss the film's heaviest talking points: white privilege in education, implicit racial bias in the classroom, and our country's long and horrific history of oppressing people not of Western European descent.

Some of the adults who watched that night admitted genuine surprise at the documentary's content. Some had no idea that students of color frequently experience the classroom in an entirely different way from their white classmates. Many were shocked to learn that kids regularly talk among themselves about race and ethnicity, prejudice, anti-immigration politics, and flat-out fear for themselves and their friends who might be targeted by haters.

"I know I should talk about race in my classroom," one teacher said that evening, "but I'm not sure how to bring it up."

I understand her anxiety. As a twenty-four-year-old practicum student, I blundered through *Adventures of Huckleberry Finn* at a private preparatory school, cringing at key words and phrases on behalf of my students and particularly the only teen of color—a seventeen-year-old black boy who rolled his eyes and joked away any obvious discomfort.

In hindsight, I wish I'd asked my supervisor to let me teach a contemporary novel, instead—perhaps Jervey Tervalon's 1994 novel *Understand This*, about two black South Central teens growing up against a backdrop of drugs, gangs, and guns just ninety minutes south of my classroom, and a lot more relevant than Huck and Jim's adventures along the Mississippi River in the 1800s.

In 2017 the FBI reported an increase of hate crimes in the US—racially and ethnically motivated attacks that targeted Muslim, Jewish, and LGBTQIA+ people. News stories across the country continue to report harassment of Latino, Indian American, and black students.

While it may be difficult—even painful—to facilitate discussions about contemporary racism in the US, it's absolutely imperative. Even our youngest kids—unless they're home-schooled without television, radio, magazines, newspapers, and the ever-present internet—observe daily acts of bigotry. Young people who have been the victims of these attacks are particularly vulnerable to depression, anxiety, and poor health.

It's harder than ever to shelter our kids from this reality. In 2017 thirteen-year-old Rosalie Avila, a Mexican American girl in California, hung herself after classmates taunted her. That same year, eight-year-old Gabriel Taye, a black boy in Ohio, hung himself after a bullying incident caught on video left him unconscious on the floor of a school restroom.

Our kids hear these stories. We must help them process their emotions and fears, and that means addressing these difficult topics head-on. Fortunately, children's and young adult authors have our backs.

Angie Thomas, who wrote the blockbuster teen novel *The Hate U Give*, was twenty-one when she learned about the BART police officer who shot unarmed twenty-two-year-old Oscar Grant in an Oakland station—his death was captured on multiple cell phones. Three years later, Florida resident George Zimmerman shot and killed Trayvon Martin—an unarmed black high school student who'd been visiting relatives in a gated community where Zimmerman patrolled on neighborhood watch.

Zimmerman's acquittal on the grounds of self-defense inspired international protests and the Black Lives Matter campaign against racism and violence. In turn, the BLM movement inspired *The Hate U Give*; the story features sixteen-year-old Starr Carter, who learns to lift up her voice in protest after she watches her friend Khalil—an unarmed young black man—be killed by a police officer in front of her.

The book's cover shows an illustrated black teen girl whose brown eyes contain a mixture of determination and rage. Her mouth is obscured by a protest sign with the book's title painted on it in black block letters. The title comes from rapper Tupac Shakur's definition of "thug life"—an existence marked by poverty and racism. The plot speaks to any teen who has grown up cognizant of the systematic murder of black men (and some women) by police in this country.

Starr is a complex protagonist. She has a wealthy white boyfriend and a black uncle who works as a police officer. She and her immediate family and friends navigate a neighborhood fraught with drugs and gang wars and shootouts. Her mother drives her an hour across town each day to a school with more money and opportunity than those in her part of the city—a school made up mostly of white students.

Starr maintains an allegiance to childhood friends from her neighborhood while spending more and more time with her classmates. But when white students stage a protest for her murdered friend Khalil—whom they've never met—just to get out of class, she's outraged. And when a white girl makes racist jokes about Starr and an Asian friend, she's had it.

"We let people say stuff, and they say it so much that it becomes okay and normal for us," she says. "What's the point of having a voice if you're going to be silent in those moments you shouldn't be?"

The Hate U Give hands teachers, parents, and other caregivers a powerful template for how to be an ally to anyone targeted by bigots. The novel is every bit as rich and thought-provoking as *Adventures of Huckleberry Finn* and—with apologies to Mark Twain—a lot more pertinent and entertaining for today's teens.

Readers witness the complicit support that they themselves offer when they laugh or stay silent over an insulting punchline or racial slur or a peer who's being harassed. They see how Starr's boyfriend supports her with humility, educating himself about how best to be of help. And they watch Starr learn to wield her voice as a weapon.

"I'm sick of this," she says among a crowd of protesters facing off with police on the night of Khalil's murderer's acquittal. "Just like y'all think all of us are bad because of some people, we think the same about y'all. Until you give us a reason to think otherwise, we'll keep protesting."

This is the message that teens need to hear—that their voices can be honed and sharpened to a powerful point. As Starr jumps on top of a police car to shout through her bullhorn, readers experience the moment viscerally along with her.

At first glance, that pivotal scene in *The Hate U Give* seems to have little in common with anything in the Harry Potter series. But researchers have found that when someone reads about Harry's first broom-flying lesson, it activates the same brain region they use when observing someone in motion in the real world.

This means that when we read fiction, we gain an enhanced ability to imagine another person's predicament—in the case of *The Hate U Give*, we feel Starr's newfound empowerment during the rally as she shouts through her bullhorn. Likewise, we feel her terror of being racially profiled and pulled over by a police officer. Fiction is the original virtual reality; a well-written novel makes us feel like we're right there in the scene, which can raise consciousness and change lives.

My friend Merie assigned *The Hate U Give* in her college literature classroom at the University of North Dakota, and she read it with her young teen too.

"Not only did we have really good conversations about the characters and their circumstances and choices, but then she got a bunch of her friends to read it too," she reports. "That was also a case where I was able to give her a little more background on the Black Panthers and food deserts than she would have had on her own. It's a great read without the additional knowledge, but seeing all the ways the story intersects with real life and history expands its influence."

Children's author Sharon M. Draper, named National Teacher of the Year in 1997, is concerned about the effects of racism on young people. She doesn't believe the actual level of racism in the US has changed significantly over the decades; it's simply become more public because of social media and smartphones. Instead of people going home and recounting, "This is what happened to me today," now twenty-seven cell phones capture and post it, she says.

Draper has twice received the Coretta Scott King Book Award for her preteen novels. She notes that many writers today put issues pertaining to prejudice into novels, which lets young people take those fictional characters with them as friends and allies.

But sometimes it's difficult to get these books into students' hands—at least in a school setting with a fixed curriculum aimed at helping kids to pass standardized tests.

Draper acknowledges that there's only so much protesting about curriculum a teacher can do. "They need their job to support their families. They need advocates who entrust them to teach the students who are in front of them in a way that those particular students will learn." The best teachers find stories that will appeal to those students.

When she visits schools, Draper tells young people to go to the library at least once a week. She knows how thirsty librarians are to help kids who walk in the door and say, "You got a good book in here?" "But we're not encouraging our kids to do outside reading," she laments. "I can't do anything about the current state of educational control, but I can encourage kids to read."

Her preteen novel *Stella by Starlight* takes place in a segregated southern town during the Great Depression. Eleven-year-old Stella and her little brother witness a gathering of the Ku Klux Klan, which threatens the lives of the people in their black community.

Kids who read the book often tell Draper, "Oh, that racism stuff was bad. I'm glad it's over now." Then they learn otherwise. If a teacher tells them to read about racism in a history book, they might read it, she says, but they won't understand. When truth is presented through fiction, they remember it.

Truth motivated Katherine Applegate to write the preteen novel *Wishtree*. In the summer of 2016, bipartisan politics dominated US media, with immigration issues at the forefront. Children saw swastikas painted on playground equipment. Teens discovered white supremacist posters on school campuses. They heard anti-Mexican and anti-Muslim rhetoric every time they turned on the television or went online. Applegate heard it as well, and she poured her heartbreak into her illustrated story about a suburban oak tree named Red who witnesses a hate crime against a newly arrived Muslim girl.

A wishtree is a tree—most often in Scotland—hung with wishes printed on rags or paper. People make offerings of coins or trinkets. If the idea of an oak tree as narrator strikes you as far-fetched, remember that Applegate is the author who penned the 2013 Newbery Medal–winning novel *The One and Only Ivan*, stunningly narrated by a silverback gorilla. Her skill in giving voice to sentient beings without human language may just transform the way an entire generation of readers thinks about both plants and animals—not as "the other," but as kin.

The writing in *Wishtree* is delicately witty, lyrically subtle. Rather than confronting young readers with violent scenes of racism, Applegate implies them through imagery. A curtain closes against the immigrant child's loneliness and pain. A hateful teen carves the word "Leave" with a screwdriver into the oak's venerable trunk. The furred and feathered residents of the tree act as a sort of Greek chorus, getting readers to think about what it means to welcome someone, and what it means to hate.

Applegate wrote *Wishtree* as a call for civility. Like *The Hate U Give*, its deeply empathetic protagonist is struggling for a voice. "There have been so many times I've wanted to speak up, to intervene, to help people," says the red oak, sworn to silence by the rules of nature. "I've never said a word, though. That's just the way the world has always worked."

But the world doesn't work like this anymore. All around us, all around our children and teens, those who've been the victims of hate crimes and those who desire to be allies are standing up and crying "enough."

I think of the twenty-five teens on the edge of their seats during an Oregon Shakespeare Festival production of *Manahatta*—a play that spans four hundred years of bigotry and cultural obliteration written by attorney and activist Mary Kathryn Nagle of the Cherokee Nation. After the performance, they drifted out to the lobby in their suits and dresses looking solemn, even stunned, and discussing the play on the walk back to their hotel.

I think of the thousand-plus people gathered on the second floor of my public library—sitting and standing wherever they could find space and packing the third-floor balcony—to hear black writer and activist Ijeoma Oluo give a presentation on her book *So You Want to Talk about Race.* Hell, yes, we want to talk about it. We should have been talking about it three hundred years ago.

We *need* to talk about it now. We need to discuss bigotry in our classrooms. We need to bring it up in book clubs, in libraries, and at home so that kids can learn how to safely confront it and put a stop to it. As black writer and professor Roxane Gay says in her TED Talk: "I recognize that even if I'm not experiencing a given struggle, that doesn't mean I shouldn't care or can't do anything about it."

Not sure how to bring up race and prejudice with your tweens and teens?

Grab a book.

PRETEEN BOOKS ABOUT RACE AND ETHNICITY

AS BRAVE AS YOU by Jason Reynolds (Atheneum/Caitlyn Dlouhy Books, 2016). Black eleven-year-old Genie Harris learns to love his blind but pistol-packing and irascible Grandpop when he and his older brother leave Brooklyn to spend a month with their grandparents in rural Virginia, and they learn the secret of how their uncle died during Desert Storm.

BETTY BEFORE X by Ilyasah Shabazz (Farrar, Straus and Giroux, 2018). Inspired by civil rights activist Dr. Betty Shabazz, this is the story of eleven-year-old Betty in 1940s Detroit who gets involved in her church and volunteers to support black-owned businesses after she hears a speech by Thurgood Marshall.

BLACKBIRD FLY by Erin Entrada Kelly (Greenwillow Books, 2015). Asian American twelve-year-old Apple moves to Louisiana from the Philippines with her mother, who cautions her not to become "too American." Caught between two identities and struggling to understand friends who aren't always what they seem, Apple saves up for a guitar so that she can immerse herself in music.

BOOKED by Kwame Alexander (HMH Books for Young Readers, 2016). In this novel in verse, black twelve-year-old Nick finds his dream of winning a youth soccer tournament threatened by bullies and problems at home, but he finds encouragement thanks to a rapping librarian who offers inspiring books.

BROWN GIRL DREAMING by Jacqueline Woodson (Nancy Paulsen Books, 2014). This author's memoir in verse is about growing up as a black girl during the Civil Rights movement and turning early difficulties as a reader into a passion for writing.

CANNED AND CRUSHED by Bibi Belford (Sky Pony Press, 2015). Eleven-year-old Sandro Zapote bullies a classmate while he struggles to balance school, soccer, and helping his underemployed and undocumented father after his mother takes his sister to Mexico for heart surgery.

CLAYTON BYRD GOES UNDERGROUND by Rita Williams-Garcia (Amistad, 2017). Devastated by his musician grandfather's death, black middle-schooler Clayton Byrd leaves school and heads for New York City's Washington Square Park, hoping to join the blues band his granddad left behind.

CONFETTI GIRL by Diana López (Little, Brown Books for Young Readers, 2009). Latina middle-schooler Lina Flores comes of age and navigates first love after her mother dies, her father becomes distant, and her best friend's divorced mother becomes obsessed with making *cascarones*—confetti-filled eggs.

THE CROSSOVER by Kwame Alexander (HMH Books for Young Readers, 2014). In this novel in verse, black twelve-year-old twin basketball stars Josh and Jordan find themselves drifting apart in their sports-focused family after one falls for an attractive girl and the other struggles with anger and abandonment issues.

DARIUS THE GREAT IS NOT OKAY by Adib Khorram (Dial Books, 2018). Teen Iranian American pop culture expert Darius Kellner suffers from clinical depression and anxiety about his first trip to Iran. There he meets a neighbor boy named Sohrab, and they develop a powerful bond based on soccer and endless conversations that help Darius to discover and celebrate his identity.

THE DREAMER by Pam Muñoz Ryan (Scholastic Press, 2010). This is a fictional biography of Chilean poet Pablo Neruda, who hides from his disapproving father and finds inspiration in his childhood forests, then grows into a teen concerned about rights for the indigenous Mapuche people.

THE EPIC FAIL OF ARTURO ZAMORA by Pablo Cartaya (Viking, 2017). Thirteen-year-old Cuban American Arturo Zamora teams up with the girl he likes in order to save his abuela's restaurant in Miami from a land developer.

THE FIRST RULE OF PUNK by Celia C. Pérez (Viking, 2017). In this illustrated story, Mexican American twelve-year-old Malú writes a 'zine (some of the pages of which appear in the novel), and struggles to fit in at her new school until she starts a band with her classmates and stands up to school administration to defend her love of punk and punk rock fashion.

FULL CICADA MOON by Marilyn Hilton (Dial Books, 2015). This novel in poems tells the story of half-black, half-Japanese seventh-grader Mimi, who moves in 1969 to a mostly white town in Vermont from Berkeley. Wanting to become an astronaut, she insists on taking shop class instead of home economics and enters science competitions with the support of new friends and her parents.

THE GREAT WALL OF LUCY WU by Wendy Wan-Long Shang (Scholastic Press, 2011). Chinese American sixth-grader Lucy Wu finds her dream of becoming a basketball star threatened when her great-aunt from China comes for a long visit and insists that Lucy attend Chinese school to learn about history and culture.

A HANDFUL OF STARS by Cynthia Lord (Scholastic Press, 2015). Motherless preteen Lily lives in Maine with her grandparents. There she meets Salma—a migrant girl in Maine for the summer to pick blueberries. The girls become friends, but when Salma becomes the first migrant girl to enter the town's Blueberry Queen pageant, Lily witnesses bigotry within her community and herself.

THE HOUSE THAT LOU BUILT by Mae Respicio (Wendy Lamb Books, 2018). Biracial thirteen-year-old Lou shares a bedroom with her Filipina mother in her grandmother's San Francisco home. On one hundred square feet that she inherited from her father, she decides to build a tiny house, depending on help from family and friends when the land is at risk of being auctioned off.

IT AIN'T SO AWFUL, FALAFEL by Firoozeh Dumas (Clarion Books, 2016). Iranian middle schooler Zomorod Yousefzadeh moves to Newport Beach, California, with her family and navigates racism and social angst during the Iran hostage crisis of the late 1970s.

LOWRIDERS IN SPACE by Cathy Camper (Chronicle Books, 2014). In this graphic novel, Latino characters Lupe Impala, El Chavo Flapjack, and Elirio Malaria transform a decrepit old car, hoping to win a cash prize so they can open their own repair shop.

MIDNIGHT WITHOUT A MOON by Linda Williams Jackson (HMH Books for Young Readers, 2017). Thirteen-year-old Rose Lee Carter joins the civil rights movement in Mississippi after a boy named Emmett Till is murdered in the town beside the one in which she lives with her grandmother in poverty on a cotton plantation.

MY BASMATI BAT MITZVAH by Paula J. Freedman (Harry N. Abrams, 2013). Eleven-year-old Tara Feinstein questions how to navigate between Indian and Jewish identities, and whether she should have a bat mitzvah if she's not sure what she believes. To add to the complexity, she may be developing romantic feelings for one of her best friends, Ben-O.

THE NIGHT DIARY by Veera Hiranandani (Dial Books, 2018). In 1947, twelve-year-old Nisha, who is half Muslim and half Hindu, writes letters to her deceased mother as she emigrates with her father away from Pakistan toward a new and safer life. Traveling first by train, and later on foot, Nisha struggles with sadness at losing her homeland and tries to feel hope for the future.

ONE CRAZY SUMMER by Rita Williams-Garcia (Amistad, 2010). Eleven-year-old Delphine and her younger sisters travel from Brooklyn to California to spend the summer with their mother, who sends them to a day camp run by the Black Panthers.

ONE GOOD THING ABOUT AMERICA by Ruth Freeman (Holiday House, 2017). Nine-year-old Congolese refugee Anaïs and her family settle in Maine where she must write one good thing about America in each letter to her grandmother. Anaïs becomes friends with other immigrant children as she embraces mysterious new traditions such as trick-or-treating and sleepovers.

PAPER CHAINS by Elaine Vickers (Harper, 2017). Fifth-grader Katie, adopted from Russia as a baby, lives life timidly because of a heart transplant. Her friend Ana—a gregarious athlete—has a Russian grandmother who moves in with her family after Ana's father leaves to become a professional hockey player and her mother sinks into depression.

THE PARKER INHERITANCE by Varian Johnson (Arthur A. Levine Books, 2018). In 1950s South Carolina, black middle-schooler Candice finds a mysterious letter addressed to her grandmother. With the help of a neighbor boy, she discovers her city's racist history, along with unexpected heroes.

PIECING ME TOGETHER by Renée Watson (Bloomsbury, 2017). Black high school junior Jade is poor and on scholarship to a private school in Portland, Oregon; she learns to advocate for herself and her art after she's matched with a black mentor with a more privileged background.

SOMEWHERE AMONG by Annie Donwerth-Chikamatsu (Atheneum/Caitlyn Dlouhy Books, 2016). Eleven-year-old Japanese American Ema lives in Japan and spends summers in California until her mother's difficult pregnancy requires the family to remain in Tokyo. From there they watch the 9/11 terrorist attacks, which throw Ema's shaky sense of identity into chaos.

THE STARS BENEATH OUR FEET by David Barclay Moore (Knopf Books for Young Readers, 2017). Twelve-year-old Lolly Rachpaul and his mother struggle to deal with the gang-related shooting death of his older brother. When Lolly's mother's girlfriend brings him two giant bags of Legos, he resists the temptation to join a gang himself and builds a magnificent Lego city at the community center.

STELLA BY STARLIGHT by Sharon M. Draper (Atheneum Books for Young Readers, 2015). In the segregated south during the Great Depression, eleven-year-old Stella and her little brother witness a gathering of the Ku Klux Klan, which threatens the lives of the people in their black community.

THE THING ABOUT LUCK by Cynthia Kadohata (Atheneum Books for Young Readers, 2013). Japanese American twelve-year-old Summer and her family experience a year of bad luck. She almost dies of malaria, and then her parents have to travel to Japan to take care of family. Summer and her difficult younger brother and grandparents are left to harvest wheat and experience a series of disasters.

THINGS TOO HUGE TO FIX BY SAYING SORRY by Susan Vaught (Paula Wiseman Books, 2016). Middle-schooler Dani Bean loses a friend and discovers the truth about her grandmother's role in the riots that started in response to the desegregation of Mississippi.

TORTILLA SUN by Jennifer Cervantes (Chronicle Books, 2010). When twelve-year-old Izzy has to spend the summer in a remote New Mexican village with her grandmother, she finds herself immersed in southwest Mexican culture and discovering truths about her father and his death.

WISHTREE by Katherine Applegate (Feiwel and Friends, 2017). When a teenager carves one hateful word into a venerable red oak, a community of people and animals—and the tree itself—conspire to support a newly arrived immigrant Muslim girl and her family by letting her know they're welcome in the neighborhood.

TEEN BOOKS ABOUT RACE AND ETHNICITY

ALL AMERICAN BOYS by Jason Reynolds and Brendan Kiely (Atheneum/Caitlyn Dlouhy Books, 2015). Black sixteen-year-old Rashad Butler is beaten by a police officer as his white classmate Quinn looks on, horrified. The media runs with the story, and the town takes sides in a battle that challenges both boys to confront the repercussions of racism and privilege.

AMERICAN PANDA by Gloria Chao (Simon Pulse, 2018). Seventeen-year-old Taiwanese American Mei Lu wants to open a dance studio, but her parents want her to attend medical school after MIT and marry a man of their choosing. She finds herself attracted to a Japanese classmate and restores her relationship with her brother, who's been exiled for dating the wrong woman.

AMERICAN STREET by Ibi Zoboi (Balzer + Bray, 2017). Haitian teen Fabiola Toussaint moves from Port-au-Prince to live with her Detroit aunt and cousins, where she longs for her mother who's been detained by US immigration and struggles to assimilate to a baffling new culture as she wonders if she'll ever be reunited with her.

ANGER IS A GIFT by Mark Oshiro (Tor Teen, 2018). After high school sophomore Moss Jeffries's father is killed by a police officer and denigrated by the media, Moss and his classmates at his West Oakland High School organize to protest random locker searches and intimidation by police officers stationed in the corridors, and he finds courage and purpose.

THE AUTHENTICS by Abdi Nazemian (Balzer + Bray, 2017). Sixteen-year-old Iranian American Daria finds that she's not Iranian after all. She keeps the results of her DNA test a secret from her adoptive mother, who's planning an extravagant Sweet Sixteen party, while she searches for her birth mother and navigates a forbidden romance.

CALLING MY NAME by Liara Tamani (Greenwillow Books, 2017). Taja Brown, a black girl from a religious community in Houston, comes of age and navigates an exploration of her sexuality while trying to please her strict parents and sustain a relationship with God.

CHILDREN OF BLOOD AND BONE by Tomi Adeyemi (Henry Holt, 2018). Informed by the author's West African heritage, this novel is told in multiple points of view by the two children of a controlling king and siblings who've suffered because of his ruthlessness. All four struggle with injustice and discrimination and unexpected love as they journey together in search of power.

DEAR MARTIN by Nic Stone (Crown Books for Young Readers, 2017). Black honors student Justyce tries to make sense of his private school classmates' scorn, his neighborhood friends' disgust with him, and then the sudden violence at the hands of a police officer through an examination of Dr. Martin Luther King Jr.'s life and writings.

DOWN AND ACROSS by Arvin Ahmadi (Viking, 2018). Sixteen-year-old Iranian American Scott Ferdowsi, rebelling against parental pressure, quits a summer internship and sneaks off to Washington, DC, to talk with a famous psychologist. There he finds new purpose among young bartenders and crossword-puzzle writers who have political aspirations.

DREAMLAND BURNING by Jennifer Latham (Little, Brown Books for Young Readers, 2017). Seventeen-year-old Rowan Chase unearths a skeleton on her family's property and investigates both the history of a seventeen-year-old boy and a brutal murder that took place in the 1921 Tulsa race riot. Both force her to evaluate race relations in the United States then and now.

THE EDUCATION OF MARGOT SANCHEZ by Lilliam Rivera (Simon & Schuster, 2017). After Puerto Rican American Margot Sanchez abuses her father's credit cards, she must spend the summer working in her family's Bronx-based grocery store, where she makes a series of bad decisions and learns hard truths about friendship and self-worth.

THE GAME OF LOVE AND DEATH by Martha Brockenbrough (Arthur A. Levine Books, 2015). Love and Death, personified, manipulate a white boy and a black girl bonded by their love of music in 1920s and '30s Seattle.

THE GIRL WHO FELL FROM THE SKY by Heidi W. Durrow (Algonquin Books, 2010). After a family tragedy, biracial teen Rachel must live with her strict grandmother in a black community that regards her light skin and blue eyes with suspicion. There she learns about how her Danish mother struggled with her own identity in a way that is similar to Rachel's questions.

GIRLCOTT by Florenz Webbe Maxwell (Blouse and Skirt Books, 2017). When the secret Progressive League orders a boycott of Bermuda cinemas in 1959 to end racial segregation, fifteen-year-old Desma Johnson becomes aware of the bigotry around her island—a prejudice that threatens her plans to get a coveted scholarship and pursue her dreams.

GIVE ME SOME TRUTH by Eric Gansworth (Arthur A. Levine Books, 2018). After his brother gets shot by a racist restaurant owner, Native American teen Carson Mastick teams up with Maggi Bokoni, who's just returned to the reservation to start a band and to stage a protest.

THE GO-BETWEEN by Veronica Chambers (Delacorte Press, 2017). When Camilla del Valle's wealthy family relocates from Mexico to the United States, she finds herself capitulating to the stereotypes perpetuated by new friends at her private school who believe that her mother is a domestic worker rather than a famous actress on telenovelas.

THE GOOD BRAIDER by Terry Farish (Marshall Cavendish, 2012). In this novel told in free verse, sixteen-year-old Viola escapes a violent past in Sudan and moves to Maine, where she navigates her mother's strict expectations of her along with exciting and confusing new freedoms and temptations.

HARBOR ME by Jacqueline Woodson (Nancy Paulsen Books, 2018). When six fifth- and sixth-graders must meet weekly to talk with no adults present, they reveal insecurities about deportation, racism, poverty, and friendship.

THE HATE U GIVE by Angie Thomas (Balzer + Bray, 2017). Black sixteen-year-old Starr Carter watches a police officer shoot and kill her childhood best friend, and then watches as some condemn his murder while others malign him. Frustrated by the reactions of wealthy white classmates, she finds her voice and begins to protest on behalf of her black community.

HEARTS UNBROKEN by Cynthia Leitich Smith (Candlewick Press, 2018). In a predominately white Kansas town, Louise Wolfe dumps her boyfriend after he makes fun of Native people and focuses on her school newspaper reporting job, which asks her to cover community bigotry and backlash after the theater teacher announces an innovative and inclusive casting of *The Wizard of Oz*.

HOW IT WENT DOWN by Kekla Magoon (Henry Holt, 2014). Black sixteen-year-old Tariq is murdered by a white man, and the story is told by multiple witnesses with various perceptions of the shooting. The police, a minister, neighbors, family, friends, and gang members add their accounts of the story to create a picture of who Tariq was alongside a nationwide narrative.

I AM ALFONSO JONES by Tony Medina (Turtleback Books, 2017). In this graphic novel, black teen Alfonso Jones finds his plans to star in the school play and confess his love for a girl ruined when a police officer shoots and kills him. He rides a ghost train guided by other victims of police shootings while his family and friends fight for justice on his behalf.

I AM NOT YOUR PERFECT MEXICAN DAUGHTER by Erika L. Sánchez (Knopf Books for Young Readers, 2017). After an accident that leaves her seemingly perfect sister dead, Mexican American teen Julia chafes against her mother's constant criticism and longs to move out of the house and attend college.

LOVE, HATE, AND OTHER FILTERS by Samira Ahmed (Soho Teen, 2018). Seventeen-year-old Indian American Muslim Maya Aziz longs to attend film school in New York City, but her parents' plans and a horrific hate crime leave her reeling in an aftermath of bigotry and fear that shatters her community.

MARIAM SHARMA HITS THE ROAD by Sheba Karim (HarperTeen, 2018). College sophomore Mariam is excited to spend the summer with her best friends Umar and Ghazala. After a shocking photo of Ghazala appears on a Times Square billboard, the three Pakistani American teens escape on a riotous road trip to New Orleans, which becomes a journey of self-discovery.

OUT OF DARKNESS by Ashley Hope Pérez (Carolrhoda Lab, 2015). Mexican American fifteen-year-old Naomi Vargas grapples with her racially divided East Texas oil-mining town in 1936 and with her attraction to Wash Fuller, who is black. This story of family bonds and racism culminates with the 1937 New London school explosion.

THE RADIUS OF US by Marie Marquardt (St. Martins Griffin, 2017). After seventeen-year-old Gretchen Asher is mugged in a parking lot, she abandons school and her friends. When she meets eighteen-year-old El Salvadorian immigrant Phoenix—who looks like her attacker—her fears return, but are replaced by concerns that he'll be forced to return to his home country with its threats of gang violence.

THE SECRET SIDE OF EMPTY by Maria E. Andreu (Running Press, 2014). Undocumented Argentinian immigrant Monserrat Thalia is a straight-A student, and with her pale skin and blond hair, she's able to hide her illegal status and her fears about her future after high school.

SOMETHING IN BETWEEN by Melissa de la Cruz (Harlequin Teen, 2016). In this semi-autobiographical novel, Filipino American teen Jasmine de los Santos gets a full college scholarship and a relationship with the funny and sensitive boy of her dreams, but then discovers that her entire family is illegal and in danger of being deported from the United States.

STARFISH by Akemi Dawn Bowman (Simon Pulse, 2017). Japanese American teen Kiko Himura feels like an outsider in her small town and longs for acceptance into her dream art school in New York. When she's rejected, she overcomes crippling anxiety and leaves her narcissistic mother and abusive uncle to tour art schools with a friend on the West Coast.

THE STARS AT OKTOBER BEND by Glenda Millard (Candlewick Press, 2018). Fifteen-year-old Alice has a traumatic past and a brain injury that causes her to have trouble speaking, but she writes poems and puts them in public places. Sixteen-year-old Manny, former child soldier and refugee from Sierra Leone, finds one of her poems, and they develop a deep connection despite opposition from their community.

THE WAY THE LIGHT BENDS by Cordelia Jensen (Philomel Books, 2018). In this novel in verse, Linc takes on a photo project based on Seneca Village in what is now Central Park and finds a new sense of self-worth after years of watching her sister Holly—adopted from Ghana—please their surgeon mother with her academic successes.

THE WAY YOU MAKE ME FEEL by Maurene Goo (Farrar, Straus and Giroux, 2018). After a prank turns into disaster, Korean American teen Clara Shin must work on her dad's Los Angeles food truck alongside a high-strung black classmate Rose while she's navigating a crush on a boy named Hamlet. Clara realizes there's more to life than jokes, and commits to helping her father.

WE WERE HERE by Matt de la Peña (Delacorte Press, 2009). Mexican American teen Miguel is sentenced to a year in a group home, where he hides from his mother's disgust and writes in a journal as mandated by the judge. Then he and two others break out of the home, and he makes a run for the Mexican border and the chance for a new life.

WHEN DIMPLE MET RISHI by Sandhya Menon (Simon Pulse, 2017). When Rishi Patel's parents tell him that the wife they've arranged for him will attend the same summer program for web developers, he's thrilled. Though Dimple and Rishi clash when they meet, they end up bonding in part because of the prejudice of a group of wealthy preparatory school kids.

X by Ilyasah Shabazz (Candlewick Press, 2015). This story of Malcolm X written by his daughter explains how young Malcolm Little sees his father murdered and his mother taken away. He abandons plans to become a lawyer in favor of smoky jazz clubs. When he's imprisoned for theft at age twenty, he develops a new faith and the determination to fight for social justice.

YAQUI DELGADO WANTS TO KICK YOUR ASS by Meg Medina (Candlewick Press, 2013). After Piddy Sanchez learns that an unfamiliar girl wants to hurt her for not looking Latina enough, she tries to avoid her assailant while trying to focus on honors courses and find out about the father she's never met. When the harassment becomes overwhelming, she must hide or run away.

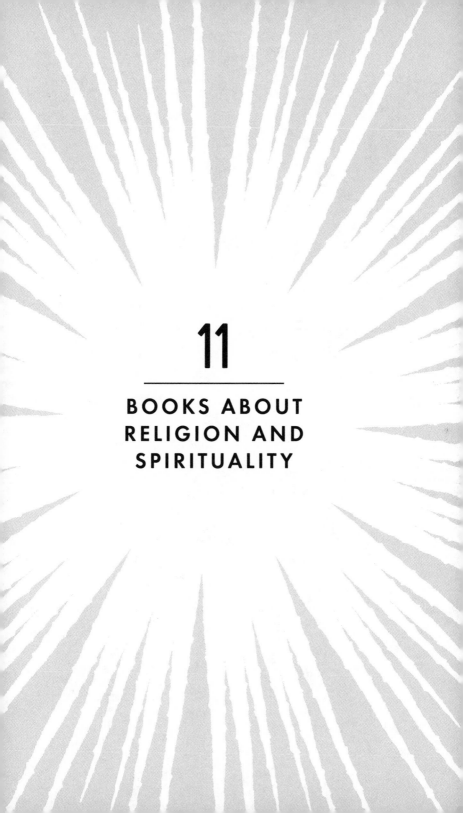

11

BOOKS ABOUT
RELIGION AND
SPIRITUALITY

On a cold, rainy evening in late winter—Ash Wednesday, to be specific—my fifth-grade daughter came home from a playdate with a friend whose parents I didn't know well and burst through the front door with a smudged gray cross on her forehead.

"My friend's mom took us to church, and we got ashed!" she told my husband and me. "And I ate the body of Christ, but it was gross so I spit it into my hand, and I told the guy who gave me wine that my mother was going to be pissed."

I washed the ashes off her forehead, quietly furious. How could another parent take my kid to their church, and especially invite her to participate in communion, without asking us first? Religion is so deeply personal; we wouldn't just take someone else's child to our Unitarian SpiritJam and ask her to light the chalice.

My husband and I want to offer our daughter a wealth of religious and spiritual experiences, but on our terms. If she's going to observe Ash Wednesday, allow us to preface the experience by reading *The Light of the World: The Life of Jesus for Children* by Newbery Medal winner Katherine Paterson. If someone invites her to a post-Ramadan feast, first let me read with her Medeia Sharif's young teen romance *Bestest. Ramadan. Ever.* Books give us context and meaning behind other people's rituals so that we don't inadvertently insult an entire congregation by spitting a representation of the divine into our hand.

Regardless of how families worship or don't, religion plays a powerful role in this country—one that many kids and young adults observe in their classrooms and communities. Approximately half of adolescents in the US practice some form of religion. One in three pray daily. While most identify as Christian, millions of Americans are Jewish, Muslim, Buddhist, Hindu, agnostic, and atheist.

I myself wasn't born into any particular spiritual practice. My mother took us to the Unitarian Church when time allowed, but I read about religion . . . a lot. Sydney Taylor's All-of-a-Kind Family series about Jewish sisters in New York City led me to *Anne Frank: The Diary of a Young Girl*, and then to Christian author Corrie ten Boom's *The Hiding Place* and Madeleine L'Engle's spiritual teen novel *A Ring of Endless Light*. From there, I moved to Herman Hesse's *Siddhartha*.

And of course, there was Judy Blume's preteen novel *Are You There God? It's Me, Margaret*, beloved of girls who grew up in the 1970s and '80s. Margaret is the eleven-year-old daughter of a Christian mother and a Jewish father. She observes how these different religions cause tension in relationships with her grandparents. Confused about her own faith, she decides to attend a variety of churches.

I loved this idea then. I love it now. I want my daughter to comprehend different religions so that she can make an informed decision about what she believes or doesn't believe. And I want her to understand what it means to her Jewish friends when they show up to school on a Monday morning—as they did in our city—to find swastikas painted on their playground equipment. I want her to grasp what it means to her Muslim friends when a man stands outside our local mosque and threatens to shoot worshippers.

Sadly, these hate crimes aren't limited to Eugene, Oregon. In a country that's seen a recent increase in anti-Semitic and anti-Muslim bigotry, kids hear and read stories about tyrants tearing the turbans from the heads of Sikh cab drivers. Haters place slabs of bacon in the doorways of mosques. Progressive Christian congregations arrive at churches on Sunday to find banners splattered with racial and homophobic slurs across their fences.

Paula J. Freedman, author of the preteen novel *My Basmati Bat Mitzvah*, is horrified. "It's clear to me that these attitudes have always existed, but it's more acceptable to air them in public than maybe it was in the past twenty years," she says.

"It makes me very sad to think we'd made a lot of progress in the world—at least paying lip service to tolerance and appreciation of others—but now even the outward signs of civility seem to be going away."

In *My Basmati Bat Mitzvah*, twelve-year-old protagonist Tara Feinstein's mother is Jewish by conversion, and members of her extended family are Hindu, so her family identifies with a variety of faiths. Tara grapples with questions about her bicultural and biracial identity. With her bat mitzvah—a Jewish girl's formal celebration of passage into adulthood—hanging over her head, she's stressed out and doubting elements of her faith.

Readers will find Tara every bit as engaging as my generation's Margaret; she's smart and feisty, set against a backdrop of charismatic friends and family members in a vibrant story about what it's like to grow up in a neighborhood with kids who identify—or whose parents identify—with a variety of beliefs. Readers who get to know Tara's classmates and relatives can't help questioning—and even surrendering—religious bias.

Research backs this up. In 2013 adult study, participants at Washington and Lee University read an excerpt of Shaila Abdullah's 2009 adult novel *Saffron Dreams*. It's about Pakistani American woman Arissa Illahi, who moves to New York City when her husband takes a job at the World Trade Center. He dies during the September 11 terrorist attacks, and Arissa is attacked by racist teens. At one point in the scene, a boy holds a knife to her throat—so closely that it itches her skin.

That scene is what researchers had volunteer subjects read. After they read the excerpt, they showed reduced prejudice and increased empathy for Muslim women. Studies like this one show just how much power a novel can hold. Still, at this point in my sixth-grader's life, she craves stories with happy endings and without the violence and tragedy that have informed many of the books we've read together. Tween novels like *My Basmati Bat Mitzvah* are perfect for her—informed by relevant social issues while also being lighthearted.

Even the cover art is fun. It's bright yellow, with the photograph of a smiling brown-skinned biracial girl surrounded by henna-like doodles of hearts and Stars of David.

That cover is particularly important to readers used to seeing white kids on book jackets. Freedman tells me about the time she did a Shabbat reading at a New Jersey synagogue, and a man rushed over after the service to introduce her to his nine-year-old daughter—a black Ashkenazi Jew who looked nothing like the people around her.

The book had resonated with her, particularly because there's a picture on the cover of a young person of color who is also Jewish. To be able to see this was, to that girl, miraculous.

Protagonist Tara's powerful response to bigotry may also strike readers as extraordinary. When a boy tells her his grandfather believes all Muslims to be terrorists, she doesn't miss a beat. "Gran once taught me a handy trick that I use all the time," she observes. "She said to take any remark that you suspect might be racist and substitute the word Jew. If you're insulted by it, it's probably racist." Readers will be tempted to likewise substitute the word that best describes themselves for a deeply felt lesson on speaking mindfully and with kindness.

At the end of the book, Tara ends up with a bat mitzvah celebration that's uniquely and joyfully her own, with her family's blessing. She wears her great-grandmother's sari, repurposed for the occasion, and selects a menu of Indian delicacies to serve her guests in a celebration that truly feels like a transition from childhood naïveté to a more deliberately examined young adult life.

Plenty of people have studied the benefits of adolescent rite of passage (I'm looking at you, Joseph Campbell), and what's lost when we don't give them a ceremony to celebrate their transition into young adulthood. Learning to drive the family car lacks the gravitas—and the heavenly buffet tables—of a bat or bar mitzvah or the solemnity of confirmation or the festivity of a *quinceañera*. In my city, secular nature-based organizations charge a hefty sum to take young people backpacking and rock climbing—the trips neatly timed with puberty—to help them make the leap from child to young adult.

But what of the millions of teens who don't have these opportunities because of economic status or absence of religious practice or caregivers too tired and tapped out to navigate rental halls and guest lists? These kids may look at their peers who talk about religious services and coming-of-age celebrations with envy. They may struggle with feeling less than, of not being a part of a group that appears to have answers to big questions, like the ones that keep my sixth-grader up at night— genuinely heartfelt questions like, "Daddy, who was Jesus's stunt double?"

Kids crave knowledge. After the publication of *My Basmati Bat Mitzvah,* a young reader wrote Freedman a long letter that included: "I used to think I had to have my whole life figured out, especially religion, before my bat mitzvah. Your book made me realize I have at least until ninth grade.'" (Freedman wrote back: "Darling, I'm forty-five, and I don't have any of it figured out.")

Novels for children and teens offer a way to figure it out, or to live comfortably with not knowing. They provoke discussion, and not just about religion and spirituality. In the preteen novel *Shooting Kabul,* N. H. Senzai tells the story of a Muslim family who immigrates to the US and deals with religious bigotry following September 11. Cynthia Leitich Smith, in the teen novel *Hearts Unbroken,* shows how Native American kids struggle with long-held prejudices against both their skin color and their beliefs.

In other books, religion intersects with LGBTQIA+ issues. Alex Sanchez's teen novel *The God Box* includes a protagonist who finds his thoughts about faith and sexual identity challenged when he meets a young gay Christian man. In *Georgia Peaches and Other Forbidden Fruit* by Jaye Robin Brown, an evangelical preacher father moves his family to a conservative town in Georgia and demands that his teen daughter keep her homosexuality a secret.

In her teen novel *Vivian Apple at the End of the World*, author Katie Coyle blends observations about organized religion, climate change, and school shootings with the story of sixteen-year-old Vivian, who loses her parents to a cult. Vivian sets off on a road trip in search of her mother and father, who have apparently levitated through twin holes in their bedroom ceiling during an event that looks an awful lot like the Rapture.

Coyle grew up Catholic but found herself disillusioned as a teenager after she learned of the sex abuse scandals within the church. Her break from Catholicism felt particularly difficult because of her close relationship with her parents.

Teens have the job of figuring out their identity, and most start to figure that out by opposing their parents and differentiating themselves, she says. "I wanted to write a book that said 'It's okay to not know what you believe; it's okay not to believe.' It can be really difficult to think about these questions and to come down on the side of not believing." Coyle explains that it can be helpful for readers to see a fictional character working through these questions.

Sometimes young readers may find that they simply have no faith—or no religious faith, anyway. "I don't believe in hate," Vivian narrates after her parents' disappearance. "I don't believe in money. I don't believe in God. I don't believe it's too late." For some teens, simply articulating what they don't believe in can be incredibly empowering.

Coyle wrote *Vivian Apple at the End of the World* in part as a response to prejudice against minority groups. In one scene, Vivian's beloved high school teacher talks to a group of bereft teens. "The way we live our lives is not sustainable," she says. "I don't just mean recycling and turning off the faucet while brushing your teeth. I mean the way we treat each other. The way we pick and choose whose lives are important—who we actually treat as human. There is nobody on this earth whose life is not of value."

Coyle believes that young people start out as open to the possibilities of human experience; they want to understand the world and the people in it. The younger they are, the more open she has found they are to the availability of stories that invite them to see the world through someone else's eyes.

Not long after the book's release, a lesbian twentysomething reader reached out to Coyle. The woman described her childhood and adolescence in a family of doomsday survivalists. "She had this reactionary family structure and belief system that was very difficult for her because she was attracted to girls," Coyle recounts. She read the book and saw so much of her life in it—especially in terms of the restricted roles of women. "It was incredible to hear her story," she says.

When we recognize our own life reflected in a book, we comprehend its validity. We see it as something worthy of being examined. And that examination helps us to answer the big questions like "What do I truly believe in?"

Paula J. Freedman is thrilled that more and more young people are recognizing themselves in the novels being published today. She hopes that children from all demographics can say, "I'm finally seeing me," and that kids who have traditionally seen themselves represented in mainstream literature can read about them too, encouraging empathy.

As Egyptian author Alaa Al Aswany notes in a piece for *The Atlantic*, "When you read a good novel, you forget about the nationality of the character. You forget about his or her religion. You forget about his skin color or her skin color. You only understand the human. You understand that this is a human being, the same way we are. And so reading great novels absolutely can remake us as much better human beings."

This is what authors like Freedman and Coyle are banking on as well—that reading novels with diverse characters will increase empathy for their various religious and nonbelieving backgrounds and make them think twice before bullying anyone wearing a yarmulke or hijab or necklace hung with a pentagram or a cross. Novels about religion and spirituality offer kids a way to make sense of an often bewildering world. They humanize people whose beliefs may look different—people who absolutely deserve compassion and respect, as we all do.

I want my preteen daughter to attend a variety of services, observe multiple rituals and traditions, so that she can make up her mind for herself about what she believes, or whether she believes anything at all. Heck, I'm fine if she returns to church on Ash Wednesday and has another sip of wine.

But first, I want her to read.

PRETEEN BOOKS ABOUT RELIGION AND SPIRITUALITY

AHIMSA by Supriya Kelkar (Tu Books, 2017). Ten-year-old Anjali's mother joins Gandhi's 1942 Indian freedom movement and asks her to give up her most beautiful clothes and challenge her prejudices against society's "untouchables." When her mother is thrown in jail, Anjali takes over her work in the independence movement.

DEVOTED by Jennifer Mathieu (Roaring Brook Press, 2015). Born-again Christian teen Rachel Walker lives in a patriarchal community. She begins to exchange emails with a girl named Lauren, who escaped their restrictive life. When Rachel is sent to a retreat to teach her to be more obedient, Lauren rescues her, and Rachel finds the courage to pursue her own dreams.

DREIDELS ON THE BRAIN by Joel ben Izzy (Dial Books, 2016). Set in 1971, this is the story of twelve-year-old Joel, an amateur magician and one of the few Jewish kids in his community. When he is asked to teach his school about Hanukkah in an assembly, he learns to take pride in his religion and his family, and in his abilities as a humorous storyteller.

ECHO STILL by Tim Tibbitts (Whole Story Publishing, 2015). Seventh-grade soccer player Fig must attend bar mitzvah classes and deal with his grandmother's extended visit. When he doesn't make the traveling soccer team because of a bully, he's forced to examine his feelings about his family and his religion.

8TH GRADE SUPER ZERO by Olugbemisola Rhuday-Perkovich (Arthur A. Levine Books, 2010). After Reggie throws up on his school principal's shoes, he's a nobody among his classmates. But his life changes for the better when he and his church youth group start volunteering at a homeless shelter. Reggie runs for class president and becomes a Big Brother for a younger boy in need.

ELSIE MAE HAS SOMETHING TO SAY by Nancy J. Cavanaugh (Sourcebooks Jabberwocky, 2017). Elsie Mae adores the swamp around her grandfather's house and spends the summer exploring and attempting to save both the land and swamper families who are being robbed. When her religious cousin shows up and thwarts her investigation into the theft, she proves herself a hero.

EVOLUTION, ME, AND OTHER FREAKS OF NATURE by Robin Brande (Knopf Books for Young Readers, 2007). High school freshman Mena is kicked out of church and shunned by friends when she embraces a science unit on evolution and protests the attempted "conversion" of a gay classmate. She's supported by a science teacher and a brilliant lab partner who introduces her to kissing and Lord of the Rings.

THE GARDEN OF MY IMAAN by Farhana Zia (Peachtree Publishers, 2013). Indian American Muslim fifth-grader Aliya worries about girls making fun of her for observing Ramadan, and so she writes letters to Allah about her worries. A new Muslim classmate from Morocco inspires her to appreciate her identity and come to a new understanding about her own faith.

THE GIRL WHO FELL TO EARTH by Sophia Al-Maria (Harper Perennial, 2012). Twelve-year-old Sophia from Seattle is sent to stay with her Bedouin father in Qatar, where she struggles with strict gender roles and the feeling that wherever she lives, she's in exile.

HEART OF A SHEPHERD by Rosanne Parry (Random House Children's Books, 2009). After his father is deployed to Iraq to fight in the war, eleven-year-old Brother cares for the livestock on his family's Oregon farm, and in the process of spiritual exploration, decides to become a military chaplain.

THE INQUISITOR'S TALE: OR, THE THREE MAGICAL CHILDREN AND THEIR HOLY DOG by Adam Gidwitz (Dutton Books for Young Readers, 2016). A Jewish boy, a boy from a monastery, and a visionary peasant girl experience witty and fantastical adventures as they deal with religious persecution.

MY BASMATI BAT MITZVAH by Paula J. Freedman (Harry N. Abrams, 2013). Eleven-year-old Tara Feinstein questions how to navigate between Indian and Jewish identities, and whether she should have a bat mitzvah if she's not sure what she believes. She ponders the religions of her various classmates, and creates a unique coming-of-age celebration with a blend of cultures.

THE OPPOSITE OF HALLELUJAH by Anna Jarzab (Delacorte Press, 2012). When Caro Mitchell's much older sister Hannah returns from years of living in a convent, Caro—angry about no longer feeling like an only child—lies to friends about why she has returned. Then Caro discovers a secret about Hannah's past, and suddenly she understands why her sister has become so quiet and withdrawn.

RUNNING THE ROOF OF THE WORLD by Jess Butterworth (Algonquin Young Readers, 2018). Tash and her family hide their Buddhist beliefs in their Tibetan village so that Chinese soldiers don't imprison them. When her parents send her away with a backpack full of mysterious documents, she travels across a mountain pass with her good friend and two yaks to India in search of the Dalai Lama.

SHOOTING KABUL by N. H. Senzai (Paula Wiseman Books, 2009). Middle school student Fadi emigrates from Afghanistan to San Francisco, leaving behind his six-year-old sister. After the 9/11 terrorist attacks, Fadi enters a photography competition hoping to win the grand prize trip to India so he can find and bring his sister to the US.

THIS IS JUST A TEST by Madelyn Rosenberg and Wendy Wan-Long Shang (Scholastic Press, 2017). Against a backdrop of the Cold War, David Da-Wei Horowitz struggles to prepare for his bar mitzvah and honor the wishes of his Jewish and Chinese grandmothers.

THE WHOLE STORY OF HALF A GIRL by Veera Hiranandani (Delacorte Press, 2012). After her father loses his job, half-Indian and half–Jewish American Sonia Nadhamuni must leave private school and forge a new identity in public school—and then her father goes missing.

TEEN BOOKS ABOUT RELIGION AND SPIRITUALITY

AMISH GUYS DON'T CALL by Debby Dodds (Blue Moon Publishers, 2017). High school junior Sam Stonesong has an absentee father, a promiscuous mother, and a longing to belong to the in-crowd. She begins dating Zach; they bond over a love of horror movies, but his strange behavior is off-putting until she finds out that he's Amish and may reluctantly have to return to his community.

AUTOBOYOGRAPHY by Christina Lauren (Simon & Schuster Books for Young Readers, 2017). When bisexual high school senior Tanner Scott's family moves from California to Utah, he is back in the closet and longing for the moment he can graduate and leave the state. Then he falls in love with Sebastian Brother—a Mormon writer—complicating his plans for the future.

BESTEST. RAMADAN. EVER. by Medeia Sharif (Flux, 2011). Almira Abdul resents having to spend a month fasting in observation of Ramadan. In the midst of wondering how to be Muslim American and frustrated that her parents won't let her date, Almira worries about a new Muslim classmate who dresses provocatively and captures the attention of her own crush.

BOXERS & SAINTS by Gene Luen Yang (First Second, 2013). In this two-volume graphic novel series, a Chinese peasant boy joins a rebellion against Western missionaries after Chinese gods visit him in visions. Meanwhile, Christian missionaries kidnap a girl who finds a welcome place among them and must choose either to become Christian herself or leave her friends.

CONVICTION by Kelly Loy Gilbert (Disney-Hyperion, 2015). Star baseball pitcher Braden is the key witness when his father—a well-known Christian radio host—is arrested for the murder of a police officer. His older brother returns home after ten years; when Braden learns of his father's drinking and abuse, he finds his faith in religion and family challenged.

DRESS CODES FOR SMALL TOWNS by Courtney Stevens (HarperTeen, 2017). Billie McCaffrey, daughter of a preacher, finds herself in trouble after she and her friends accidentally burn down a section of their church. She grapples with her own gender and sexuality, and that of her friends, while doing community service and trying to save the local Harvest Festival.

DRIVING BY STARLIGHT by Anat Deracine (Henry Holt, 2018). Sixteen-year-old Saudi Arabian best friends Leena and Mishie share gossip about their crushes, listen to forbidden music, and hoard Western clothing on the sly. Leena wants to go to college and longs for independence in a world in which women can't drive and religious parents have rigid expectations of teen girls.

EDEN WEST by Pete Hautman (Candlewick Press, 2015). Seventeen-year-old Jacob has almost always lived inside a gorgeous fenced religious compound in Montana, but when a new kid arrives and begins questioning The Truth, and then Jacob finds himself attracted to a forbidden girl who lives nearby, he struggles with his faith and his sense of reality.

A GAME FOR SWALLOWS: TO DIE, TO LEAVE, TO RETURN by Zeina Abirached (Graphic Universe, 2012). In this graphic novel based on the author's childhood, Zeina grows up Christian with her parents and little brother in Beirut during the civil war in Lebanon. When her parents visit the Muslim section of the city and don't return, neighbors create a sanctuary in their apartment.

GEORGIA PEACHES AND OTHER FORBIDDEN FRUIT by Jaye Robin Brown (HarperTeen, 2016). High school senior Joanna Gordon's father is a radio evangelist. When he relocates the family to a conservative town in Georgia, he makes her promise to keep her homosexuality a secret. She agrees, but then she finds herself falling in love with a girl.

HERETICS ANONYMOUS by Katie Henry (Katherine Tegen Books, 2018). Michael, the new kid and an atheist at Catholic school, bands together with other outsiders—a pagan, a feminist, a Jewish homosexual—to expose hypocrisy. But when Michael takes the protesting too far, he finds his friendships and his freedom challenged.

I'M NOT MISSING by Carrie Fountain (Flatiron Books, 2018). Miranda's mother abandons her to join a religious cult, her prom date stands her up, and then her best friend runs away. Miranda has the support of her kind father as she searches for her best friend and discovers the truth about her prom date, with whom she falls in love.

LIKE NO OTHER by Una LaMarche (Razorbill, 2015). Devorah, an obedient Hasidic teen in Brooklyn, falls in love with Jaxon—a smart non-Jewish black boy—after they're stranded together in an elevator during a hurricane. They defy Devorah's family and community to meet secretly in this story told from two perspectives.

LIKE WATER ON STONE by Dana Walrath (Delacorte Press, 2014). Forced to leave their mixed religious community in Armenia after the genocide of 1915, twins Shahen and Sosi must flee with their little sister toward an uncle who lives in the United States in this novel told in verse.

LOVE, HATE, AND OTHER FILTERS by Samira Ahmed (Soho Teen, 2018). Seventeen-year-old Maya Aziz has a crush on a boy and a dream of going to film school, but her parents ask her to attend a different college and date the Muslim boy they've chosen.

THE MISEDUCATION OF CAMERON POST by Emily M. Danforth (Balzer + Bray, 2012). After Cameron Post's parents die, she moves to Montana to live with her conservative aunt. She sends Cameron to religious conversion therapy camp in order to "cure" her of homosexuality after she falls in love with a beautiful bisexual cowgirl.

THE NAMES THEY GAVE US by Emery Lord (Bloomsbury USA Childrens, 2017). Lucy Hansson is excited to work at Bible camp and spend time with her boyfriend and parents, but then her mother's cancer returns. Suddenly Lucy finds her faith tested, especially after her boyfriend asks to take a break from their relationship and painful secrets about her family emerge.

NEIGHBORHOOD GIRLS by Jessie Ann Foley (HarperTeen, 2017). After Wendy Boychuck's father, a Chicago police officer, is imprisoned for brutality, she abandons her best friend and becomes part of a dangerous clique at Academy of the Sacred Heart. Wendy ponders the meanings of faith and forgiveness as she makes bad choices that nearly destroy what she loves the most.

NO PARKING AT THE END TIMES by Bryan Bliss (Greenwillow Books, 2015). After Abigail's parents sell their house and give the money to a faux preacher, they move into their van and travel to San Francisco to his so-called church, where they anticipate the end of the world. Abigail attempts to protect her angry brother, who falls in with a group of homeless teens and their street drama.

NOT THE GIRLS YOU'RE LOOKING FOR by Aminah Mae Safi (Feiwel and Friends, 2018). Arab American Muslim teen Lulu Saad is bold and determined to succeed, with the support of her three best friends. But after she creates a scene during Ramadan and almost drowns a boy at a party, she struggles to mend the injured feelings of both family and friends.

ONCE WAS LOST by Sara Zarr (Little, Brown Books for Young Readers, 2009). Samara Taylor's father is a well-loved pastor preoccupied with his congregation. When her mother ends up in rehab after a DUI and a thirteen-year-old girl in her church is kidnapped, Sam pulls away from her friends and begins to question both her family and her faith in God.

PLAYING BY THE BOOK by S. Chris Shirley (Magnus Books, 2014). Seventeen-year-old Jake Powell spends the summer in New York City, where he becomes attracted to his Jewish classmate Sam despite the misgivings of his fundamentalist Christian father.

THE POET X by Elizabeth Acevedo (HarperTeen, 2018). Dominican American teen Xiomara Batista, who lives in Harlem, channels her anger at growing up in a patriarchal community and her questions about religious faith into poetry. She defies the strict rules of her mother and the church after she falls in love with a forbidden boy and secretly joins her school's slam poetry club.

P.S. I MISS YOU by Jen Petro-Roy (Feiwel and Friends, 2018). When Evie's strict Catholic parents send her pregnant sister to live with a distant relative and forbid them to talk, Evie begins to write her letters. In them, she worries about their dysfunctional family, questions their religion, and tells her sister about a new female classmate on whom she's developed a crush.

RUMBLE by Ellen Hopkins (Margaret K. McElderry Books, 2014). Matt blames his friends, family, and teachers for his gay younger brother's suicide. Several of the bullies belong to the same youth group as his girlfriend, who has begun to distance herself from Matt while her father works to ban books containing homosexual content from their school.

THE SACRED LIES OF MINNOW BLY by Stephanie Oakes (Dial Books, 2015). After Minnow Bly's hands are chopped off by members of the polygamous cult in which she was raised, she runs away and nearly kicks a man to death. In juvenile detention, she learns to read and admits to a forbidden romance, then reveals what happened in her community the night their prophet was killed.

SAINTS AND MISFITS by S. K. Ali (Salaam Reads, 2017). Teenage Jenna, who has a Muslim Egyptian mother and a secular Indian father, wears a hijab and feels like a misfit in a school where students question her religion. She struggles to maintain her faith after her parents divorce and the cousin of a close friend attempts to rape her at a family gathering.

TIFFANY SLY LIVES HERE NOW by Dana L. Davis (Harlequin Teen, 2018). When black teenager Tiffany Sly loses her mother to cancer, she moves in with her father—a strict Jehovah's Witness—and struggles with his rules until another man shows up claiming to be her true father.

A VERY, VERY BAD THING by Jeffery Self (PUSH, 2017). Christopher, the teen son of a famed homophobic preacher, falls in love with an aimless boy named Marley and gets sent to a conversion retreat. Marley becomes suddenly famous and finds himself lying to cope with the public attention as he struggles to remain faithful to Christopher.

VIVIAN APPLE AT THE END OF THE WORLD by Katie Coyle (HMH Books for Young Readers, 2015). When sixteen-year-old Vivian Apple loses her parents to a cult and they vanish—apparently through twin holes in their bedroom ceiling—she takes off on an epic road trip across a country newly paranoid, accompanied by her best friend and a mysterious boy harboring a dangerous secret.

WRITTEN IN THE STARS by Aisha Saeed (Nancy Paulsen Books, 2015). Pakistani American high school senior Nalia can chose her path of study and her career. But when she attends the prom with her sweetheart, her conservative and hyperprotective parents whisk her away to Pakistan, where she's expected immediately to marry the man they've chosen for her.

YOU'LL MISS ME WHEN I'M GONE by Rachel Lynn Solomon (Simon Pulse, 2018). Jewish eighteen-year-old Adina wants to become a viola soloist, while her twin, Tovah, hopes to attend medical school and become a surgeon. When a rare degenerative disease ravages their Israeli mother's body and mind, they undergo genetic testing and find that one twin has tested positive for the disease.

ACKNOWLEDGMENTS

I'm deeply grateful for the time and insight offered by the authors I consulted for this book. Thank you to An Na, Angela Cervantes, Beth Vrabel, Brian Tashima, Carrie Mac, Chris Crutcher, Donna Gephart, Eric Gansworth, Holly Goldberg Sloan, Katie Coyle, Kelly Milner Halls, Martha Brockenbrough, Paula J. Freedman, Sharon M. Draper, and Thanhha Lai.

Thanks to the young adults who shared their insight and enthusiasm for literature—Annie, Celina, Emma, and Leyda. I look forward to reading the books that you'll surely write.

Librarians have been my heroes since the day I signed up for a library card in the fourth grade and eagerly checked out piles of books from the Wiseburn Library in Hawthorne, California. Thanks to librarians Anna Monders and Kerry Sutherland, who shared their booklists, anecdotes, and love of reading and children with me.

A special shout-out to the children's and young adult staff at Eugene Public Library—Chuck, Claire, Hadley, J, Jay, Patricia, Rob, Vicki, and others: you answered a barrage of my bizarre questions for months on end and pointed me in the direction of much of the literature that ended up in this book. The library is my daughter's and my second home, and you are family.

Thanks to brilliant teacher Gillian Esquivia-Cohen, therapist Emily Mendez, and *Kazoo* founder and editor Erin Bried for your stories and your inspiring work with young people.

So many of my friends checked in with me weekly on the progress of this book and cheered me along as I wrote it. Thanks especially to Amy Samson for the warm chocolate chip scones delivered to my front door during deadline week. So much gratitude to Jamie Passaro and Merie Kirby for your friendship and literary/parenting wisdom.

Boundless appreciation for my agent, Jennifer Unter. She knows me so well now that whenever I email her to complain, she wisely counsels me to go for a long run. Works every time.

Thanks to Sasquatch Books executive editor Susan Roxborough for helping me shape this book into something that I hope will benefit and inspire thousands of young readers, teachers, and caregivers of all sorts. You saw the potential in the early draft of this manuscript and brought it to life with your insight both as an editor and as a mother. Deep gratitude to my eagle-eyed project editor, Rachelle Longé McGhee, who helped me polish up the final draft of the manuscript with tremendous insight into how it would best serve readers. I'm grateful to sales director Jenny Abrami for early support. Tony Ong, what a splendid cover you've designed.

To my mother—who let me open her boxes of books and also taught me to write and submit my own stories at her electric typewriter—an eternity of thanks for your energy and inspiration.

To my daughter, who cheered me on endlessly as I worked on this manuscript—even when I disappeared into my office for hours at a time and ate all the chocolate in the house— thank you for your kindness, and for bringing me more chocolate hearts.

Special thanks to my husband, Jonathan B. Smith, who's been reading novels aloud to our daughter since she was two, and does a mighty impressive Gollum. Without your constant support in so many, many ways, this book could not have been written.

APPENDIX

Resources for Parents, Teachers, Librarians, and Young Readers

Nonprofit Organizations Devoted to Diversity in Literature

Africa Access Review

AfricaAccessReview.org
Devoted to helping schools, libraries, and caregivers discover children's and young adult books on Africa. Includes booklists and teaching resources.

America's Battle of the Books

BattleoftheBooks.org
Nationwide reading incentive program with teams and competitions in each state. Features extensive booklists and information on how teachers, school administrators, and/or parents can start a Battle of the Books team.

Children's Book Council

CBCBooks.org
Trade association of North American book publishers promoting children's books and reading. Provides information about new book releases and award winners.

Common Sense Media

CommonSenseMedia.org/book-reviews
Searchable database of children's and young adult book reviews designed to give parents insight into each book's educational value, positive messages and role models, presence of violence and/ or sex, consumerism, and drinking and/ or drugs.

National Book Foundation

NationalBook.org
Highlights North American literature and emphasizes the importance of books in our culture. Lists National Book Award winners for children's and young adult fiction.

Young Adult Library Services Association

ALA.org/yalsa
Supports librarians in helping all teens to find success and sponsors Teen Read Week. Includes extensive booklists and a teen book finder database and app.

We Need Diverse Books

DiverseBooks.org
Helps change the publishing industry by promoting literature that reflects the lives of all young people, through internships and financial assistance. Features numerous booklists organized into diverse categories.

Websites Devoted to Diversity in Literature

African American Literature Book Club

AALBC.com
Curated collection of more than 11,000 titles of black literature. Includes reviews, awards, excerpts, and purchasing options.

American Indians in Children's Literature

AmericanIndiansinChildrensLiterature .Blogspot.com

Provides book reviews, booklists, and critical analysis of the representation of indigenous peoples in children's and young adult literature.

The Brown Bookshelf

TheBrownBookshelf.com

Black writers and illustrators showcase children's and young adult books, providing reviews and booklists.

Disability in Kidlit

DisabilityinKidlit.com

Publishes book reviews, articles, and author interviews from the disabled perspective on the portrayal of disability in middle grade and young adult literature.

GayYA.org

GayYA.org

Publishes booklists and blog posts about books with LGBTQIA+ characters.

Literature Review Publications

The Horn Book

HBook.com

Independent magazine featuring articles, reviews, and editorials about children's and young adult literature. Features extensive information about diverse fiction for kids of all ages.

Kirkus Reviews

KirkusReviews.com

Provides independent book reviews, and maintains a blog exploring children's and young adult titles.

School Library Journal

SLJ.com

Publication for librarians and information specialists who work with children and young adults. Provides book reviews and the Teen Librarian Toolbox, with in-depth information on diverse titles.

Voice of Youth Advocates

VOYAMagazine.com

Library journal serving young adult librarians and promoting literature and reading. Provides booklists and interviews with young adult authors.

Other Websites of Interest

BookRiot

BookRiot.com

Searchable database of children's and young adult titles, including reviews, podcasts, articles, and interviews.

Epic Reads

EpicReads.com

Book reviews, a searchable database of young adult fiction, and author interviews and information on public appearances.

Goodreads

Goodreads.com

Offers searchable databases for diverse children's and young adult literature, including both professional and reader reviews.

A Mighty Girl

AMightyGirl.com/Books

Contains a vast searchable database of diverse children's and young adult literature, including award winners, reviews, and purchasing information.

YA Books Central
YABooksCentral.com
Professional reviews for middle-grade
and young adult literature; readers are
also invited to review favorite books.

Book Awards

Browsing the following websites can
be an excellent way to identify diverse
quality children's and young adult books.

**The American Indian Youth
Literature Awards**
http://ailanet.org/activities/american
-indian-youth-literature-award

The Americas Award (Latinx)
http://claspprograms.org
/americasaward

Arab American Book Award
www.arabamericanmuseum.org
/bookaward

**Asian/Pacific American Award for
Literature**
www.apalaweb.org/awards
/literature-awards

Coretta Scott King Book Awards
www.ala.org/rt/emiert/cskbookawards

**Dolly Gray Children's Literature
Award (autism and developmental
disabilities)**
DollyGrayAward.com

**The Green Earth Book Awards
(nature and environmentalism)**
www.natgen.org/green-earth
-book-awards

**The Jane Addams Children's Book
Awards (social justice)**
JaneAddamsChildrensBookAward.org

Lambda Literary Award (LGBTQIA+)
www.lambdaliterary.org/complete-list
-of-award-recipients

**The Michael L. Printz Award for
Excellent in Young Adult Literature**
www.ala.org/yalsa/printz

**NAACP Image Awards for
Outstanding Children's Literature**
http://aalbc.com/books
/image-award-winning-books
.php?year=NULL#Children

**New Voices Award (authors of
color and native nations)**
www.leeandlow.com/writers-illustrators
/new-voices-award

Newbery Medal
www.ala.org/alsc/awardsgrants
/bookmedia/newberymedal
/newberymedal

Pura Belpre Award (Latinx)
www.ala.org/alsc/awardsgrants
/bookmedia/belpremedal/belpreabout

**Schneider Family Book Award
(disability)**
www.ala.org/awardsgrants
/schneider-family-book-award

South Asia Book Award
http://southasiabookaward.wisc.edu

Stonewall Book Awards (LGBTQIA+)
www.ala.org/rt/glbtrt/award/stonewall

Sydney Taylor Book Award (Jewish)
http://jewishlibraries.org/content
.php?page=Sydney_Taylor_Book
_Award

**Tomás Rivera Book Award
(Mexican American)**
www.education.txstate.edu/ci
/riverabookaward

FURTHER READING

Bal, P. Matthijs, and Martijn Veltkamp. "How Does Fiction Reading Influence Empathy? An Experimental Investigation on the Role of Emotional Transportation," *PloS ONE*, Volume 8, Issue 1 (2013).

Djikic, Maja, Keith Oatley, and Mihnea Moldoveanu. "Reading Other Minds: Effects of Literature on Empathy." *Scientific Study of Literature*, Volume 3, pages 28–47.

Hammond, Meghan Marie, and Sue J. Kim. *Rethinking Empathy through Literature*. New York: Routledge Taylor & Francis Group, 2014.

Hogan, Patrick Colm. *What Literature Teaches Us about Emotion*. Massachusetts: Cambridge University Press, 2011.

Johnson, Dan R., Brandie L. Huffman, and Danny M. Jasper. "Changing Race Boundary Perception by Reading Narrative Fiction." *Basic and Applied Social Psychology*, Volume 36, Issue 1 (2014): 83–90.

Kidd, David, and Emanuele Castano. "Different Stories: How Levels of Familiarity with Literary and Genre Fiction Relate to Mentalizing." *Psychology of Aesthetics, Creativity, and the Arts*, Volume 11, Issue 4 (2017): 474–486.

Leverage, Paula, Howard Mancing, Richard Schweickert, and Jennifer Marston William. *Theory of Mind and Literature*. Indiana: Purdue University Press, 2010.

Oatley, Keith. "In the Minds of Others," *Scientific American Mind*, Volume 22, Issue 5 (Nov/Dec 2011): 62–67.

Simmons, Andrew. "Literature's Emotional Lessons." *The Atlantic*, 5 April 2016.

Society for Personality and Social Psychology. "Can Fiction Stories Make Us More Empathetic?" *ScienceDaily*, 11 August 2014.

BIBLIOGRAPHY

Introduction

Castano, Emanuele, and David Comer Kidd. "Reading Literary Fiction Improves Theory of Mind." *Science*, 18 October 2013.

Chiaet, Julianne. "Novel Finding: Reading Literary Fiction Improves Empathy." *Scientific American*, 4 October 2013.

Flood, Alison. "Literary Fiction Readers Understand Others' Emotions Better, Study Finds." *The Guardian*, 23 August 2016.

Hudson, Cindy. Personal Interview. 30 May 2018.

Kirby, Merie. Personal Interview. 1 June 2018.

1. Books about Adoption and Foster Care

Castellitto, Linda. "Holly Goldberg Sloan: A Kooky Kid Finds a New Family." *BookPage*, September 2013.

Children's Rights. "Foster Care." www .childrensrights.org/newsroom /fact-sheets/foster-care.

Covenant House. "Teen Homelessness Statistics." www.covenanthouse.org /homeless-teen-issues/statistics.

Crutcher, Chris. Personal Interview. 15 May 2018.

French, Agatha. "In Her Sixth Book for Teens—*Far From the Tree*, a National Book Award finalist—Robin Benway Strikes at the Heart." *The Los Angeles Times*, 9 November 2017.

Garcia, Leyda. Personal Interview. 19 July 2017.

Piccadilly Press. "*Counting by 7s* by Holly Goldberg Sloan." 3 June 2015. YouTube video, 3:34. www.youtube .com/watch?v=Fg4MmKi8s_E.

Sloan, Holly Goldberg. Personal Interview. 14 May 2018.

Suma, Nova Ren. "Author Interview and Book Giveaway: *Counting by 7s* by Holly Goldberg Sloan." *Distraction No. 99*, 28 August 2013.

2. Books about Body Image

Bell, Cece. "Cece Bell: How I Made *El Deafo*—in Pictures." *The Guardian*, 4 August 2015.

Bried, Erin. Personal interview. 8 June 2018.

Brody, Jane E. "Bias Starts Early and Takes a Serious Toll." *The New York Times*, 21 August 2017.

Kazoo Magazine. "About." www .kazoomagazine.com/about.

Mendez, Emily. Personal Interview. 11 June 2018.

Pai, Seeta, and Kelly Schryver. "Children, Teens, Media, and Body Image: A Common Sense Media Research Brief." 21 January 2015. www.commonsensemedia.org /research/children-teens-media -and-body-image.

SmartGirls Staff. "Interview with *Dumplin'* Author Julie Murphy." Amy Poehler's Smart Girls. 15 September 2015. http://amysmartgirls.com /interview-with-dumplin-author -julie-murphy.

3. Books about Immigration

Cervantes, Angela. Personal Interview. 30 May 2018.

Child Trends. "Immigrant Children." 2014. www.childtrends.org /indicators/immigrant-children.

Esquivia-Cohen, Gillian. Personal Interview. 6 May 2018.

Fontana, Francesca. "Eugene Rallies for Refugees." *The Register Guard*, 29 January 2017.

Lai, Thanhha. Personal interview. 11 April 2018.

——. "Raising Children Inside a War." *The New York Times*, 21 April 2017.

Lamiell, Patricia. "The (Therapeutic) Value of Being Heard." Teachers College Columbia University Newsroom, 14 May 2012.

Merchant, Nomaan. "Hundreds of Children Wait in Border Patrol Facility in Texas." *The Chicago Tribune*, 18 July 2018.

Miroff, Nick. "A Family Was Separated at the Border, and This Distraught Father Took His Own Life." *The Washington Post*, 9 June 2018.

Morris-Young, Dan. "Put a Human Face on Immigration, Declares San Francisco Archbishop." *National Catholic Reporter*. 9 January 2018.

Russo, Maria. "Children's Books That Tackle Race and Ethnicity." *The New York Times*, 23 September 2016.

4. Books about Learning Challenges

Centers for Disease Control and Prevention. "Autism Spectrum Disorder (ASD): Data and Statistics." www.cdc.gov/ncbddd/autism/data .html.

Learning Disabilities Association of America. "Types of Learning Disabilities." http://ldaamerica.org /types-of-learning-disabilities.

Logsdon, Anne. "The Link Between Learning Disabilities and Depression." *Verywell Family*, 28 January 2018.

National Center for Learning Disabilities. "The State of Learning Disabilities." Third edition, 2014. www.ncld.org /wp-content/uploads/2014/11 /2014-State-of-LD.pdf.

Passaro, Jamie. Personal interview. 30 May 2018.

——. "Talking to My 8-Year-Old about Her Dyslexia." *The Washington Post*, 17 October 2017.

5. Books about LGBTQIA+ Youth

Acker, Lizzie. "2nd School District Scraps Oregon Battle of the Books Over Novel about Trans Child." *The Oregonian*, 2 May 2018.

Blad, Evie. "How Many Transgender Children are There?" *Education Week*, 7 March 2017.

Crutcher, Chris. Personal Interview. 15 May 2018.

Gephart, Donna. Personal Interview. 12 May 2018.

Martin, Michel, and Benjamin Alire Saenz. "Discovering Sexuality through Teen Lit." *Tell Me More*. National Public Radio. 20 February 2013.

Waters, Michael. "A Brief History of Queer Young Adult Literature." *The Establishment*, 3 August 2016.

6. Books about Mental Health

American Academy of Pediatrics. "Children's Hospitals Admissions for Suicidal Thoughts, Actions Double During Past Decade." *AAP News and Journals*, 4 May 2017.

American Psychological Association. "Children's Mental Health." www .apa.org/pi/families/children-mental -health.aspx.

Anxiety and Depression Association of America. "Children and Teens." http://adaa.org/living-with-anxiety/children.

Centers for Disease Control and Prevention. "Children's Mental Health: Data and Statistics." www.cdc.gov/childrensmentalhealth/data.html.

——. "How Much Physical Activity Do Children Need?" www.cdc.gov/physicalactivity/basics/children.

Child Mind Institute. "Anxiety and Depression in Adolescents." http://childmind.org/report/2017-childrens-mental-health-report/anxiety-depression-adolescence.

——. "Children's Mental Health Report." http://childmind.org/2015-childrens-mental-health-report.

Denizet-Lewis, Benoit. "Why Are More American Teenagers than Ever Suffering from Severe Anxiety?" The New York Times Magazine, 11 October 2017.

KidsHealth. "Anxiety Disorders." http://kidshealth.org/en/parents/anxiety-disorders.html.

Mac, Carrie. Personal interview. 8 May 2018.

McCullough, Meghan. "10 Things I Can See from Here: Carrie Mac on Anxiety, Platitudes, and More." Signature, 16 March 2017.

National Book Foundation. "Jason Reynolds." www.nationalbook.org/nba2016finalist_ypl_reynolds_ghost.html#.WyL1OFVKjIU.

National Institute on Drug Abuse. "Ohio Opioid Summary." February 2018. www.drugabuse.gov/drugs-abuse/opioids/opioid-summaries-by-state/ohio-opioid-summary.

The New York Times Editorial Board. "An Opioid Crisis Foretold." The New York Times. 21 April 2018. www.nytimes.com/2018/04/21/opinion/an-opioid-crisis-foretold.html.

The Telegraph Staff. "Reading 'Can Help Reduce Stress.'" The Telegraph, 30 March 2009.

7. Books about Nature and Environmentalism

Annie. "10 Ways You Can Help Save the Planet/Want by Cindy Pon Review and Discussion." Blossoms and Bullet Journals, 13 March 2018. http://blossomsandbulletjournals.wordpress.com/2018/03/13/want-by-cindy-pon.

Brand, Madeleine. "Hoot." All Things Considered. National Public Radio. 27 October 2002.

Doyle, Brian. "Brian Doyle on His New Novel: 'I Was Trying to Write What We Don't Know.'" The Oregonian, 27 May 2015.

Halls, Kelly Milner. Personal interview. 11 May 2018.

Kirby, Merie. Personal interview. 15 April 2018.

Louv, Richard. "The New Nature Movement, After 11/8." Huffington Post, 22 December 2017.

Matthews, Celina. Personal interview. 20 May 2018.

O'Rourke, Ciara. "The 11-Year-Old Suing Trump Over Climate Change." The Atlantic, 9 February 2017.

Phyu, Lei. "17 Ways Young People Are Changing the World." Medium, 8 August 2016. http://medium.com/@UNDP/17-ways-youth-are-changing-the-world-505a489e91dc.

8. Books about Physical Disability

Disabled World Disability News. "2017 US Census Bureau Disability Statistics Facts for Features." www.disabled-world.com/disability/statistics/cbfff.php.

Draper, Sharon M. Personal Interview. 16 May 2018.

Guarisco, Martha S., and Louise M. Freeman. "The Wonder of Empathy: Using Palacio's Novel to Teach Perspective Taking." *The ALAN Review*, Fall 2015.

Kraus, Lewis. "2016 Disability Statistics Annual Report." Durham, NH: University of New Hampshire. 2017. http://disabilitycompendium .org/sites/default/files/user -uploads/2016_AnnualReport.pdf.

Mastre, Brian. "Basketball Player with Down's Syndrome Makes Spectacular Shot after Moment of Kindness from Opposing Team." NBC 4 NY. NewYork, NY: WNBC-TV: 10 January 2018.

McKnight, Amanda. "Engineering Students Team Up to Make Accessible Products." *Shakopee Valley News*, 17 May 2018.

Mirfendereski, Taylor, and Susannah Frame. "Oregon School District Includes All Students with Disabilities in Regular Classes." KING 5 News. Seattle, WA: KING, 23 May 2018.

North Carolina Bookwatch. "Sharon Draper, *Out of My Mind*." Public Media North Carolina. Public Broadcasting Service. RTP, NC: UNC-TV, 14 September 2012. http:// video.unctv.org/video/nc-bookwatch -sharon-draper-out-my-mind.

Rought, Karen. "Josh Sundquist Shares the Various Inspirations Behind 'Love and First Sight.' *Hypable*, 8 February 2017.

Vrabel, Beth. Personal Interview. 14 May 2018.

Vrabel, Emma. Personal Interview. 14 May 2018.

9. Books about Poverty and Homelessness

Ehrlich, Hannah E. "The Diversity Gap in Children's Book Publishing, 2017." Lee & Low Books blog, 30 March 2017. http://blog.leeandlow .com/2017/03/30/the-diversity-gap -in-childrens-book-publishing-2017.

National Center for Children in Poverty. "Child Poverty." www.nccp.org /topics/childpoverty.html.

Pao, Maureen. "Dolly Parton Gives the Gift of Literacy: A Library of 100 Million Books." *NPR Ed*. National Public Radio. 1 March 2018.

Rowe, Claudia. "Student Homelessness in Seattle Growing at New York City Rates." *The Seattle Times*, 9 November 2017.

Running Strong for American Indian Youth. "The Poverty Cycle." http:// indianyouth.org/american-indian-life /poverty-cycle.

Yorio, Kara. "A Fifth Grader's Mission to Save His School's Librarian." *School Library Journal*, 24 May 2018.

10. Books about Race and Ethnicity

Bergland, Christopher. "Can Reading a Fictional Story Make You More Empathetic?" *Psychology Today*, 1 December 2014.

Berman, Mark. "Hate Crimes in the United States Increased Last Year, the FBI Says." *The Washington Post*, 13 November 2017.

Butler, Shakti, dir. *Cracking the Codes: The System of Racial Inequity*. World Trust, 2013. DVD, 75 min.

Draper, Sharon M. Personal Interview. 16 May 2018.

Garcia-Navarro, Lourdes, and Angie Thomas. "*The Hate U Give* Explores Racism and Police Violence." *Weekend Edition Sunday*. National Public Radio. 26 February 2017.

Gay, Roxane. "Confessions of a Bad Feminist." Filmed May 2015 in Monterey, CA at TEDWomen 2015. TED video, 11:29. http://www.ted.com/talks/roxane_gay_confessions_of_a_bad_feminist.

Haber, Leigh. "How Black Lives Matter Inspired a No. 1 Best-Selling Book." *O, the Oprah Magazine*. July 2017.

Lodge, Sally. "Four Questions for Katherine Applegate." *Publishers Weekly*, 17 August 2017.

Panko, Ben. "Racism Harms Children's Health, Survey Finds." Smithsonian.com, 5 May 2017. http://www.smithsonianmag.com/science-nature/racism-harms-childrens-health-180963167.

Slate Staff. "Hate in America: An Updating List." *Slate*, 8 February 2017.

Spice, Byron. "Reading Harry Potter: Carnegie Mellon Researchers Identify Brain Regions That Encode Words, Grammar, Character Development." Carnegie Mellon University News. 26 November 2014. www.cmu.edu/news/stories/archives/2014/november/november26_computationalreadingmodel.html.

11. Books about Religion and Spirituality

Coyle, Katie. Personal Interview. 30 April 2018.

Fassler, Joe. "How Literature Inspires Empathy." *The Atlantic*, 18 August 2015.

Freedman, Paula J. Personal interview. 19 April 2018.

Johnson, Dan R., Daniel M. Jasper, Sallie Griffin, and Brandie L. Huffman. "Reading Narrative Fiction Reduces Arab-Muslim Prejudice and Offers a Safe Haven from Intergroup Anxiety." *Social Cognition*: Vol. 31, No. 5, pp. 578–598 (2013).

Spector, Carrie. "Religiously Engaged Adolescents Demonstrate Habits That Help Them Get Better Grades, Stanford Scholar Finds." Stanford Graduate School of Education News Center. 15 April 2018. http://ed.stanford.edu/news/religiously-engaged-adolescents-demonstrate-habits-help-them-get-better-grades-stanford-scholar.

Wilson, Reid. "The Second Largest Religion in Each State." *The Washington Post*, 4 June 2014.

Winfrey, Kerry. "We Interviewed Katie Coyle, Author of *Vivian Apple at the End of the World*." HelloGiggles. 4 January 2015. http://hellogiggles.com/lifestyle/interviewed-katie-coyle-author-vivian-apple-end-world.

INDEX

ABOUT THE AUTHOR

Melissa Hart grew up in Los Angeles with two mothers and a younger brother with Down syndrome. She's the author of the award-winning preteen novel *Avenging the Owl* and *101 Ways to Love a Book,* as well as two memoirs for adults.

Melissa works as a contributing editor at *The Writer* magazine. Her essays have appeared in the *Washington Post, Boston Globe, Los Angeles Times, Chronicle of Higher Education, Advocate, Rumpus, Orion Magazine, High Country News,* and *Woman's Day.*

She lives in Oregon with her husband and daughter, plus a flock of chickens and cats and one very patient terrier. When she's not reading and writing, you can find her on the hiking trail or kayaking rivers or swimming in mountain lakes.

Find out more about the author and her work at MelissaHart.com.